PEE UP A TREE:

A Mental Health Memoir
by Jim Henson

Arborwood Press

This book describes the author's experience while living in the Umpqua Valley in the years 1970 through 1973 and reflects his observations and opinions relating to those experiences. Some names and identifying details of individuals mentioned in this book have been changed to protect their privacy.

Cover Photo by Jim Henson, Upper Rogue River, August 2010

ISBN: 1453713883
EAN: 978-1453713884
Library of Congress Control Nunber: 2010911098

Published by Arborwood Press
1937 SE Arborwood Ave.
Bend, Oregon 97702
arborwoodpress.com
arborwoodpress.blogspot.com
arborwoodpress@aol.com

Dedication

To my loving and supportive wife who encourages my writing process even when our memories differ and to Kenneth Fenter and the Writing for Fun gang who keep me going and help me clean up my (literary) act. A special thanks to Jim Lobitz, whose insights and feedback have been a source of inspiration.

Contents

Forward:

Why does one choose to read a memoir? The reasons are as varied as the colors of a Caribbean sunset. Grant's memoirs of the Civil War—new insights into military leadership? Maybe. Madeleine Albright's memoirs of her life as the first female Secretary of State—understanding of a woman's approach to international affairs or tidbits about the way the Clinton administration functioned? Perhaps both. Whatever the motivation leading you to pick up this memoir, you will find a multi-layered commentary on the first few years of someone dedicated to his clients, dedicated to the community, who is not afraid to laugh at himself or at the irony in his environment.

Perhaps you are interested in how a newly minted, very well educated social worker deals with the reality shock of real clients needing real relief while they are living in less than supportive circumstances. If so, you will not be disappointed. You will meet Hugh, whose approach to orienting new staff is a unique blend of good-humored cynicism, common sense, and a focus on the importance of getting the job done. Micromanaging, never. Hands off, hardly. Responsive when asked, always. He was ready to give practical advice to keep Jim from really messing up. What a gift! Many of us would have had a far easier adjustment to professional life, and would have been more effective professionals sooner, had we been blessed with a Hugh on our first real job.

Perhaps you are a student of social work theory and are interested in what University of Chicago was teaching as state of the art social work theory in the late 60's? If so, you will not be disappointed.

Forward:

Vignettes illustrating key social work principles abound. Honoring the client's definition of the therapeutic agenda, facilitating a focus on behavior change, a practical approach to empathy, learning from non-verbal expression, and avoidance of enmeshment are but a few of the social work concepts illustrated here in humorous and delightful stories. All of us who graduated from that august institution in the 60's knew we were going to save the world and knew we had the tools we needed to succeed. We did not end up saving the world but the stories here show that the concepts we were taught, when used skillfully, could help.

I have worked in community-based programming for over thirty years. It is hard work. It requires patience, respect for those you are trying to serve, and a clear focus on the community or client's definition of the problem. It requires the willingness to spend the time and energy necessary to form quality relationships and it requires a high degree of skilled professionalism. The stories in this memoir illustrate all of these concepts.

What the stories most illustrate however is that a key requisite is the ability to have fun while valuing the effort required. Whatever your reasons for picking up Jim Henson's memoir, what you will find most worthwhile is the sense of enjoyment and of fulfillment that comes when community based programming is done well.

You can expect to find good humor, good will, a healthy dose of common sense and a very good read.

Well done, Jim!
Mary Lee Fitzsimmons, PhD
Executive Director of One World Health Centers (retired)

The Landing
1

Visually and culturally, Chicago and Southern Oregon have almost nothing in common. To fly out of one and land in the other can create serious emotional shock for the uninitiated. But that is exactly what we did. On our first Friday of the year 1970, we took possession of a brand new Toyota Corolla Mark 2 sedan deluxe at the dealership in Medford, Oregon. It was a beautiful shade of pale blue. Before saying good-bye to Chicago, we had sold our old gray Volkswagen camper bus, a microbus conversion actually, to a Lutheran pastor and his wife. Bob and Joyce Davis were Vietnam anti-war tax resisters who could intuitively feel the close breath of the FBI, CIA, Treasury Department and IRS agents. At times, as members of the American Friends draft counseling services, we could imagine that breath coming our way as well. Bob and Joyce took their commitment to civil disobedience several notches above our own. They had, as a consequence of their activities, decided it was time for them to leave the USA while they still had freedom to choose. Therefore, they systematically closed their bank accounts, sold their home and made all preparations necessary for a move to French Canada. This of course included an active study of French. Our camper van appealed to them as the ideal escape-mobile. I made no effort to discourage them on any of these beliefs.

Leaving Chicago, as we did on the first day of January, I was not keen to drive any vehicle across the rolling frigid plains or over the snow blown Rocky Mountains to Oregon. Visions of the Donner party come to mind! We had already taken this trek in both directions in much more hospitable months. The deal was struck. The Davis family gave us some of the cash from under their mattress, took possession of the camper and set sail for Quebec. While we, on the other hand, took that cash and booked a flight out of Chicago that would in a matter of hours land my wife, infant son and me in Oregon.

Just days after the landing in Oregon, with what was left of the car-cash added to the money from the insurance company for our two bicycles, stolen from the back porch of our Dayton Street flat, we strolled into the Toyota dealership in Medford. It was my contention, based upon a thorough reading of a recent Consumers Report magazine, that the Toyota would be far more reliable and efficient than the microbus camper van. In the years to come, this educated guess would prove to be half-correct. That Corolla would go twice as far at twice the speed for half the money. How were we to know that this little beauty would try to kill us on three occasions! There was one omen to which in retrospect we should have paid more attention. As we left the car dealer, we noticed that the gas gauge was on "E." Trying to reach a Shell station less than a dozen blocks away, we coasted to a very quiet stop about half the distance to our goal. Perhaps we drove too hard a bargain! We had plenty of exciting experiences with the camper van over the years we owned it.

For example, on one occasion, the brake master cylinder went out, and since I could not afford a tow truck, I crept half way across Chicago on side streets to the VW dealer relying solely on the emergency brake.

I can't remember any time when I had to leave it and walk just to go 12 blocks.

You might ask what would possess a man with a beautiful wife and a three-month-old son to pack up all worldly goods and parcels, and leave behind a vibrant diverse city in the middle of winter. And, to top that off, to leave behind a full time position with decent pay and very good professional growth potential seems like personal folly.

Not one event by itself was the tipping point to my decision to lobby for leaving the big city. It was more like an avalanche of experiences that came tumbling through our lives. One such experience was the death of a young black man who had the misfortune of losing his entire exhaust system after hitting a pothole a block from the clinic where I worked. Chicago streets in mid-winter could be a maze of potholes. The prevalent de-icing method on the highways and byways of the mid-West was to spread salt on the roadway surface. Salt and metal are not all that friendly. In fact, the former tends to eat the latter, so it was not unusual for a car with a decade or more of history on it to suffer massive amounts of rust on it and under it. On this particular night, salt, corrosion, and being black in a certain white neighborhood in the middle of the night turned out to be a lethal combination. The sagging tailpipe and muffler assembly came flying off the car right after being disturbed by the pothole. It very likely made quite a racket as it bounced across the pavement. A trail of sparks, as well as the now completely unmuffled engine roar could also have drawn attention to the scene as the young black man got out of his car to inspect the damage and consider his damage control options. He never had time to explore his options. Getting out of his car turned out to be the last decision he would ever get to make.

Perhaps I should give just a brief word of explanation about the location of the Chicago Family Service Bureau where I found employment. It was located in the lily white pond known locally as "Back of the Yard" which referred to a certain south side neighborhood of tough, hardworking blue collar white folks who felt threatened as this small ethnically pure enclave became surrounded on all sides by growing black and Hispanic communities. The "Yard" aspect of "Back of the Yard" was a historical reference to the adjacent Stockyard. Though I never met the man in person, this was Richard J. Daley's own neighborhood. Chicago was and may still be a city of many separate and distinct villages. That which was unique or unusual about this particular office of Family Service Bureau was the fact that it was located in the pure white lily pad, but like the neighborhood schools, it also had the mission of serving the lily pad and all of the surrounding villages. Tension arises from the fact that residents of all the surrounding villages had to enter the lily pad to access almost any of life's basic services, including food, supplies, healthcare and education. This branch of Family Service Bureau was located in the eye of the intercultural storm. Many school days quaking elementary age children of color found refuge in our office lobby until their parents could pick them up and ferry them home to safety.

Our own mid-north Lincoln Park neighborhood was not exempt from the ethnic wars and common thievery of urban life. An eight-foot high solid wood fence with a well-secured gate was no barrier to the people who coveted our bicycles, which were chained to an eye-bolt fastened through the wall of our home.

One day as the postman was making his rounds down our street, he came upon twin toddlers toddling along the sidewalk in their pajamas. He recognized that it was quite odd for unsupervised toddlers to be out and about on the sidewalk mid-morning in their pajamas. On closer inspection, these nightclothes were blood spattered and so were the feet of the children. These observations set off a chain of inquiry that led to the discovery of the toddlers' parents. The pastor of Armitage United Methodist Church and his wife were found in their home in bed. Multiple stab wounds were determined to be the cause of death. No one was ever arrested, tried or convicted.

Only in retrospect can I acknowledge the extent to which these two deaths altered my sense of comfort and direction. We did not know this couple in any intimate sense of the word "know". We knew who they were by title, activity and proximity. But I have come to believe that these deaths became commingled with nascent fatherhood protectiveness feelings within me. In ways that I cannot yet fully understand and describe, my sense of comfort and resolve to seek change was profoundly altered. With much resolve and very little understanding or communication, I began to explore the notion of escape. Escape? How had I so suddenly changed from attraction, interest and desire to be in the city of Chicago to a sense of urgency to be elsewhere?

From city to town to burg, mother, father and infant flew out of the windy city and within what seemed like a few hours were headed north on an Oregon freeway to Roseburg... with emphasis on burg. Which of these three do you think will make the best landing, the infant, his mother or father? Perhaps if we had taken the camper bus across the prairie and over the frigid winter mountains we might have had more time to adjust and navigate this transition.

Someone is bound to say that this "best landing" contest fails to meet any basic test of fairness. One party to the contest is a much loved and cherished cherub with no significant worldly experience beyond the arms of his parents and the ample breasts of his very attentive mother. So long as these other two fawning faces, these comfort giving creatures who keep showing up on demand or by shear uncanny anticipation, then life could be nearly perfect almost anywhere. A hill, a plain, a river valley or an ocean shore, they all look pretty much the same from inside the bassinet.

Then into the contest comes the city slicker who never lived in a village smaller than San Diego, who is moving from a city with three times greater population than the entire State which will soon become her home State. And, there were 80 times more people in her old Lincoln Park district of Chicago than reside in the burg to which she is now driving. No small wonder that she asks strange questions like: "Where are all the people?" and "why are there so many trees?" And also, "where is the bookstore?" The burg did not have a bookstore, and the movie house burned down after the popcorn machine caught fire.

"But sweetheart," I said," There's a good restaurant up the road not more than 65 miles in the town of Eugene." Somehow, these words failed to comfort or console the city slicker. Nor did the fact that the University just up the road about 65 miles was about to close its graduate school where she could have completed the education she had begun before the arrival of the cherub. Then there is the leaving behind of the familiar. Brownstone buildings covered with the smoke from a century of coal fired furnaces. Gardens, some no bigger than a planter box on the side of a flight of stairs. Friends refined to gold in the fiery crucible of antiwar activity and neighborhood politics. Yes, trading this for a tiny apartment on the mossy side of the hill in the near industrial part of the burg, and knowing not a soul in this sparsely populated lumber mill dominated place, and being essentially isolated by virtue of job description... mother of a three month old, this was quite an elegant trade.

The third participant in the "best landing" contest grew up in a lumber and pear dominated village one river valley south of the new landing zone. With the trees coming out of the woods by the perpetual truckload, this native son of the State of Jefferson (as southern Oregon and northern California was known by locals) was conditioned to believe that all this bountiful harvest was taken to provide the world with shelter. It would be decades later before many of us came to believe that the most important product to come from trees was air to breathe.

Having worked in the pear packing and canning operations of the Rogue Valley, contestant number three had come to believe that pears had two basic purposes: exporting and throwing! Exporting means get them out of here so that we don't have to look at them again until next year. The throwing has to do with alleviating or mitigating long hours of tedious boredom, which results from the excruciatingly monotonous cannery work. If you happen upon a really juicy rotten ripe pear, it's always fun to toss it in the direction of some poor unsuspecting fool... preferably one just out of site behind the next monster machine. You can see, I hope, how this kind of activity would help break up the monotony and at the same time prepare one to live in such a place. These are just a few of the opportunities that tend to give contestant number three a distinct advantage over contestant number two.

Finding the right burg, when you are looking for one from Chicago, doesn't take much genius. It's actually a simple process of elimination. One day, the social work profession quarterly journal came in the mail. In the back of this esteemed publication could be found some personnel recruitment advertisements. These ads were listed State by State and there for all to see was a notice placed in the journal by Tillamook County Mental Health Department. "For more information, contact Robert Wilson, program director." As strange as it may sound to any normal person sitting at his desk in Mayor Daly's neighborhood with an entry room full of elementary age refugees, I got to thinking about the tranquility of cows chewing green grass in a misty field. Cows making milk and world famous cheese, doesn't this sound terrific? Of course, I didn't have any manure or flooding in my daydream to dampen or stink it up. Don't sweat the details!

In no time at all, I am dashing off a query letter to Bob Wilson "for more information."

Dear Mr. Wilson:

At this moment as I am writing to request more information about the position for mental health specialist, the police have blocked off the streets surrounding our clinic to deal with a situation at the adjacent high school. Suffice it to say, water cannons are in position and helicopters are making a lot of racket over head, making it difficult to attend to the counseling process.

Having read your ad in the latest quarterly journal, I found myself having a pleasant daydream about your job offering and its pastoral setting. I am interested in relocating and would greatly appreciate receiving more details about your open position and the compensation and benefit package that may come with it.

Sincerely,
Urban Warrior

In a matter of days, a response arrived from Bob Wilson. The upshot of his reply was that he had hired a person to fill the vacancy in his program. Then he extended a courtesy I have never heard of before or since. He asked if he might share my letter with other county mental health directors with position openings. Even before he received my response, he began shopping my letter around the network of his peers, generating several job offers. The counties of Oregon, with matching money from the State, were growing their community mental health system. With Bob's help, I just fell into it.

Medford and Roseburg offered immediately available positions, and between these two, Medford (place of my birth and first 18 years of life) just seemed a bit too close to "home." The Medford I remembered not only had the giant wigwam burners, but multitudinous smudge pots as well. The wigwam burners received, via conveyer belts, all the wood tailings of the sawmill operations. Most mill towns sported several wigwams to burn up bark and get rid of anything that was not marketable lumber. A relative few clever operators used this waste wood to fire steam generators to create the power to run the mill. The idea of landscape bark had yet to present itself. As if the wigwams couldn't put up enough smoke by themselves, a thousand plus smudge pots would kick in each spring.

Those rascally pear trees would persist in flowering each spring before winter's frost had subsided, putting the whole crop at risk before it could even get set. Smudge pots were the answer! At some ungodly hour of the late night or early morning when the temperature dropped below freezing, my teenage peers would get up, go out into the orchards of the valley, get drunk and light up the crude oil pots. This process left the sky a deep blue/black color, a stinking pale cast over the early light of day so penetrating that one could not see from one end of the hall to the other on the inside of Hedrick Junior High School. To be fair about this description, every spring day was not this bad, but the geography of the place created a toilet bowl effect. With the Coast range to the west and the Cascade range of mountains to the northeast, and the Siskiyous to the south, all that smoke had no place to go... so it settled into the bowl!

"And so," I thought, "I'll take my chances on the burg." Did it have wigwams, the Coast range and the Cascade Range? Yes, but no pears and no pots. And on the positive side of the ledger, there were stories in the local newspaper about intelligent life in the vicinity of Roseburg. I'm referring here to the Mt. Nebo weather goats, which were said to have the uncanny ability to forecast the weather more accurately than the local meteorologists. If a storm were coming in, that renegade pack of goats would head down the hill. Conversely, if high pressure was building and a clearing was on its way, up the hill they scampered. Local public-spirited folk were up in arms at the very idea that hunters might take to the hill and make sausage and jerky out of these pesky weather predictors.

Another story that added to the attractiveness of the burg was one told about the largest employer in the area, a family owned mill that hired the deaf to work in the high noise areas of the mill. These were still the macho days of mill operation generally. People expected to go deaf while working in a mill, especially around the head rig, trim saws or planer operations. They also seemed to accept the idea that emphysema was an acceptable outcome of employment, since no one would dare wear a respirator in the high dust areas of the mill. On the day when one self-respecting mill worker tried to protect himself with a proper lung saving device, coworkers heckled and teased him about wearing a Kotex on his nose. It seemed like rather forward thinking to hire the deaf to do some noisy and reasonably well paying work in the mill. This very same farsighted employer scholar shipped some engineering students at the university to explore the feasibility of a blower/pipeline system that would blow sawdust over the Coast range to the port of Coos Bay, thereby eliminating the use of hundreds of diesel trucks daily traversing the same mountains on windy, narrow and treacherous roads. Unfortunately, the blowpipe did not meet some cost effectiveness test and was never built. With two rivers running through it, and lots of timber revenue going into public health and mental health, the burg seemed to have a lot going for it. I had a feeling of genuine optimism about the whole place as we rolled into town.

The Initiation
2

The architecture wasn't anything special. The Health Department and its subordinate, the Family Service Clinic, were housed in a 1950s era Nazarene Church purchased by the county and expropriated for this use approximately five years previous.

I must say that my newly assigned space in it was almost palatial in comparison to the renovated mop closet that was my office on Chicago's south side. There were no hypnotherapy options in that Chicago closet, since it adjoined the men's restroom with very little sound insulation, but you could expect the newest staff member to be assigned the least desirable office space.

Here in the burg, however, offices in the mental health section had formerly been used as Sunday school classrooms. It would be eight reasonably long years before I would again have an office this spacious and comfortable.

Hugh, my boss, was an affable sandy haired fellow with a nicely trimmed beard of the same color except for a few small streaks of gray that had snuck into it. His handshake was firm and his smile genuine as he welcomed me, introduced me and showed me around.

"It's the administrative staff that is truly in charge around here," he said in a manner leaving no doubt that he meant it. "So, I am going to introduce you to them first. Jim, this is Betty. She has been here longer than any of us and knows where all the bones are buried. If you need anything, she is your best bet. A wise person would check with Betty first no matter what the topic!"

Betty extended her hand in greeting and a great big radiant smile as she said, "Welcome aboard the good ship 'Personal Repair.' Did you and your family find a place and get moved in all right? If you need anything just let me know, cause my husband Herb and I have way too much stuff!"

I could sense that this somewhat short and somewhat round woman possessed a rare combination of warmth and savvy, of generosity and practical bearing. "Yes," I said. "We are all moved in... over on the mossy side of Winchester Street, in the 24 Karat apartment complex. I think it will work pretty well in the short run, while we look around to see where we really want to be. Thanks for the offer of stuff, but I think we have that covered for now also. But I will keep your offer in mind in case something vital comes up missing."

And so it went, from Betty to Diane to Stacy as the introductions continued around the administrative team. All were welcoming and positive, I felt.

After we were well out of ear shoot of the admin pool, Hugh said, as an aside as we proceeded down the hall toward the counseling offices, "Those women are in charge of case assignments. You understand what I am saying? They are going to determine which clients are assigned to you. My advice to you is never piss 'em off." This sage information was given as calmly and matter of factly as if he had just informed me that 100 watt light bulbs were installed in all the ceiling light fixtures.

On went the introductions for the rest of the morning. Gary, a tall gentle man with an honest Abe beard waved us into his office. We discussed group therapy and transactional analysis and family experiences. I could tell that we would likely team up on lots of interesting situations. Perhaps we would do a group together, or do case consultations back and forth. Then there was Denny, the staff psychologist. Of the three other men on the clinical staff, Denny was the youngest and most recently arrived. Even at the tender age of 30- something, he was practically bald. He was at once serious, adventuresome and impractical. He and his wife had one child, a preschooler named Gabe. He was sharing with Hugh and me his plan to take his new canoe down a section of the Umpqua River, which he hadn't scouted and about which he knew nothing.

The last stop, going north down the clinical wing of the converted church building, Hugh introduced me to Iris, the senior most member of the staff in terms of age. With a long and distinguished career behind her, she was beginning to make some retirement plans. Iris was modestly forgetful, but usually in benign ways. And, what she had lost in memory, she made up for in warmth and caring.

In this clinic, there was no shortage of cases to assign. So, having established a working connection to the various players on the team, the second day on the job found me preparing to see my first client in this new setting. In the back of my head, still rang the prophetic words of my new boss. "The administrative staff is in charge of case assignments," he had said. At the appointed hour, down the stair I went to greet my new client in the waiting room, which was located at one end of the administrative area. I must say that it was with a great deal of confidence that I skipped down the stairs to the waiting room. As a recent graduate of the Clinical Social Work program at the University of Chicago, who could be more qualified to meet the next client assigned by the administrative team? There could be no mistaking the fact that I was about to meet a young woman who was within a year or two of my own age. I say, no mistaking because she was at that moment the only person in the waiting area, and Betty had just notified me by intercom that my client had arrived.

Brandy, or possibly Candy, was her name. In her hand was a tissue, and she was holding it just beneath her left eye as tears were streaming down both cheeks. Outside of San Francisco's north beach, I had never seen anyone dressed like Candy. The outfit included a see through blouse with a push up bra, accompanied by a red mini skirt, fishnet panty hose and high heels. The whole ensemble struck me hard, as I tried to maintain my University of Chicago professional composure in the moment before introductions were made. "Focus on the face of grief," I told myself, as I worked at steadying my breath, even though the air smelled of lilacs or some such.

"Good morning Candy," I said, as brave as I could make it sound. "I'm Mr. Henson. I have been assigned to be your counselor. Would you please follow me back to my office where we can address your issues with more privacy?"

"Yes," she sobbed, as she rose from her chair. She looked prepared to follow wherever I led, so without another word we both proceeded up the stairs and down the hall to my spacious new office.

I was thinking all the way down the hall, "What have I done already to piss off Betty!" Once the door was closed and we were both seated, and keeping my focus always on the face of grief, I began the interview. "Tell me about your tears or about what brought you to the clinic today," I said, with what I hoped that she would hear as a voice of compassion, of concern.

"It's men," she said, "They just treat me like a sex object... Like a piece of meat or something." She sobbed even harder, so I handed her the whole box of tissues, hoping that she would place the box in her lap, which she thankfully did. After she took a nice big blow on her nose, she resumed her story. "They just don't see me for who I am. All they want to do is grab me, and force themselves on me. It's disgusting, really. As if I don't have a brain in my head ...," she sort of trailed off at the end and seemed a bit calmer.

In the quiet space, I offered these words, "What are the characteristics, the parts of yourself that you want men to see? The part of you that men don't seem to notice?" I don't know what she heard, or just when she stopped listening. But it was right in there somewhere that she let out an angry roar.

Candy suddenly stood up, the tissue box flying off her lap as she did. She glared at me with astoundingly raging eyes, and shouted, "You're just like them! You're one of them!" And she headed for the door in a rush, both opening it and slamming it before I could even get up.

It's probably just as well, because I certainly didn't want to get between Candy and the door.

With the same ferocity, she zoomed down the stairs and slammed the waiting room door hard enough to jiggle the fillings in the teeth of each admin area employee. Then, out in the parking lot, I could not hear her open her car door, but everyone in the building could hear it close.

"Good going," I thought. "You have really screwed up your first case." I took a few slow, deep breaths, and stretched a little, then began to contemplate what to do next. The whole building was quiet. Not a creature was stirring, not even a mouse! What could I have done differently? How did I so famously blown it? And to think it is the first crack out of the box. And, what did I do already to piss Betty off! And, what must they be think about me, and what could have happened up stairs to cause such an explosion. And the other therapists... what were they thinking? Boy, I'll bet I blew their trance.

The contemplation in my mind was so long and so loud that I didn't hear it at first, the very gentle and quiet almost imperceptible knock at the door, but there it was again. I got up from my reverie, went to the door and opened it. Standing in front of me with tissue still in hand was Candy, not sobbing, not raging Candy.

"Can I come back in?" she asked in a whispery little voice that seemed to have some trust and hope mixed into it.

"You are more than welcome to come in and complete the hour, which if my clock serves me correctly, we have more than half an hour to go," I said to the quiet grieving face. The rest of the hour went remarkably well. She decided that I was genuinely interested in the process of helping her to find the parts of herself that she wanted others to see. She even let me say to her that she had done a pretty terrific job of covering up the parts of herself that she wanted to know and wanted others to find. The hour came to a blessed end and Candy rescheduled to continue her personal discovery process. And, best of all, I never got any more grief from the admin staff.

Envy

3

That first evening, as I was preparing to head home, I had a very scary experience, which would become commonplace, but until that moment I had never before witnessed. The experience to which I am referring is 5:00 PM in the public employee's parking lot. Every one, it seemed, was pouring out of the county offices at the same time, hustling to their respective cars and pickups, jumping in and backing up at once. It was like some kind of a bizarre stock car race or a demolition derby in which someone was silently mouthing the words: "Ladies and gentlemen, start your engines." Then that same someone waves an invisible flag, and all the drivers put their rigs in reverse and begin to back up! That's when I noticed that half the cars were missing a head light or a tail light lens. It was nuts. Everyone wanted out of the parking lot at once. Observing this self-inflicted public mayhem, I decided to just sit there quietly until at least 5:07 P.M.

"Perhaps I'm the odd one," I thought. I was trying to put this social behavior into some kind of mental context. My dad, for instance, was a self-employed optician in a downtown upstairs office. He parked his car blocks away from his office building to an area that had no parking meters to feed. The metered parking close to the building was reserved for customers. And, he didn't leave his office until the job he was working on was finished. We never owned a car with a missing head light or a broken tail light lens. And, in Chicago, the CTA bus dropped me off just a block or two from the clinic. Going home was just as easy. Our VW camper bus stayed in the garage.

Soon the momentary chaos around me was beginning to subside.

Out of the corner of my eye, I caught some pedestrian movement and turned my head in that direction. It was Hugh, and it appeared that he was headed toward my Toyota. As he approached, I rolled down my window. He put his hand on the roof of the car and leaned down toward me and gave me one of his rogue smiles.

"Nice going today," he said.

"Thanks," I replied.

"Fran and I would like you and your family over to our place for dinner Friday evening if you can make it," he continued. "Say about 6:00 or so."

"That sounds great. I'll check with headquarters to be sure that we're not otherwise committed. It's not like we have established a terrific social calendar yet. What would you like us to bring?" I asked.

"Just yourselves and that sweet little baby, which reminds me, do you know what penis envy is?" Hugh said, with that devilish smile on his face again.

This change in the conversation caught me somewhat off guard, but I decided to just pitch it back at him. "If memory serves, Sigmund Freud decided that men were superior because they had one, and women were stuck with insecurity and neurosis because they didn't have one. But in Medford where I grew up, the story went 'round that girls were jealous 'cause they couldn't pee up a tree on a picnic, or even write their names in the snow," I said with a straight face.

"You're on the edge of it. You're skirting around it some. Penis envy is a father with five daughters!" he said with the ring of certainty.

Then it hit me right in the gut. He had envy of our sweet baby son. Sensing that there was some pain hiding behind his winsome smile, I said, "Are you familiar with the work of Anna Fromm the psychoanalyst?"

To my relief he answered, "Not particularly."

"It's her contention that 40 to 50 percent of men suffer from womb envy, since they lack the patience, creativity and nurturing capacity of women, thus leading to depression and other neurosis.

She has reported in the Journal of Contemporary Psychiatry that an even higher proportion of men suffer from unacknowledged breast envy which leads to a condition of obsessive lust instead of normal admiration."

"I think you're full of unmitigated bull. You are going to fit with perfection into this group!" he said. "By the way, Doc Gray has called for a department-wide meeting for first thing Friday morning to introduce you to all of Public Health: nurses, vector control, sanitarians, V.D. checkers, everybody. You must be pretty damn special. I don't think he did that for me, and I know he didn't do it for Denny or Gary."

"I'll try to remember to wear a clean shirt and underwear. See you tomorrow," I said as he straightened up and waved me adieu.

Anatomy of the Earth

4

The days flew by and Friday came very quickly, but I guess that's the way it is when anticipation and curiosity are running at full tilt. Betty and the admin team kept assigning interesting people to my case load ... a crop duster who crashed his plane after clipping a power line ... a young woman in Douglas Community Hospital was on a two physician hold after a suicide attempt ... and an eccentric California refugee who lived up the far reaches of the Little River where he ran a small mom and pop grocery store until mom ran out on him. Now it was just pop and his dog.

My plate was full to over flowing from the beginning, and I was enjoying every minute of it. More about these terrific yet wounded people later, but first I wanted to bring you up to speed on the Health Department staff meeting.

If I grew an inch for every time Hugh pulled my leg, I'd be 10 feet tall by now. The truth of the situation is that a Health Department staff meeting occurs on the first Friday of every month, come rain or shine. Yes, I had my 30 seconds of introductory fame. And, yes, Dr. Gray was very kind and even enthusiastic about my arrival on his staff. It turns out he did his residency at Cook County General Hospital in Chicago, and had a high regard for the University of Chicago and its graduates, but the guts of the staff meeting concerned the provision of services by each section of the department. The sanitarians presented their report on restaurants that were in and not in compliance, and the failure of septic drain fields in South County. Vector control gave a report on rabid rodents and preparations for the upcoming mosquito abatement season. Contagious disease section brought out a graph that charted the rise and fall of the 10 most popular diseases, like flu and STD's. And round and round it went until it finally came to focus on mental health.

Hugh took his turn to present as the Director of the Family Service clinic. "Now that we are fully staffed again, we are in a position to reconsider a satellite clinic in the north county area. I plan to send Jim up to Yoncalla and Drain to put that service together. I believe he has the energy and the vision necessary to accomplish this long needed goal."

What the heck was he talking about? Energy maybe, but vision, for crying out loud?

From across the room, during Hugh's presentation, I could over hear some chuckling and more than a few snorts. This noise seemed somewhat disruptive or even impolite to the presenter, but I was just an ignorant observer and didn't really know what Hugh was up to or how he was regarded by employees of other health department sections. I have to say that I was surprised to hear at this meeting, for the first time, that I was going to be in charge of something. At the close of the staff meeting, which came suddenly, Hugh was the first one out the door. With the congestion and confusion of moving people and chairs, I hadn't a prayer of a chance of catching up with him then.

Standing in front of me, and between the exit and me stood Agnes, the supervising home health nurse (also known as Aggie and The Enforcer) extending her hand in welcome. She was a sturdy, large and unadorned middle aged no nonsense kind of woman. A very muscular grip it was, as she shook my hand, giving my arm a good work out. As she had been sitting in the middle of the gang of nurses that had led the laughing and snorting, I couldn't help but ask what their apparent humor was all about. "Agnes, I think I missed something funny during Hugh's part of the meeting. What was going on? I think I missed out on a joke," I said.

Aggie busted out laughing again, and then when she got herself under control, she said, "I know you are not in on the joke. You are the butt of the joke!"

"What do you mean?" I asked.

"Let me put it to you as delicately as I can because you seem like a nice young fellow. If God decided to give the earth an enema, she would insert the tube in Drain. That's all I can say about it, Honey," she said, never losing her grip or smile. "A hearty welcome and all that. I hope you will enjoy working with that loopy mental health bunch," she said before she hustled on about her business.

Aggie, I could tell, was a decisive person with strong opinions about most things. In just a few words, she had filleted my new colleagues and my upcoming assignment, whatever it was going to be. "Whew," I thought," if ever I want a quick x-ray of something, I now know just where to go to get it."

It almost goes without saying that I left the conference room with considerable confusion, but the inference was that I was not going to like what I would find in Drain. I suspected I was going to have to do my own research on the communities of Yoncalla and Drain to determine why God had given it such a strategic location. Later that day, with the dinner invitation ahead, perhaps I could get some answers.

Within seconds of our arrival at Hugh and Fran's house, baby Aaron was surrounded by seven adoring females, the two mothers and the five girls. Hugh and I wisely stepped to the side and backed away so as not to get knocked down by the incoming stampede. That baby boy couldn't have attracted more attention if he had been a baby jaguar. What caught my attention during this introductory period of cooing and cuddling was the foot-sized hole in the bathroom door. My curiosity having gotten the better of my manners, I couldn't help but ask Hugh about that hole.

"What's the story behind that hole in the door there, Hugh?" I ask.

"The five girls share this one bathroom, and when the timer goes off, sometimes so do the tempers. I think that one is a Julie size hole, but I may be wrong. When you get a houseful of kids, you'll understand. That's not the original bathroom door, by the way." He said.

Dinner was exciting, with all those chattering and vibrating young people at the table. Annis, my bride, took in all of this youthful energy far better than I did, of that I am sure. While she is the oldest of four siblings, I am the youngest of two with a sister four and a half years older. Right in front of me, I could see that the rules of operation for larger families were different than for small ones. There was the timer for the bathroom one. Then there was the one about taking only one piece of chicken until the plate comes back around, a rule from which guests were evidently exempt. I ask Hugh and Fran, "are there any other important survival rules for full size families?"

"When each girl reaches the age of 18, we have the favorite meal of the birthday child. When the table is set, beside the knife, fork and spoon we set a hammer. After dessert, and after all the presents have been unwrapped, the birthday girl will take the hammer and break her plate, and prepare to make her way in the world as an adult. Meaning, if they stay home after that, they pay rent!" Fran said.

It seemed to me that the girls were quiet and pensive after Fran's comment, though she had said the whole thing with a pleasant smile.

Hugh added, "If any parent were to leave the home when there were still children in it, that parent would have to take all the kids with him."

This thought seemed to please or reassure Fran, but the kids were still quietly chewing with their mouths closed and eyeballing each other as if to ascertain the meaning of these expressed rules.

Later in the meal, we learned that Hugh and Fran had been studying sign language, and had begun a parent group for the deaf adults who worked at the sawmill in those high noise jobs. Most of these parents had hearing competent children, and they were likely very appreciative of the offering of this specialized parenting class. I could tell just by looking around me that Fran, Hugh and the kids were all involved in music or the arts in some way. Here and there were instruments, sheet music, paintings, sculpture and the like. It was a fully lived in home.

I didn't have the courage or the inclination to ask Hugh more about the Yoncalla-Drain satellite clinic idea before we left for home. Why break up the fun with work? That topic and my curiosity about it could wait until Monday.

Stuff Flows Downhill

5

Hoping to catch the boss well before the client schedule commenced, I rolled into the staff parking lot a good half an hour early. Only one other car graced the lot and it belonged to Hugh. "I'm in luck," I thought. All was quiet in the waiting room area as I passed through it. No admin people and no clients had arrived. Heading up the stairs to the consult office area, I could see that Hugh's door was ajar, so I just said, "Is anybody home?" from outside the door.

"Come on in. I've been waiting for you," he replied. "We need to talk about your new satellite assignment."

"Have we got ESP (extra sensory perception) or what?" I thought." But what I said was, "Good, good. I wanted to get that straightened out in my head before diving into the people part of the day. Tell me what it's all about."

"Surviving as a clinic director requires never forgetting two important things," he began. "The first is to always take an interest in what your boss takes an interest in and the second is to always try to make the program look like it reflects the interests of your boss. And, as you may have guessed, I've been in this job a long damn time, so it must be a winning recipe! Are you following me?"

It really sounded to me, as I was carefully listening, a lot more like mentoring than a lecture. I couldn't quite imagine it, but it was as if he was suggesting that someday I would become a clinic director and would need to know some things about survival that they don't teach in graduate school. At that moment, I didn't know that Dick, my predecessor in this job, had taken exactly that route and had become the new clinic director in La Grande.

"Yes, I think so," I replied.

"We're talking about what is important to Doctor Gray. What kind of interests does he have?" I said.

"Same song, second verse," Hugh said. "For Doctor Gray to survive, he has to know what pleases his employer and to limit his liability on the dark side of what could happen to the Health Department."

"The Board of County Commissioners?" I ventured.

"You are a quick learner, my man!" He said. "And what do you think pleases the County Commissioners?"

"Getting re-elected!" I guessed with a growing sense of where this conversation was headed. "So, what makes the voters happy that keeps the Commissioners in office and helps Doctor Gray, you and me employed here? Let's see now, the public would think that we civil servants are out there doing a terrific but efficient job."

"Yes, out there and visible is what they want. And nothing is more visible than a service in the voter's own neighborhood. And, we are going to call it a satellite clinic, placing it in the neighborhood that thinks it is the most underserved," he concluded.

"Ergo, north county. What about protecting Doctor Gray from the dark side, protecting against his or the Department's liability," I'm asking, but I'm feeling like a bird being led down a breadcrumb trail.

"To doctors, nobody is more important than another doctor. Doctor Gray, because he's the only doctor in the whole Department, has to double as the medical director of the mental health clinic. He's very knowledgeable, experienced and wise, but he is not a psychiatrist. More than anything else in the world of his liability, he wants to hire a psychiatrist so that he can dump off that responsibility on someone else. And, as soon as he gets the chance, he's going to hire one," He said. Then he added, "Just to make Doc feel better, we meet for lunch once a month with Doctor Forrest Miner from the Veterans Hospital. We call it due diligence. Even though it's more of a food gathering than a clinical enrichment thing, it's good to do now and again, and I hope you will come along with us next time."

"Sure thing. Well, I think it's time to get myself together for today's client population, but there's a lot more that I need to know about the people and situation of need in north county. So let's pick a time later this week for that. OK? I will be glad to take an interest in what interests you, though I guess we're pretty well at the bottom of the proverbial pyramid, aren't we?" I said.

"Yes you are!" he said with that grin on his face, as I headed for the door.

On my way down the hall to my office, I ran into Denny. I had to do a double take, because something was amiss about him. What was it? Oh yes, his shiny baldhead was the same, but his wire rimmed glasses were missing and there were serious scratches running down the right side of his face. Wanting to be observant though also diplomatic, I asked, "Where are your glasses Denny?"

In a mildly dejected tone, he replied, "Down the river some flippin' place, with all the rest of the stuff that was in the bottom of my canoe when I turned it over. And, my paddle is also down river some place, probably near Reedsport by now."

"Geez, that's a shame. Are you hurt badly?" I said, because one of the scratches looked like it could have gone right across that right eye.

"No, it's more of a pocket book and pride kind of injury. I hate to get beaten by the river. And I lost a bunch of stuff, binoculars, camera, back pack, and some miscellaneous. Plus, my expensive non-water proof watch is trashed. Doubt it will ever run again.

"But my boat's OK. I had to float and swim quite a ways before I caught up to it soze I could grab it and dump the water out. I'm gonna try that stretch of river again next weekend. You know, I can't let it beat me. You wanna go?" he asked.

"Naugh, with the new baby and all, Annis would probably kill me if I drowned, but good luck to you," I said.

Always Something Interesting
6

First client of the day on Monday was, you guessed it, Candy. But when I trekked down to the waiting room, I almost didn't recognize her. She was wearing blue jeans, genuine Wranglers held up by a serious rodeo belt and silver buckle. She topped that off with a red plaid western shirt, the kind with fancy snap down pockets.

Her hair was pulled back into a neat ponytail. On her feet were highly polished riding boots too clean to have ever left the sidewalk. She was still a stand out for appearance, but all traces of streetwalker had left her outfit. When she turned to greet me, there was no make-up mask at all, just a fresh scrubbed country girl face with a pleasant smile on it.

"Are you ready to go to work this morning?" I asked.

"No, I came to see you instead," she responded.

"It's a figure of speech, Candy. By 'go to work' I mean are you ready to keep searching for the authentic, genuine, real you in your session today?" I shot back.

"Oh that," she said. "That's what I came here for!"

We proceeded up to the counseling space where we commenced the session. The truth is that you can never be sure how a counseling session is going by just observing the client in a single session. If anything, my first interview with this young woman had shown me that much. "Keep humble and look out for surprises," has become my motto of late.

Hugh told me his motto was, "Never die with a hard on or a dollar in your pocket."

All people, it turns out, have a significant amount of skin and bone in front of their brain, and you can't even get at what they are really thinking by looking in their ears.

After we had settled into our respective chairs, and before I had a thought about how to begin the session, Candy said, "I'm sorry for all the trouble I caused last time I came here. All that door slamming and stuff, "she added.

"Somehow, I think it was all part of our necessary get acquainted process, Candy. You established that you were a volunteer here, and that you can come and go whenever you want to within our allotted time. And, I hope we also established that I am interested in helping you achieve the goal or goals that you set for your counseling. Also, I want you to know that you have my attention. I'm awake, alert and listening, wondering what you'll do next!" I said.

"We're OK then?" She asked.

"I believe we are," I replied.

Candy said that she couldn't remember ever being in a relationship like ours before, like the one I had described at the beginning of the hour. "You know. Where I was a volunteer, and could go and come as I please. Usually I can get into a relationship, but I can never get out before there's a lot of grabbing, shouting and shame."

I assured her that there would be none of that in our relationship of counselor and client. As the session rolled on, I couldn't help but ask if her new attire was a different costume or an outward representation of the new Candy.

"I'm kind of trying it out, actually. The silver buckle belongs to Kenny, my stepbrother. He got drafted into the army and is over in Viet Nam right now. However, before that, he was on the Rodeo circuit as a bull rider, and he was really good at it. I suppose it is just sort of another costume. But I have decided for sure that I don't want to continue my life as an exhibitionist," she said quietly but with some dignity.

"Where the heck did you come up with a big word like

'exhibitionist?'" I asked.

"From my loud-mouthed stepmom. She calls me all kinds of bad things, but that one is the least nasty. So I looked it up and I kind of think it fits, don't you think?"

"I'll agree to go with you on that description of the old Candy if you promise not to use it against yourself as a put down or a weapon to hurt yourself with from now on. And, as far as the cowgirl thing goes, you have a perfect right to try out many things before you settle more comfortably into yourself. As a matter of fact, you'll need to give yourself lots of room to try out things. I myself was a cowboy once, but it didn't work out very well," I said in a half teasing manner.

"Why didn't it work for you?" she asked seriously.

"Well, first of all, I was only five or six years old at the time. And, we lived in town on a city sized lot. And, I didn't have a horse. What I did have was a Hopalong Cassidy radio and two six guns with genuine pearl imitation handles and leather holsters that I was mighty proud of. They shot roll caps, and could make enough noise to rouse the cat and chase her outside. There was an electrical short in the radio, and every time I went to turn it on or off, it would shock the shit out of me! I didn't want to tell my mom or dad, because I was afraid they would just get rid of my radio. And then, how would I be able to listen to the 'The Shadow' and the 'Lone Ranger.'

"But the final chapter in my cowboy days came when my California cousins and their parents arrived for a visit right after my birthday, right after I got my six guns. Those cousins always got into my stuff and messed it up. So, in anticipation of their visit, I hid the guns and holsters underneath my clothes in the bottom drawer of my dresser. The sad thing is that I was off at a swimming lesson when they arrived, so I couldn't see what was going on. I wasn't there to protect my turf. By the time I got home, my youngest cousin had not only found the guns and holsters, he had taken them outside, shot all the caps out of both guns, lost one gun, and had broken the genuine imitation pearl handles off the remaining gun. He was using it like a hammer to pop the caps that hadn't popped when the roll of caps went through the gun!"

"What did you do then?" she asked, which only served to encourage me to plunge on.

"I tackled him and wrestled him to the ground, to the sidewalk actually. And, I got on top of him and was intending to beat the poop out of him. That's when my uncle Jack showed up. He pulled me off my cousin and asked me why I was so angry. And, I told him in no uncertain terms that his son was a sneak, a thief, and a vandalizing scoundrel. And that I wanted to pound some restitution into his hide as any good T.V. cowboy would have done. I guess Uncle Jack didn't like my plan, so he said I shouldn't be so upset. He said if I let my cousin go, he'd replace my missing and broken six guns and holsters. He hasn't replaced 'em yet, so I had to give up on the idea of being a cowboy," I said.

"That's so sad. What's all this got to do with me becoming the genuine me?" she asked.

"That's a very good question. What do you think?" I said.

"I think it means I can explore all kinds of ideas, outfits and stuff, and that not all of my experiments will turn out the way I want or expect. Or maybe the story just explains why you are a little bit wacky," she said with a bit of an impish smile, as if implying that 'wacky' was a good thing.

"I think you are way ahead of me. My first thought was that I'm glad I got that story off my chest. And thank you for that. And, my second thought is that I predict you won't be a cowgirl for long either."

Perpetual Motion

7

On the way back up the hall, I caught a glimpse of Doctor Gray. So I hustled to catch up with him before he disappeared altogether. "Have you got a second for me?" I asked.

"Probably two, if you make it quick," he replied.

"OK then, quickly, who is the most important contact I should make in north county as I try to figure out how to get the new satellite clinic up and going?" I asked.

"The name's Doctor William Wiltse. He has medical privileges in Cottage Grove, but he has a highly regarded practice in Drain and been there a long time. You'll like him," he answered without the slightest bit of hesitation.

"Thank you," I said, but I was remembering what Hugh had earlier mentioned. Doctors are important to Dr. Gray. And, in a world of professional responsibility, doctors are the people with whom he shared responsibility for the health of the greater community that is Douglas County.

When you look at it on a map of the United States of America, noticing how it runs from the Pacific Coast all the way to the Cascade Divide west to east, and from below Glendale to above Curtin south to north, the county is larger that several of the States. That's a lot of acres and souls to be medically responsible for. Then I thought that even though Doctor Gray felt a special bond of importance and connection for other physicians, I also felt that he held us mental health types in pretty high regard too.

"You're welcome," he said, just before he disappeared around the corner.

The next client of the day was Jordon Johnson, a Southern California refugee who had landed up on the far reaches of Little River. Just a few years back, he had been an inspector of some kind for Lockheed Aerospace Company, overseeing the construction of flying war machines. An intelligent man in his mid-50s, something in him had snapped as he watched the news night after night streaming out of Southeast Asia. Agent Orange falling out of aircraft, defoliating the forests ... napalm falling from the sky ... burning villages and people of all ages indiscriminately in its wake ... planes coming out of his factory or others just like it ... young men coming home, broken in body or spirit ... others coming home in flag-draped coffins. These were the images passing in front of Jordon on his television set.

And one day he just couldn't take it any longer, and one part of his brain went to war against another part of his brain. He took early retirement from his job, packed up his Dodge Ram pickup and headed north, with his wife Mavis, and his dog Ringo. After about a thousand miles of Interstate 5, Jordon inexplicably turned right and followed the North Umpqua highway east until he came to the town of Glide, where the Little River collides with the North Umpqua. It's a very unusual site, two rivers colliding head on and forming one, so he and Mavis had to stop and take a look.

While Jordon and Mavis were standing there, hanging over the metal rail enthralled with the mist of colliding rivers wafting over their heads, a local realtor just happened to slip up beside them. Actually, Ringo was the first to detect the realtor's presence and let out a distinct "woof" that was not really threatening, but startling enough to bring Jordan and Mavis to an awareness of this other person hovering near at hand. The realtor had a large welcoming smile on his face, but I am sure if one had looked closely at his eyes, they were beady as a snake's.

"Hi there folks. Where you all from?" He said, as if he hadn't just looked over their Dodge Ram with what was left of their worldly possessions piled high in the one-ton truck bed with a tarp over holding it all down. As if he hadn't noticed the California license plates screwed to bumper for God and everyone to see.

Mavis wasn't about to talk to this glad-handing stranger, but Jordan thought the man was only being friendly. So, he shook the hand being offered to him, and replied that he and his wife were from California.

"That's wonderful," said the realtor. "What brings you this way?"

This greeting and inquiry should have been received as a certain warning that they were about to be lined up for a shellacking. Hadn't they seen the sign at the border that boldly announced "Welcome to Oregon? We are glad you came to visit, but don't stay." How could they have missed all the bumper stickers clearly stating, "Don't Californicate Oregon?"

Well, I guess they didn't see any of that, or it just didn't register. At least the meaning of it all didn't dawn on Jordon. He fully embraced the realtor's friendliness as genuine beef jerky, with Mavis looking on skeptically.

"This part of the country is so beautiful, so pristine, so unlike San Pedro," said Jordon." We are going to move up here somewhere and start a small business of some kind, me and Mavis."

"That's wonderful. That's just wonderful," replied the smiling, beady-eyed salesman, "There' a lot of opportunity right around here. You're going to love it here," he went on.

"Opportunity right here, you say!" Jordon said, with his eyes beginning to twinkle.

"Oh sure, you bet there is. For instance, as luck would have it, a neat little place right up Little River here came on the market that might be perfect for you two. It's a one of a kind, once in a life time situation." The slick salesman knew he had left someone out of the deal, but he noticed that Ringo wasn't paying much attention to these proceedings. "It's a combination business and home property, smack on river front, with a couple or more acres. Honestly, it has the makings of a resort from what I can tell." Even without an x-ray, a sane person could have seen that this character didn't have an honest bone in his entire body.

Mavis poked Jordon in the ribs with her elbow, hoping against hope to wake him from the trance encapsulating him. Even Ringo began a slow stroll back toward the pickup. "Time to get back on the road," she encouraged. Mavis had no idea where they were going, their actual destination. Jordon had never been very clear about that. She knew he was fragile, mentally troubled, and needed to find a slower, easier life pace. But she felt no attraction to Glide, and she could smell corruption seeping from the pores of the beady-eyed hand-shaker. Her sympathy and support were generally behind Jordon, or she never would have agreed to sit in the passenger seat of the northbound Dodge Ram. She was perhaps eight to 10 years older than Jordon and they were hard years that left her looking even more haggard and shop worn than her actual age. Her phobia for dentists might explain part of it. "Come on," she said again.

Now seemingly transfixed by the mesmerist's spell, Jordon begged for Mavis to be patient with him and the sales pitch he wasn't even aware that he was getting. "Tell me more about this place that's for sale up the river here, smack on the river, couple of acres."

"I think it might be just what you and your wife are looking for. But don't take my word for it. I know the people who own it. I think I could arrange with them for you to see it. What they have there is a historically significant property, which comes with a general store complete with a large upstairs apartment and sort of an RV park out on the riverside of the store. So you'd have residence, income and paradise all for one modest price." What the salesman was thinking didn't come close to this description. A true picture would have shown a ramshackle old two story shingle sided wooden building with a fairly fresh coat of paint holding it all together. The RV park was more of a squatter's perch of old camper and trailer rigs with lots of flat tires indicating little if any movement in or out. There were even a couple of aging retrofitted yellow school buses with wood stove pipes poking up through the roof. The "general store" was stocked with pop, beer, chips, cigarettes and out of date magazines, a few canned goods and not much else. During the all too short summer season, the store also carried fishing tackle, bait and licenses. The salesman also forgot to mention that the Little River Store had been on the market for over five years, or about one year after the previous flat land suckers bought it. None the less, he thought the coat of new paint and the upstairs apartment, which had been remodeled when the present owners took over and sunk all their remaining cash into it, these two items just might sell the place to the Johnsons. As a matter of fact, so long as he could keep the subject of profit and loss out of the conversation, he figured that he had finally found his buyers.

"How far up the road is this place? About how long would it take us to get there from here?" Jordon said, trying to subdue and control the excitement in his voice. He didn't want to sound as eager as he knew he probably looked.

"Maybe 10 or 15 minutes, not much more than that," was the salesman's sly reply, even though he was fully aware that this little jaunt would take at least double his higher estimate.

"What do you think, Mavis? It sounds exactly like what the doctor ordered. A nice residence, a small business, both in one package alongside this river here! I say we've got to go see it." Jordan's question was entirely rhetorical and Mavis knew it. So, she agreed to take half an hour out of her day to take a side trip up Little River.

Neither before had Jordon or Mavis ever owned or run a private enterprise. They knew about working hard and collecting wages for their labor. Neither one asked to see the books on the income and expenses of The Little River Store. Neither one thought to consult an accountant to determine if the business activities of the property would cover their underlying mortgage. By five o'clock that evening, Mavis and Jordon had signed the papers to become the next owners of The Little River Store and imaginary resort property.

The foregoing information Jordon had given to me in a rambling and disjointed narrative during his first session. And today's session was approximately fifty-three weeks downstream from the date of their purchase of the store. Mavis had left Jordon and Ringo just under three weeks ago because they had not been able to cover their expenses for over six months. Their life savings were fully depleted. Mavis now knew what the previous owners had gone through, and she knew that the Johnson pockets weren't deep enough to last until the beady-eyed salesman could help them find another sucker. Under the stress and strain of it all, Jordon continued to emotionally unravel. His grasp of reality had been marginal when first he pulled into Glide to examine the colliding rivers. Now he was spending his days hallucinating, having imaginary conversations with Bill Lear, the inventor of the Lear Jet, and the eight-track tape player. Together, Jordon and the invisible Bill Lear were inventing a perpetual motion machine that would revolutionize all modes of transportation worldwide.

Also, I needed Doctor Gray's prescriptive help.

Worlds Apart

8

In my few spare moments, I'd been wondering what might make Drain and Yoncalla think they were the most underserved and in need of mental health services. From Doctor Gray I now had the name of the person he thought would be invaluable to my entering and understanding this neighborhood. Yet I still didn't have a clue about the mental health needs of these two small rural communities. What was going on in these places that would inspire them to lean on the Board of County Commissioners for locally delivered services?

While puzzling on these curiosities, I carried my brown bag lunch into the break room where Hugh had already landed and parked behind one of Tom Robbins's novels, avariciously devouring the book in one hand and the tuna salad sandwich in the other. Hugh looked up from his book as I pulled a crummy metal stack chair free from a four high pile and plunked it down none too gracefully beside him. "May I join you?" I asked.

"Too late for permission. You're already here." He accurately observed. His smile was inviting even if his response was somewhat terse and ambiguous.

"Since I've unfortunately interrupted your concentration, would you be open to some further conversation about the satellite project?" I ventured, "If I'm not asking at a bad time."

"This is as good a time as any. Your interest and pursuit of the idea is terrific. A weaker person might just procrastinate, in an attempt to ditch the whole notion. I sure don't want to dump any cold water on your interest," he said. "It is totally amazing to me how two little towns less than 10 miles apart could be so strikingly different. With all the school district mergeritis that's going on all around the country in the name of efficiency, you might think that the schools in Yoncalla and Drain would be ideal candidates for something like that. But they wouldn't even consider it. The families that comprise the population of Yoncalla District are pioneer farmers, with family roots going back to the covered wagons traversing the Oregon Trail. They think of themselves as established and possessing a bit of cultural refinement. Their school board meetings are held on tractors out in the middle of somebody's pasture. When the local paper pressed them about adhering to the open meeting law, their public information officer pointed out that you just can hardly get more open than a pasture. Anybody with a tractor is welcome! On the other hand, the citizens and taxpayers of the Drain School District are hardworking, hard drinking, tobacco chewing loggers and mill hands who consider the landed residents of Yoncalla as rather uppity. They think of themselves as inhabiting two different worlds."

"OK, but why in the world are they asking for locally delivered mental health services? I would have guessed that the one would want a first class feed and seed store and the other would be trying to track down saw filers. Where did they each come up with the idea that they want to see more of us?" I asked.

"That's what is so blasted interesting about these parallel requests. In each case, the Mayday requests are howling out of each school district office. Each has a slightly different problem to address. And you know darn well that they haven't been talking to each other about their in-house problems. So it is simply amazing synchronicity that we are receiving simultaneous requests for support services from each district." Hugh said.

"Amazing indeed. What can you tell me about each presenting problem?" I replied.

"The story we got from the Yoncalla Superintendent centers on the salesmanship of the foster parent recruiter for Children's

Services, who evidently knows how to play a masterful guilt trip on the hearts and minds of the good Christian farmers up there. I mean, so masterful is his pitch that Yoncalla High School now has a 20 percent foster kid population. The classroom discipline has gone out the window. Some of these troubled teens are tough customers, runaways from drug-affected families and the like. Simply put, this little country high school doesn't know what hit it or what to do about it. They think we, I mean you, are going to fix it. You are aren't you?" he asked.

"What about Drain?" I asked, ducking his question by tossing him another question. That's the oldest trick in the mental health domain, but I needed to buy some time before trying to steal the cheese from his trap.

"Their concern is more endogenous in nature. The rate of alcoholism in the households of the Drain District is the highest of any place in the country. It's probably a badge of honor to work hard all day and drink all night among some loggers and mill workers; however, intoxication tends to really foul up parent discipline and domestic harmony. In Drain, the elementary school is taking the brunt of this dysfunctional family stuff. The little kids come to school from a culture of chaos, and the school expects them to sit in their little seats and keep their hands to themselves, etc. A couple of teachers have been reduced to tears in their attempts to manage the classroom. One of them says it's like trying to create order in a room full of woodpeckers overdosed on caffeine. Anyway, they are looking to us, I mean you, to fix it. OK?"

"I think there are some Jesus sandals in my closet, but I don't have them with me today. On second thought, they probably wouldn't do me much good anyway. I suppose they wear steel toed boots in Drain and cow shit brown farmer boots in Yoncalla. This is going to be exciting," I said.

"All kidding aside, now that you know the total load, are you still willing to tackle these red ant piles? If so, what would be your strategy.

I hope you realize that we don't want to devour or run you off in this first month!" Hugh had a bit of protective father in his delivery just then.

"I do have a strategy, as a matter of fact. And it comes from my personal survival philosophy. Part one of the strategy is to take no greater interest in these problems than each district does. In other words, they have to participate in the solution attempt on an equal and full partner basis. I'm not going to Lone Ranger either one. If they don't come up with a Tonto, it would be a no go. My off the cuff plan would be a counseling group in each school, co-lead by the person they designate to be my partner. One being at the high school and one being in an elementary school, they will each have a distinctive focus and flavor. If we get shot down, at least we can spread the blame around, keeping some of our dignity intact," I said.

"I like it. I like it a lot. If the districts don't partner up with you, it will be a non-starter. And, we'll tell the Board of Commissioners that the schools are not serious about their requests," he said, as if he really thought my plan had a chance.

In the afternoon, I was scheduled to make my first visit to Douglas Community Hospital. I'm finding that one of the things I really like about this new job is the variety. The Family Service Clinic of Douglas County just happens to be the only mental health services provider between Eugene and Grants Pass. That's 64 miles north and over 80 miles to the south. And, east to west, the territory would run from the Cascade divide to Kona, Hawaii, assuming that the Big Island had a clinic. Private practice in Douglas County would be non-existent for another decade.

You think I'm kidding about our western reach, but in truth, Reedsport has some nautical types who venture well beyond sight of the lighthouse. And, they were all our potential clients. Alcohol and drug dependent, anxious or depressed, broken marriages and fractured families, suicidal or schizophrenic or bi-polar, learning disabled or oppositional, they sought us out because we were all they had.

As hospitals go, Douglas Community was no beauty. It was all on one floor, with the rooms strung out along several long drab antiseptic hallways that were painted a light institutional shade of green. The long tube fluorescent lighting scheme didn't do anything to warm up the stark corridors. I'm thinking as I my stroll down the B wing, "If you're not depressed before your admission, just wait until you are confined to this impersonal space for an uncertain stretch."

Monica was on a two-physician hold in Douglas Community Hospital, which meant that she was an involuntary patient, and in her case, it was a result of an attempted suicide. In her mid-twenties, so roughly my own age at that time, she had ingested a massive amount of prescription medication, a full month's supply of her mother's painkiller. It was hard to judge her height as she was in a reclined position in her hospital bed, but I could see that she had wavy light brown hair and appeared to not be particularly skinny or over weight, and she was not unattractive in spite of the dark circles under her eyes and the frown on her face. I am, by nature I guess, curious about what thoughts and beliefs were waiting to be discovered behind that frown and those heavily circled eyes that my grandmother would have referred to as two burnt holes in a mattress pad.

Depression is one thing. Suicide ideation and activity are something else. My meager experience tells me that depression is the emotional result of being overly serious, overly responsible, and usually unrealistically perfectionist, or all of the above. In other words, eventually we get pretty beaten up by our own mistaken beliefs that we can and should be a lot more than we are. In the words of Alcoholics Anonymous, some of us imagine that we should be our own "Higher Power." Recovery from depression comes when we can give up unrealistic beliefs about ourselves, and accept the fact that we are mortal, imperfect and limited by our simple-minded humanity. On the other hand, I have come to believe that suicide carries with it the underlying notion that for some reason or another life is a mistake. Very early in life, certainly before we have enough data to dispute the idea, someone or the situation strongly suggests that we are in the way, unnecessary, and shouldn't be here in the first place. In transactional analysis theory terms, a "don't be" script gets implanted. It is through this lens that I am seeing Monica for the first time.

"Who the hell are you, and maybe you should just get out the way you came in." That was her cheery greeting as I knocked on the door and then, hearing no reply, stuck my head into the room.

"Good afternoon, Monica. My name is Jim, and I'm the fortunate, tall skinny guy they sent over here from the Family Service Clinic to find out why you are trying to kill yourself." No reason to pussyfoot around, I thought.

"You sure are Mister Tact," She replied.

"Probably a poor choice of words on my part. I apologize if you think I'm too abrupt, but I don't know how much time we have for you to reconsider the self-harm thing you have going on here. Would you commit to the idea of no more self-harm while you are in this hospital? I would appreciate it, as it would give us some time to see if together we could improve on your situation or mind-set to any degree."

"Yeah, OK. I'll behave until after discharge, but I don't really expect to feel any different when I leave here than I did when those EMTs and that policeman brought me in," she said.

"All right, no promises, we'll just do the best we can," I replied. "How long have you felt depressed?"

"My entire life, right up 'til and including this very moment... I cannot remember a time when I didn't feel depressed," she said, just as a matter of fact with no inflection whatsoever.

"And, how long have you felt so despondent or hopeless that you would consider yourself to be suicidal?" I asked.

"The desire to end it all comes and goes in intensity, but it never really goes away either," her response continuing to just sound like an objective fact, with no drama mixed in at all.

"Thank you for being so honest with me. That gives me hope that we can really work together to figure this thing out. It's kind of like a puzzle... To figure out how or where you came to believe that your life was a mistake, that you aren't wanted, that you are in the way or worthless. We have to find out where this poison comes from... and come up with the effective antidote," I said.

To my surprise, she asked me how much time I had, because she had a lot to say on those topics.

"Well, today we have about another 20 minutes, but you are on a 72 hour hold, so we can meet every day for the next three days if you would like. And then you would have to help me decide what to do after that."

"That suits me just fine. I can't remember a time when someone took an interest in what I am thinking and feeling. My mom's favorite expression was, "Why don't you shut the f... up and quit your whining. Guys usually just want sex."

First Candy and now Monica. Do wounded women have a certain magnetism for abusive men, or are men generally abusive and I just hadn't been paying close enough attention to notice? I decided to address the mother side of her presentation and ignore the "men are thoughtless users" portion.

"Ouch! That's part of the poison right there. Part of the 'Don't feel, don't bother me and go away' script. Your mom sounds like a very angry or unhappy person. Do you know anything about her story? Like why is she so unhappy and not wanting to be a mother to a beautiful little girl?"

"I don't know much about her, except I hate her and haven't seen her in a couple of years. I kicked her out of my life because she has been a hateful, mean and neglectful bitch to me," she said.

"You may have kicked her out of your life in a physical sense, but you haven't kicked her out mentally. You seem to still be living out her attitude about your worth and the value of your life. If you hate her so much, does it make any sense to let her define you? Does it make any sense to let her and abusive men decide what you and your life are good for?" I finally had the courage to bring the men back into my response.

"When you put it that way, I guess not. But getting shed of her influence on me doesn't seem to me like it's going to be that easy." That was her very reasonable reply.

"OK, you have a point there, because she started sending out her angry, hurtful and rejecting message before you could even comprehend language perhaps. However, even babies can read body language and pick up the sense of welcome or its absence. Don't you think so? Neveretheless, you certainly do have the power in the present to begin to dispute her idea for your identity. Which means you can put some energy into what you want to be, instead of wasting all your energy into hating the hater." I saw Monica nodding in the affirmative, though she remained quiet as if she was taking time to chew on and perhaps digest some of what I'd suggested.

It was in this pregnant pause that something as yet unidentified was screaming for my attention. "Hold on a moment. I think my mind is failing me, or perhaps I misheard something you said. It's about your mother. It's the part about not having seen her for a couple of years. If I remember correctly, the admitting chart notes stated that you ingested a huge amount of your mother's pain pills. How do all these pieces fit together?" It's her mystery, I thought, and she can help me with it.

"I broke into her house when I knew she would be at work. She is such a creature of habit; I knew when she'd be gone and exactly where to look. And, I stole them," she said without the slightest apparent touch of guilt or remorse.

"Oh my gosh, I am so dense, but I think I am starting to get it. You are so hurt and angry at your mother that you wanted in your death to send her the message that she was in some way responsible for your death. Is that somewhat correct?" I found myself saying.

"You got it. That's why when you said I needed to stop wasting my time hating the hater... I mean, I never ever thought about it that way before."

In the next few moments, I found my brain looking for a strategy, a way forward for Monica.

"If it's all right with you, I would like to give you some homework for tomorrow's session before we wrap up for today," I said.

"OK. I'm not going anywhere, and I can't stand watching crap on television. So, what is it?"

"I'm going to loan you this spiral notebook and my pen. I want you to write the first chapter of your biography. And, I want you to title it: 'On the Day of My Birth.' On that topic, I want you to write anything that comes to mind. Then, tomorrow we can take a look at it together."

Monica took a firm hold on the notebook and pen. And, after another minute of silence, she said, "I'll see you tomorrow then. Will it be about the same time as today?"

"As close to it as possible. If for any reason it won't work at this time, I'll get a message to you about the change," I said. There was a handshake offered and received. Then I was out the door to finish the day at the clinic before heading home.

Namesake

9

Things were winding down when I arrived back at the clinic. The waiting room chairs sat quietly by themselves, unoccupied. Of the administrative staff, only Betty and Diane remained. Betty inquired about my hospital visit. I responded that my patient was still alive and wanted to see me tomorrow. "Thanks for asking," I said as I bounded up the stairs, intending to finish the chart notes before heading home. Dr. Gray was just entering the second floor hall from the east end as I arrived at the door to my office.

"Mind if I stop by for a moment?" he asked.

"I'd be honored. Come have a seat if you like," I replied. "What brings you by my humble suite? I didn't mess up on something, did I?"

After gently lowering his very substantial frame into one of my cushy seated stack chairs, he said, "No, it's nothing like that. Just an update on a couple of things is all. Item number one, I wrote out the prescription for your patient out on Little River. Do you want me to call it in, or do you want to hand it off to the gentleman yourself?"

"If it's not too much trouble, please call it in to Harvard Avenue Pharmacy, you know the one that sells all those cartons of cigarettes at a discount. By the way, that really sounds like a conflict of interest to me, but they must think of it as seeding the lungs of future customers. Anyway, I think Jordon is coming into town again tomorrow afternoon, and could swing by there before he heads home. Thanks a lot for helping us out... again. What might be your other items?"

"Well," he began, "Hugh and Gary are gone, and I am dying to tell someone. This afternoon, a woman psychiatrist from Colorado stopped into my office. She is from Pueblo, Colorado... the State Psychiatric hospital in Pueblo. I looked over her resume, and it looks pretty good. Medical degree from Penn State, and a residency in Kansas, she has seven or eight years post residency experience. I told her to come back tomorrow so that Hugh and I can interview her together. We may not have her references by then, but we can pull them in later."

I could see a gleeful spark in his eyes, as if he had just spotted a 20-dollar bill in the bushes. "I hope this works out for you tomorrow, but between you and me, you are a lot better psychiatrist than most that I've met," I said with quiet certainty.

"Thank you for your vote of confidence, but I'm spread way too thin. Two years ago, I managed to talk the Commissioners into including money to hire a psychiatrist in the Department budget. If we don't land, one before this fiscal year ends, that would be June 30th, we may not have another shot at it for who knows how long.

Oh yes, on another topic before I forget it. I saw your namesake today. I've got a patient, an old World War II Vet, who is commonly referred to as Frenchy. I don't exactly know how he came upon that handle. Well, perhaps it's because he is a non-stop wine drinker, and he wears that funny type of hat made famous by French winos. Anyway, he came by this morning holding his groin with an old blue bath towel. I could see straight away that there was a significant quantity of blood on the towel and he was clutching it to himself as hard as he could to stave off the blood flow. His considerable self-sedation notwithstanding, I could see that the poor old boy was in a lot of pain. 'What seems to be the problem, Frenchy,' I ask him.

"'Oh Doc, I think I've really done myself in this time. You see here, I've got myself a terrible gash right here beneath my testicular sack. I'm bleeding. I came over here as quick as I could hobble and hold this towel at the same time!' That's what the old boy said."

"Let me take a look at that wound. Let's unwrap this situation and have a look," I told him. And there it was, this nasty puncture wound squarely between his scrotum and ass. In all my years as a physician, I have never seen anything like it. "That wound is going to need a good cleaning and a few stitches, then tetanus shot for good measure," I told him. Then, I couldn't help myself. I said,"Frenchy, how in the world did you get this wound?"

"'It was my masturbation machine what did it,'" he told me.

Doctor Gray let out a small sigh, and said, "I asked him about this masturbation machine of his. He told me it was his own invention, and that right up until the accident he was thinking about getting a patent on it! He said it was a combination of a sheepskin and a saber saw held in a vice. He said everything was proceeding in a very pleasant manner until the vibration of the saber saw set it loose from the vice and then the saw came after him! Can you believe it?"

"Who needs fiction when reality has so much bite!" I replied. "This was a very entertaining tale, and I certainly have enjoyed it. But what prompted you to tell it to me?"

"Oh yes, I left off that part. Frenchy's given name is James Henson. I don't think you have too much to worry about though. Beyond the staff at the Veteran's Hospital and myself, I doubt that anyone else in the County knows what his name is," he concluded.

After Doctor Gray gave a conciliatory nod and left my office, I had a lot to think about as I gathered files, put them away and made my way to the now empty parking lot.

As it turned out, I had something to worry about because a few weeks later I received a letter from a collection agency on behalf of the 24 Hour Mini Mart. They had extended credit to Frenchy, AKA James Henson.

Guilt Socks

10

It is only eight or 10 blocks to the 24 Karat Apartments from the Family Service Clinic, and if I had the brains God gave a cootie, I'd leave the car at home and walk the distance. At times like this I miss my English three speed road bike... the one stolen from our back porch on the north side of Chicago. They were secured to a large metal pipe that held up the roof over the porch by means of a heavy-duty steel chain and master combination padlock. The gate between the two houses and the backyard fence stood eight feet high. How in the hell did someone know the bikes, mine and my wife's, were there for the taking? And how did they cut the chain and loft the bikes over the eight-foot fence or locked gate? How did we sleep through the entire episode? How could this have possibly been a noiseless operation? I shouldn't complain. The insurance money went to a good cause. The move and the Toyota fund got a boost from the sale of the camper bus and the insurance check.

I pulled myself out of this rumination as I rolled to a stop in front of the 24 Karat. As I may have implied earlier, this building is no gem. The name comes from the fact that it had been built and was still owned by a now retired jeweler. But this beauty had seen better days, and better tenants, and the moss on the roof is now thicker by far than the composition shingles. This place is just a pit stop in the race to get relocated and begin to orient ourselves to our new situation.

"I think I heard gun shots in the parking lot last night. Did you hear the gunshots?" Annis Rae said to me after I got in the door. There was a distressed look on her sweet, innocent, trusting face.

"You know me. I'm the guy who could sleep all the way to San Diego on a Trailways bus." Also the one who could fall asleep in the middle of a sentence with my college roommate, whether he or I was the one making conversation! "I didn't hear a thing. Perhaps it was a car back-firing down Winchester Avenue," I said reassuringly.

"Maybe," she said," but there is a lot of activity going on in that parking lot during the night. Believe me, there is!" She's a light sleeper, and can tell if our baby's breathing pattern changes, or if he lets a fart.

Whether we were any safer on the premises of 24 Karat than we were on Dayton Street, in Chicago's Lincoln Park continued to be the topic of conversation until our weary heads hit the pillows, and gravity pulled our eyelids shut. It was agreed that tomorrow, one of us was going to hot foot it down to the newspaper office while the ink was still wet, so that we could get a jump on new rental listings.

Back at the office the next morning, I could hear the plans being made for Hugh and Doctor Gray to meet with the potential new don't-look-the horse-in-the mouth staff psychiatrist. Hugh looked as skeptical about the deal as I felt, while Doctor Gray seemed to bubble with enthusiasm over our sudden good fortune. It didn't take them long to arrive at a deal to meet with Dr. Etta Puhak (pronounced Poohawk) about 2:30 in the afternoon. The whole mental health staff was buzzing with curiosity. No one but Doctor Gray had even seen this mystery woman.

My morning was a blur of profuse activity. Candy called and left a message that she had survived a meeting with Umpqua Community College admissions personnel, and was scheduled to take the Strong Vocational Aptitude test. "Maybe they can help me figure out what my talents might be!" That was her closing line.

After his meeting with Dr. Gray, Hugh found me in records storage pulling the day's files. "Say," he said, "I think you and I should consider doing an adult therapy group together. What do you think of the idea?"

"I think I would like that. How did you come up with that idea," I replied.

"It was your resume and specifically the reference page that put me on to the idea. Back when I was scanning your employment application, I noticed that Gene Aronowitz from Jane Adams Hull House was one of your references. He's a pretty famous fellow, past president of the AGPA and all that. And a published author to boot. I called him to see if he really did know you from a pile of sticks. And, you know what he told me? He said you helped him create a neighborhood elementary therapeutic classroom with both student and parent therapy groups and that you were his co-therapist in both of those groups."

"I hate to shoot down your bubble about what a great catch I am, but have you actually read any of Gene's journal articles?" I asked.

"Uh, no. But none the less, that is, I think, a mighty impressive reference. How are you going to shoot down my bubble?"

"Gene was my field supervisor at Hull House. He invented the therapeutic classroom idea with kid and parent groups, but Gene is as strict a behaviorist as I've ever met. We were doing beanbag therapy in the kids group and the parents were on a token economy reward system for time spent reading to their children. Even though Hull House had quite a bit of success with this model, I personally hope never to replicate those types of groups again in my lifetime. Make no mistake, I love and admire Gene, but it just isn't in me to be a strict behaviorist... especially in an adult group with people of average or better intelligence," I said.

"Let me put it another way, then." Hugh said. "I believe you have some valuable group therapy background. And I would like us to do an adult therapy group together, no bean bags! OK."

"If you say so, but believe me, it will be a learning experience for both of us," I replied.

A full tilt schedule took care of the remainder of the morning, and

after lunch, my thoughts were on two divergent paths. One part of my brain was preparing to head back to Douglas Community Hospital for round two with Monica, while another part of my brain kept drifting off to the meeting scheduled with a prospective new psychiatrist, an interview at which I would not be present, but about which I was having some ominous premonitions.

At 2:31 PM, I rapped on the door to the secure patient room. I was surprised to see that the hospital staff had propped the door to a half-open position. People on hold seldom are given that option. Monica acknowledged my knock and invited me in with a very special greeting. "You're late. We have a lot of work to do!"

This was not the welcome I expected. Gone was the edgy negative tone of voice. There was by no means a playful quality to it. It was, I could feel, serious and business like. Somehow, Monica had charmed the nursing staff into allowing her to wear civilian clothes and into bringing two chairs into the room. In addition, staff had allowed her to have something of a lapboard apparatus, upon on which she had evidently been writing up a storm. Ordinarily, the secure room was pretty much full of nothing.

"Hello to you too!" I said, while making my way to the unoccupied of the two chairs. "How did you manage to round up chairs, a lap desk and get the door to spring open? I've never seen anything like this in the hold room?" I asked. And it hit me immediately that Monica seemed less vulnerable. She possessed a shade of take charge to her manner that was surprising. And, the snarl was missing.

"I just told Reggie, she's the RN in charge of this area, about my writing assignment. I can't write while lying down, and then it didn't feel right to be writing with the door closed. And, as you can see from this pile of scratch, I have been pretty much writing non-stop since you left yesterday afternoon. I did sleep a little." She paused for a moment when she observed my wrinkled forehead and questioning gaze. I believe she was trying to read my mind, and perhaps expected that criticism might be coming. "I think she checked with the doctor

whose supposed care I'm under to get the 'official approval.' I don't want to get Reggie in trouble. She is a kind person and was only trying to help. You're not mad at me are you?" She asked with worried, searching eyes.

"Not in the least, I am not upset with you at all. What I am is totally astounded at your powers of persuasion. Never have I seen a person turn a hold room into an office. You must have been incredibly convincing to Reggie," I ventured.

"I suppose we will be getting to that when we start looking at what I've written. I have made a few discoveries since last night, but I think part of it was your fault too. Reggie said that there was a note in the hospital chart from you. And, it described my homework as well as the fact that I promised not to injure myself further while in the hospital. So she said she thought it would be all right if she helped me get set up to do my homework," she said. Again, she was trying to read my expression, and concluded, "I didn't get Reggie in trouble, did I?"

Monica seemed extraordinarily sensitive to the possibility that I may not be happy with her and or with her in charge nurse. In short, she appeared to have a very strong resident pleaser inside of her. "To be honest with you, I am going to have a conversation with this Reggie person, but she's not in trouble either. As long as we are all on the same team, the one aimed at putting you on sturdier feet before you leave the hospital, then all is well with me."

"I'm so glad. You had me worried with that puzzled expression you were wearing. Would you like to see where my writing is taking me?" She asked.

"Of course I would. Where do you want to start?" I asked.

"On the day that I was born, which was December 26th, 1944, Mom and Grandmother Wilson were at Mercy Hospital awaiting my arrival. My dad was out in the South Pacific ... on a ship somewhere I think. As I was writing, I discovered that I couldn't understand my story without backing up to a point almost a year before the day of my birth. That's because Mom and Grandmother seemed to be enemies.

It's as if they hated each other long before I got here or my arrival created their hatred. Could it be that I heard them arguing with each other while I was still in my mother's abdomen? Anyway, I have this feeling that their fight with each other started long before my birth. As early as I can remember, they were always hissing and verbally bashing each other, and I didn't know what it was about. For the longest time I tried to understand, and I guess I tried to be a pesky little peacemaker. And, it always seemed like my mother was furious with me. Always, except when Grandmother was angry with me. In that one instance, she would kind of come to my defense. It's always been confusing to me. Why did she hate me so much? So, do you know what I decided to do last light?" She took a pause to breathe.

"I can't guess," I said to Monica, but to myself I thought that she was making a huge effort to reconstruct and understand her history and the motivations behind mother and grandmother's antipathy.

"Reggie let me get on the phone and call my mom!" She spoke with some confidence and enthusiasm. I could tell that she was still trying to read my face for approval again, but there was also present a sense of self-approval that she had done the right thing.

"That darn Reggie! She seems to be your co-conspirator. All right, and I can guess that, since your mother is such a complete creature of habit, you knew that in two years' time she would still have the same phone number and you knew when you could find her at home," I said, with my detective face on. "You look like you survived this self-appointed adventure in pretty good shape. Are you better off now than before the call?" I wanted her to know that I was listening and paying attention, but I didn't want to hurry or bias her telling of her story.

"Well, it wasn't easy or all nicey nice, but I think I might be better off. I went right at her from the get-go. I asked her why she hated me so much, and I think it surprised her and put her a little off balance. She usually seems so self-righteous, and certain about everything. But she just stammered around for a while, and finally asked me where

I was and why I was calling. And, I told her ... that I broke into her house, stole her prescription, tried to kill myself, and was calling from the hospital. Might as well give her the entire load, I thought. It was very quiet on her end of the line for a while after that. Then, almost in a whisper, she said she didn't hate me. She said she hated her mother and she hated the situation, back then, all those years ago. She said maybe we should talk. Maybe we should, I told her. She's coming in this evening after she gets off work. What do you think about that?" she said calmly.

"If you and Reggie like this idea, I won't stand in the way, but be prepared for the fact that it may be the most difficult conversation you've ever had. You are an adult now. That makes a big difference. I believe you can handle it, no matter what she has to say. By the way, your involuntary hold is up tomorrow. The hospital can't keep you here past noon tomorrow without your consent. I'm only going to ask one thing of you. Please finish your own history, 'The day I Was Born,' before discharge if you go home tomorrow."

"Yes I will, but would you please come by here sometime in the morning to help me decide if I am ready to be discharged," she asked.

"I'll make it a priority to be here before 11:00 AM. Thanks for asking. See you then," I said. Very delighted with the spirit of this last exchange, I made my way down the long antiseptic smelling hallway and out the door into the fresh afternoon air. Well, OK, there was the aromatic scent of wood smoke, but it still beat the stinky cocktail that passed for air inside the building.

Meanwhile, things were beginning to quiet down at the clinic when I returned in the late afternoon. Denny greeted me with a pleasant smile planted halfway between his chin and shiny dome. "How was Douglas Community?" he said.

"If I knew how to roller skate, and if I wouldn't look out of place with a respirator on my nose, it would be perfect," I said, hoping he would catch my allusion to the long hallways and air quality.

"The ambience of the place doesn't appeal to me either. How goes it with the woman on hold?" he asked, not wanting to be diverted from the intent of his initial inquiry.

"Who knows if she'll be ready for discharge or a commitment hearing tomorrow, but I think she has made tons of progress since her admission. Before the clock strikes 12 tomorrow, I'll have to make up my mind." I don't know what kind of an answer he was looking for, but he seemed satisfied that I wasn't just ducking him as I might have been in the first instance. My sense of patient confidentiality extends to everyone not authorized by the patient, even other staff unless there is a clear and convincing reason to share, even if it's an involuntary case.

"Good luck in the morning then. By the way, I have that river all figured out now. The third time's going to be the charm. You want to come with me this Saturday?" he asked playfully.

"I did check with my better half, and she said I was correct in my assumption that she would kill me if I became a blue floater in the Umpqua." It was easier to put this decision on Annis than to admit that I did not have the requisite skills for this misadventure. And, since he was a two-time loser on this stretch of river, I certainly had no reason to trust in his skills to protect us.

"You're going to miss out on a lot of fun," he said, but he knew he'd lost the sale.

There was only one more topic that I wanted to pursue before heading home, and I thought Denny might have the answer. So I asked. "Denny, do you happen to know how the hiring interview went this afternoon with that psychiatrist from Colorado?"

"Oh, they hired her, all right. And Doctor Gray bounced out of here as happy as if he was Tigger, out of Winnie the Pooh. Hugh, on the other hand, looked a little nauseous and went home early." Denny seemed to pick up on the same dichotomy that had struck me earlier. It was as if they were looking at the same subject through opposite ends of the telescope. Could the new psychiatrist be more than Hugh thought or less than Doctor Gray imagined? "I guess we'll just have to wait to see how it turns out," he said.

"Thanks for your observation. See you tomorrow," I said before we parted ways and headed for our respective consultation rooms. I thought about dropping in on Gary for his opinion, but his door was closed and I couldn't even tell if he was still in there, or whether he had a client with him. So, I finished scribbling my chart notes, stuffed them in the file cabinet, and headed for home.

Annis greeted me at the door to our upstairs apartment in the 24 Karat building. "The police were here today looking for witnesses to the break-ins and fight we heard last night. I told them we heard it, but decided not to stick our noses out the window in the middle of the night. I called up several of the people with houses to rent in yesterday's newspaper, and they had already found tenants. Aaron was asleep at one o'clock when today's paper came off the press or I swear I would have marched right down there to get a jump on any new listings in today's classified section. The first day he's awake after lunch, we are going to charge down there, I swear."

"Hi, honey. How was your day," I said cheerily, but I could tell that this transition to the burg wasn't going that well for her. Aaron was thriving, eating, pooping, sleeping and making sweet noises. She didn't answer. In truth, I knew this was not Chicago, with friends, classes, diversity, culture, colleagues and hustle-bustle. Yes, it was also short on culture and diversity, even if Drain and Yoncalla thought they were polar opposites. "Getting that newspaper is a great idea. This place is just temporary," I said hoping to more closely match her sentiments.

I slept pretty well that night, though I know Annis did not. She hears every sound the baby makes and everything outside as well. Thank God, Aaron was a good sleeper from early on. I was really no help after 10:00 PM unless Annis physically rousted me to take a turn.

At work the next morning, Hugh announced that Dr. Puhak had been hired and would begin as staff psychiatrist on this coming Monday. His presentation didn't have any animation or sparkle. I was hoping he was just tired from the previous night with Fran and the five girls, but, deep down, I thought it had more to do with his lack of enthusiasm for the hiring of Doctor Puhak. He indicated that we would all be introduced to her on Monday morning, first thing, and that was that. We all dispersed to do our thing. On my way through the admin area, Diane handed me a message. "Jordon Johnson called. Says he wants an appointment, so I scheduled him in to see you on Monday. I hope that's all right," she said.

Sometimes the efficiency of this place takes me by surprise. "Thank you, Diane. I'm sure that will work out nicely. How did he sound?" I wanted to know.

It seemed to be her turn to be surprised. Perhaps other staff members didn't ask her what could be construed as a clinical question. "In my lay opinion, Jim, he sounded more coherent than I've ever heard him sound. He may not be out in left field any more, if you get my drift."

"Thanks again … for your wonderful help and off the cuff diagnosis," I said.

Before heading off for the Hospital, Hugh and I talked some more about creating a therapy group. Slowly some ideas were taking shape. A mutual commitment to confidentiality was rule number one. It would be a mixed gender group, if we could find any men with the courage to participate in it. It would not be a symptom specific group, but rather a group of men and women with a variety of presenting concerns and symptoms. In this way, we hoped to assemble a group with a variety of strengths. Unlike a 12-step group, group members could ask each other questions, but no one would be required to answer a question they were not prepared to answer. Throughout this conversation, I could see that Hugh had his sparkle back.

Soon, I was back on the road to Douglas Community Hospital.

After getting my exercise walking down that long corridor to Monica's room, I could see that her door was wide open from some distance away. Either she and her pal Reggie had completely removed all pretenses of "secure hold," or Monica had eloped from custody. Both ideas struck me at about the same time, but when I arrived at the open door, I was much relieved to see Monica, all showered, shampooed, and dressed in a pair of new jeans and a crisp white button up blouse. She was sitting in her "office," eagerly awaiting my arrival. "Knock, knock," I said, seeking permission to enter.

Monica played along as if we were enacting a knock, knock joke and said, "Who's there?"

"The same tall skinny guy they sent over here two days ago to find out why you were trying to bump yourself off. But you don't look a thing like the bedraggled person they sent me over here to see back then," I said.

"I have my mother to thank for the new jeans and shirt. But I have you to thank for putting me in a different life perspective. Please sit down. I have so much to tell you, I hardly know where to begin," she said.

"Do you want to start with your mother's visit, or your homework assignment... or someplace else," I prompted in a vague kind of way.

"It really all goes together and it's starting to make some sense. Mother said she didn't hate me, but she did hate my grandmother and the situation she found herself in on the day of my birth. When she was a teenager, she and grandmother used to have all out hissing, screaming fights. Mother said that my grandmother was so controlling, that she had to run away to get room to breathe. I didn't know this, but she ran away from home three times, the first time when she was 15. The third time she was 17, she ran away with my dad. He was two years older. Grandmother didn't go looking for her that time. They married the day she turned 18, and I think she must have gotten pregnant immediately because I was born seven months later."

"You were born two months short of full term?" I asked, as if naively.

"All right, you stickler for details, maybe they got a small head start. The important point is that my father was drafted into the service three months after their marriage. And pregnant, without a job, and trying to live on a Private's pay, she landed right back at grandmother's house!"

"The very situation she hated and tried so hard to leave... now she was back in it and trapped tighter than before," I chimed in. I couldn't help myself, honestly.

"You got it Sherlock. Then, to top it off, my father, who I never met, gets killed in the Pacific. So on the day of my birth, Mother tells me; her fate to live in perpetual hell is sealed! Anyway, that's how it looked to her. And I was right about Mom and Grandmother being at war with each other, but what I think I'm beginning to learn from this history is that Mom and Grandmother fought about everything, not just me. Their war with each other included me, but it actually began more than a decade before the day of my birth."

"Wow, and all this time you thought you caused this fight and created the perpetual hell?" I asked, hoping to underscore what seemed to be the conclusion to which she was coming. "And now you know it was there all the whole time, and you didn't cause it!"

And Monica murmured, "Yes," and "Yes."

We both sat quietly for I don't know how long. Then, when she finally broke the silence, she said, "You know, I am never going to try to kill myself again." And I just nodded gently in the affirmative. And, in the same soft but sure voice she asked, "Can I come see you at that clinic where you work?"

I didn't want her to see that I was choking back tears of joy, and I wasn't sure words would come out of my mouth right then, so I just blinked and nodded again. They teach you all that professional detachment crap at the University, don't you know. Finally, I recovered enough to say, "Sure." I handed her one of my newly minted cards. "You can call that number on the card before you even check out of here. Ask for Diane. She seems to be my guardian angel in the scheduling department." And I knew in my gut that she had turned a huge corner.

No sooner that I arrived back at the clinic, after a bite of lunch, than Betty said, "Better call your wife...as soon as possible," she urged.

"Thank you. I will," I said, as I took stairs two at a time. It's one of the advantages of being tall. The disadvantage, of course, is an open kitchen cabinet door that you don't know about until it's too late! Whatever the call is, I am figuring that it's important, because I don't believe that she has ever called me in the middle of the day at work before.

After scarcely more than two rings, I'm hearing Annis's excited voice. "I've got it. And we have an appointment to go see it, and it is ours, if we like it and can get there within the hour," she said, all in one breath.

In Annis's version of English, a pronoun is just as good as a noun any day, because they are shorter and therefore quicker. Her brain cells work much faster than those of an ordinary person. Nouns are a pokey waste of time. For normal people listening, sometimes it's hard to keep up. "Woe there, sweetheart. You got what? And we are going where in an hour if we like what?" I asked, knowing that, once again, I am miles back in the dust someplace, struggling to catch up.

"The newspaper, silly. And, there is a little house for rent. She says that it is less than three years old. It's clean, she says, and has recently been all repainted inside. Oh, and the location sounds good. The address is two or three blocks east of northeast Stevens. Do you know where that is?" Again, all in one breath!

At risk of wasting more precious time and sounding even sillier, I didn't bother asking if this "she" had a name. So, I said, "I am on my way home. There is a hole in my client schedule. This might just be a providential find."

Passing back through the admin area on my way to the car, I let Betty and Diane know what all the excitement was about, and where I was headed. Betty suggested that perhaps I should check with Roger in sanitation before signing any lease papers.

"There are some creative builders out in that neighborhood who are not very zealous about permits and building codes. Water and septic problems, and dubious construction techniques are common place out there," she warned.

Forewarned is forearmed, they say, but I knew that if the little house looked cleaner, safer, and seemed like an improvement on 24 Karat, we would not be sweating any jive building code violations. We would be moving. It wasn't like we were going to buy it. We just needed to live in it for a while, until we could save up a down payment for a place of our own.

Aaron was all bundled up, and the folded stroller was parked by the door next to the diaper bag. Annis was completely ready to roll out on the Stevens Avenue expedition. Soon, she was saying, "I see it on the map here. Two or three more blocks ahead, we'll take a right onto Follett Street. She said that it's a little yellow and white place with lots of windows, and it's at the end of the street, with a fairly steep driveway. She will be waiting for us."

Again, I refused to break the spell by asking Annis if this woman had a name, because I decided it was a detail I didn't need to know. I saw no one around the little house as we rolled to a stop. In the distance, out in an adjacent field, someone in a red plaid shirt and bib overalls was stirring up the dirt on a D-8 Cat. From what I could tell, it looked like excavation was under way to notch another home site into the hillside. The Cat was headed our way, and eventually it came to rest immediately across the street from our little house. Annis and I, without a word spoken between us since we coasted to a stop, had decided that it was our little house. It wasn't until after Donna had climbed off the D-8 and removed her hard hat, that we realized that there was a woman inside that plaid green and black shirt and overalls outfit.

"I'm Donna," she said, pulling off her glove and offering her hard working, calloused hand for a shake. "You would be the people who called about the rental." It was more of a statement than a question. We changed greetings and names, and then we took the tour. It was clean, freshly painted and absolutely rock solid safe. As Donna later proved on her backhoe, she was tougher than a scrub oak stump, and was not about to stand for any nonsense on her street. And, she didn't have much time for any "nincompoop building code inspectors" either! Yes, we would be safe from transients, drug pushers, smash and grab thieves, and code enforcement types. It was a secure and quiet neighborhood except when Donna was operating heavy equipment..., which as it turned out was only most of the daylight hours. We didn't have to sign a lease. Donna said a payment of first and last month rent plus a cleaning deposit would be all we needed to move in. It would be month to month after that. I had the distinct feeling that Donna liked this arrangement in case she decided to remove a tenant.

Some people dread Mondays. I love them. It's a trait that is attached to my basically curious nature. I can hardly contain my eager curiosity about Denny's third Umpqua River trip, and I imagine what kind of flowers to buy for Mary, his soon to be widow. And, Dr. Puhak, who is she, and what is she really like? And, will Jordon keep his appointment? Will Candy reschedule? Will Monica follow through with her post discharge plan? Things are revealed on Mondays that set the tone for an entire week. Who needs soap opera when real life is your viewing screen?

Denny wandered into the clinic at almost the precise moment that I did, and he looked none too happy. He still wore the battle scars of the previous two weekends, but something was different about his appearance, though I had not quite figured what it was that made the difference. "How was the river trek, Denny," I asked straight out.

"I lost my damn canoe and everything that was in it. That's how it was. I can't even go downstream to recover the damn thing. It got caught sideways headed into a chute, and the boat was essentially torn in half... nearly the same spot that I went over last week," he said, with his smooth baldhead down dejectedly.

I had to struggle to keep on a sympathetic face and suppress the giggle that wanted out of my throat. "That's a shame, Denny, but look on the bright side. I won't have to buy Mary flowers. You can still do it yourself."

"And that's not the only good outcome," he said. "As I went floating passed the brush that thrashed me weekend before last, I found my glasses clinging to an overhanging limb. So it was a good thing I took one more pass by there!"

"I knew you looked different this morning. That's it. You have your glasses back. Well, I am glad to see you made it back, and found your spectacles as a bonus. Where will you be paddling next weekend?"

"I'm going to give it a rest for a while. It will take some time and cash to line up a new boat," he said with grief but no remorse.

Within a few minutes, we were all gathered in the conference room, awaiting our much anticipated introduction to Dr. Puhak. I say all, but I mean all but Dr. Puhak. Hugh managed to ad-lib an agenda for about 30 minutes to put the best possible face on the situation, but everyone took turns glancing at the empty guest of honor chair... the one with the padded seat still intact. He was about to toss in his top hat and cane and end meeting when in walked the good doctor. I don't know how Hugh actually felt about the situation, but he appeared more relieved than disgruntled. He proceeded as the perfect and gracious host, and introduced us each to Dr. Etta Puhak. And, she advised us all that we could just call her Dr. Puhak (to heck with formality). Dressed entirely in black, perhaps five feet two or three inches in height, she presented as a serious if not somber soul. There wasn't much inflection in her speech or animation in her manner. There certainly was not a stitch of humor to be seen. I usually proceed with caution around people who are unable to laugh at themselves. And, whereas Hugh gave her a nutshell description of each of us, both as persons and employees, when he encouraged Dr. Puhak to share something about herself with us, she seemed to have little to tell beyond the bare facts that she was a medical doctor, and had most recently left a position of importance at the State Hospital in Pueblo, Colorado.

"Don't be too judgmental," I said to myself. "Don't judge a book by its cover." However, all that I could see was cover, and I was truly hoping for Doc Gray's sake that there was more to Dr. Puhak than camouflage. The fact that she had been hired before any of her references were in hand made me a bit skeptical.

After the meeting, the day rapidly began to pick up speed.

Monica, in her new jeans and blouse, was sitting on the edge of her chair in the waiting room, and stood up to greet me the moment I stepped down into that area. Exchanging brief and pleasant greetings, the two of us headed back up the stairs to my consultation room.

"I am completely delighted to see you out in the real world. Hospitals, courthouses and jail are my three least favorite places. It's better not to go there if you don't have to," I said.

"We are in total agreement there, except for the fact that I wouldn't be here if I hadn't been there. But I do not think I will be headed back, at least not for anything self-inflicted. Also, you should know that I have been giving considerable thought to your script idea. You know, the 'Don't be, you're in the way, not wanted' script. And, the more I've thought about it, the more it makes sense. For example, I can remember mom saying 'I wish you weren't here. I wouldn't be stuck in this hell hole.' That takes me a long way toward understanding why I was depressed and suicidal so much of the time. But what I can't figure out is why I have this chronic guilty feeling, even when there is no particular reason to feel that way."

"Can you remember a time early in your life when you felt this guilty feeling? Someone may have planted the seed 'Monica you should feel guilty,'" I suggested.

"Well, perhaps I can spot a few thousand early memories when I felt guilty. I think I learned very early on that Mother and Grandmother were enemies and in some weird kind of combat. I don't like to admit it out loud, but I think I learned how to play them against each other. Maybe that's where my guilt comes from."

"How did you play them against each other?" I asked.

"One time I can remember, I must have been three or four years old and it was winter time, my feet were cold and I didn't have any socks. Maybe I couldn't find any, or maybe they were all holey. I am not sure of the details any more, but, I remember asking Mother if I could have some new socks. She said, 'No you can't have new socks. Do you think I'm made out of money?' Actually, she screamed it. I know she did because Grandmother, who was several rooms a way, heard Mother's words and my sobbing.

"Grandmother came running into my bedroom, where all this commotion was going on, and said, 'Don't cry little Monica. I will get you some socks.' I think from that moment forward, I knew that if I really wanted something badly enough, all I had to do was to pit my mother against my grandmother. And, it could work either way. If Grandmother gave me an adamant 'no', I could pretty much count on a 'yes' from Mother. I knew I shouldn't do it, but that didn't stop me from doing it. On the one hand, I got the object that I thought I wanted. While on the other, this would always heighten the hatred and the ugliness exchanged between them. I won, sort of, and I also lost because I felt terrible after I had done it. Don't you see? It's kind of crazy. I hated how I felt afterward. I hated myself for doing it, but then I would do it all over again."

"You were having a fine war with yourself! The logical, practical you said, 'My feet are cold. I need socks.' Then, the little manipulator said, 'I could play Mother against Grandmother to get my socks. 'Then you would feel..."

"Tremendous guilt," she said.

"Would you consider doing a brief reenactment? Would you consider being the three or four year old version of yourself for a few moments?" I asked. "I would help you to relax and revisit that time and place, if you are willing."

"If you think that would help me, I would try it. What do you want me to do?"

"First, rest both feet on the floor. That's good just like that. Next, take a nice big breath, and as you do this, raise your arms up over your head. Then, as you slowly exhale, gradually lower your hands so that they comfortably rest in your lap. In this position, you will be supported by the chair and feel comfortably balanced. Now I would like to direct your attention to your breathing, gradually deeper, slower. Make it nice and full coming in. Then let it flow out smoothly as you exhale. Again, enjoy a wonderful full sensation as you breathe in, and pure relaxation as you slowly let it all out. And, your body will tell you when to resume that nice full breath, and when to let it go. If you feel relaxed now, just raise a couple of fingers on your right hand. Good. Now, as you enjoy your slow relaxing breath, when you are ready, I would like you to allow your chair to become a time machine. When you are comfortably seated in your time machine, again raise those two fingers on your right hand. Good. When you are ready, let your time machine take you slowly back to a place where, as an adult, you can observe your four-year-old self. When you can clearly see your four-year-old self, please raise those two fingers on your right hand. Good. When you can clearly see her bare feet, please raise those two fingers. Good. Notice how cold those little feet are. ("Very cold," Monica murmured.) Now, notice how small she is. ("Only four, very small," she whispered clearly.) Please let her know that you, as an adult, understand her needs, and that you will work hard to provide for her all the things she really needs. ("I am an adult now, and I can take care of you," she said in a quiet, confident voice.) Let her know that you forgive her for manipulating her mother and grandmother, and she does not ever have to do that again. ("I forgive you for being little and needy and tricky," she continued.") From this time forward, you will listen to her whenever she identifies a real need, and find a healthy way to meet that need. And together you will agree to leave the old guilt in the past, where it belongs. ("We both agree to leave the old guilt in the past... where it belongs," she whispered.)

"Monica, when you are ready to come back to the present time, please raise those two fingers," I said, very quietly.

Several moments passed without a sound or motion, but then she raised her fingers. "All right then, I am going to begin slowly counting backwards from four as your time machine chair returns to the present. At the count of zero, you will be back to the present with the new knowledge you have gained. Four, three, two, one, zero..." I said.

In a brief few moments, Monica opened her eyes. A small smile came to her face, and it kept growing until her entire face lit up. "Thank you," she said, with warmth I had never before seen in her.

Lay Diagnosis
11

It was the last appointment of the morning, and in walked Jordon Johnson. I mean, he bypassed the waiting room and all the staff in the admin area and strolled right into my consultation room. How he did this without anyone noticing, I will probably never know. He picked up on the quizzical expression on my face, and asked if he had arrived on the correct day, at the appointed hour. I reassured him that his timing was perfect, but usually the downstairs staff members, also known as the waiting room mafia, would signal me when a client had arrived, so that I could come down to the waiting-room to make the greeting, in case the previous appointment ran over, or I happened to be on the phone or something.

"Oh, sorry," he said. "I thought maybe I could be efficient and save you a few steps. I found a shortcut up the east end stairs. Next time, I promise, I'll behave better."

"That was very thoughtful of you to go with efficiency, but it would be better if you let the waiting room mafia do their thing. If it's OK with you, I will close the door so that we can have some privacy and get our session under way," I said. "Now bring me up to speed. How are you feeling, what are you thinking, and what's going on in your life?"

"Physically I am feeling better than I have in years, but mood wise, I'm all over the map. The bank is going to foreclose on our property, Jim. Mavis saw it coming way before I did. Or maybe I saw it coming too, but just couldn't get my mind around it. I couldn't accept the fact that my dream was falling into the crapper. That's probably why

I ended up on these here pills. I couldn't take reality and had to go someplace else for a while. Mavis, she went back to Long Beach. Me, on the other hand, I guess I went a little bit crazy, didn't I? On the bright side, though, I have been talking to Mavis every day on the phone," he said. The frown lines left his forehead, and a smile moved in to replace the look of despondency.

"That's wonderful," I said in response to the change in affect.

"Yes indeed, it is wonderful. She loves me, you know, and wants me back. She said this morning that I sounded real good, that I was getting my shit together and such. I am much in debt to you and Doc Gray for all you have done for me," he said.

"No you are not in debt, Jordon. If you didn't have a need that we could help with, we wouldn't have a job. We are, as they say in Fiddler on the Roof, a perfect match. We were just in the right place at the right time to be of great help to each other," I said.

"Boy, I sure never thought about it that way. Anyhow, you guys are pretty great in my book. And, I won't ever forget you either," he said.

"Jordon, believe me, you are going in my book also. Now, tell me what your plan looks like going forward."

"The 30 day notice came in a package I had to sign for on Tuesday, I've got slightly more than three weeks to get packed up and out for good. Realistically speaking, packing up should not pose much of a challenge. I don't have much left. The old Dodge should handle it. Ringo and I are headed back to Long beach to hook up with Mavis, if she'll have us, and I think she will. I called my old boss. He left Lockheed not too long after I did and bought a Service Master franchise. He says I have a spot with him, if I want it. It's a start," he said. "So, guess I'll be around here another two, maybe three weeks."

"Jordon, you not only look good, you sound good! You have perspective. You have your dog. You probably have Mavis, and you definitely have a plan. Could you do one thing for me before you leave this valley?"

"Anything for you, my friend. Do you want me to shoot and dress a deer for ya?" he asked. "There are some big trophies right outside my kitchen window."

"It's nothing like that, and it may be the most valuable thing you could do for Doctor Gray and me. The county has hired a new psychiatrist. I need you to schedule an appointment with her and let me know how it went before you go," I said.

"Jim, I am very happy with Doc Gray. I don't think I need another doctor. Do you really think I need another doctor?"

"You do not need another doctor, Jordon. What I need is a big fat favor from you. If you will make an appointment with our new psychiatrist and tell me how the session went, then I would have some insight about how she works. This would help me get to know her, through your experience," I said. Not wanting to bias his experience of our new shrink, I didn't want to put any of my misgivings out there.

"This I can do for you, but I am sticking by what you and Doc Gray have done for me. I'm not changing a thing."

"Perfect. And, Jordon, thank you," I said. On his way out through admin, Jordon made two more appointments, one with Dr. Puhak and one more with me.

The rest of the morning, I gave more thought to the satellite clinic idea for Yoncalla and Drain. I tried to envision a logical sequence for approaching this assignment. I want to keep my curiosity and eagerness in check long enough to see if the school districts will come through with staff and ideas to partner with me. Perhaps the best approach might be to send off an introductory letter to the superintendent of each district, informing them that I have been assigned to be the chief respondent to their requests for community based mental health services. And, furthermore, that I would vision the service to be a team effort, staffed by myself and whoever the district might designate to work with me to create and implement an appropriate response to the need they have outlined to our department. That sounds all right. And the closer will be something about looking forward to meeting as soon as possible with this person that the superintendent would choose to work with me on this much needed new resource. That will put the ball back in their court. Then my mind drifted to Dr. Gray's suggestion that I get acquainted with Dr. Wiltse, the local physician practicing in this community. There is no reason that I can think of not to make an appointment to go see him now. That way, I can sneak a peek at these neighborhoods, and get an insider's view without committing to anything or without giving the impression that I was willing to Lone Ranger it with either school district. That's what I will do... send out two letters and make a call to Dr. Wiltse. I think this will also fit nicely with Hugh's philosophy and administrative survival strategy, taking an interest in what your boss thinks is important. Dr. Gray would appreciate the fact that I would commence my community research with Dr. Wiltse.

With a draft of each letter scratched out on the yellow legal pad in front of me, the phone rang just as I was about to pick it up, causing me to jump and momentarily wonder if the thing was possessed. "Jim," Diane announced, "someone calling herself Candyce is calling to see if you can see her this afternoon. Is it OK if I give her your 2:30 slot?"

"As far as I know, that would be fine. Is it someone new?" I asked.

"No, no. I'm pretty sure it has to be our Candy, the slammer."

I didn't know that the admin staff had a nickname for Candy, but if I had been a gambling man, "the slammer" would not even have been on the list options. "Wow! Candyce you say. I can hardly wait until 2:30. Please tell her she has a 2:30 appointment time. I better get out of here now for some lunch while I can. Thank you Diane." I said.

Before heading out to lunch, I made the call to Dr. Wiltse's office, hoping to arrange a future appointment date.

A pleasant and very professional sounding woman answered the phone. Cecilia was her name. I briefly told her who I was, and to my surprise, his receptionist/nurse/medical records technologist said, "Hold on for a moment please. I will get him. I know for certain that he wants to talk to you," she said.

"My God," I thought, "Dr. Gray has greased the plank that I am walking out on here!" But all I could say was, "OK. Thank you."

It was a short wait in medical parlance, perhaps two minutes at most, when I heard a very strong, warm, clear, authoritative baritone voice say, "Jim, is that you?"

"Yes, it is," I replied, feeling a very unusual immediate sense of welcome and connection.

"Drain, Yoncalla and I are looking forward to meeting you," he said in a manner that sounded like he was preparing to greet a visiting astronaut. And I am hoping there won't be a parade. "Word is out here that you are going to invest some of your professional time with the two school districts, which I think is fabulous. If you can figure out how to fit it in, I would also like you to see some of my patients from time to time right here in this office. Dr. Gray sings your praises, and suggested that between the schools and this medical office, we might keep you pretty busy one day per week. When can you head up this way?"

I think I have just been offered a drink of water from a fire hose! I know for certain that the two good doctors are far ahead of me in shaping what services might be offered in north county. "That Dr. Gray is a dynamo, and he sets the bar pretty high for all of us to jump over. Though we are in the earliest stages of visioning services for Drain and Yoncalla, I'm hoping that you and I could have a get acquainted brain storming session sometime next week."

"Let's do it. Wednesday afternoons and Friday mornings are best for me. Would either of these fit in your schedule?" he asked.

"First thing Friday sounds the best to me. I will check out a county car on Thursday night and not check back in until Friday afternoon.

That way I can avoid getting ensnared by some crisis on this end. Also, I have crafted letters to the school districts which should go out this afternoon. There is a remote chance that I could hear back from them by next Friday. If I had a response in hand from one or both districts by then, that would be a big plus for our conversation."

"Friday morning, 9:00 o'clock sharp, it is then. See you then." And he was gone.

After a late lunch and return to work, Betty sent up the signal that my 2:30 appointment has arrived. My telephone call to Dr. Wiltse had been far longer and substantial than I had anticipated, giving me much upon which to reflect. He seemed so encouraging and supporting of the north county outpost idea.

Candy, now Candyce, was cheerfully visiting with Diane when I arrived on the landing just above the waiting room. But, rather immediately, she spotted me, stood and turned in my direction. After she quickly concluded her conversation with Diane, we exchanged greetings and headed up the stairs. She led the way in her new student ensemble costume of tight blue jeans and baggy heather gray Lane Community College sweatshirt. Once settled in with the door closed, she let me know that she had a great deal to share. "The admissions people at the Community College are really nice. And, I think I must have aced my placement and vocational aptitude tests. You won't believe it... I do not even have to take any remedial math or English. Just start right in on my AA degree in business and accounting they said."

"Are you saying you have already upgraded your career plan from bookkeeping to accounting?" I asked.

"Well yeah, that's where the money is," she said with robust, confident smile. "The Aptitude and placement test results say I should go for it. Hey, I want to go for it!"

"What does your old boyfriend think of all your changes and progress?" I asked.

"That four handed grabby asshole. I dumped him like a sack of dirty laundry. The only thing I ever got from him besides a hicky on the neck was enough grief to show up in your office to start my life over again. He's history. I'm not looking back now," she cheerfully declared.

I told Candyce that she was a gigantic source of inspiration to me, and she said the feeling was mutual. At the conclusion of the session, we decided on an "as needed" contract for her return. We both acknowledged that she had made phenomenal progress. Rather than a specific appointment date of return to the clinic, she agreed to let Diane and Betty know if or when she wanted to return.

Several perfectly normal days passed by without my noticing. It seems to be the exceptional that stands out, while usual and customary just slides on by without recognition, which is pretty scary if you think that you are trying to make a difference in the world that is passing you by.

Before I was prepared, Jordon was back on my schedule for a farewell session.

"Don't let me forget that I have something for you in the cab of my pickup. I'm not heading south to the land of fruits and nuts until this item is safely moved from my truck to your trunk. So when we finish our session, you've got to follow me down to the parking lot out back.

"OK, we'll save a couple of minutes for that, but first, how goes your mind, and life plan. And second, what kinds of data have you gleaned for me from our psychiatry research project?"

"I couldn't be happier if you put cranberries beside my turkey and mashed potatoes. You know and I know that the bank is foreclosing on our Little River store at month's end, but that makes no difference to me now. What is important this that Mavis loves me and that the three of us will soon be together again, even if it is Long Beach. It is also very nice to have my mind back, thanks to you and Dr. Gray," he said.

"My presumption is that the threesome to which you are referring includes Ringo. I hope I am correct on this."

"I don't know who Mavis loves more, but I am not about to ask her to choose. It's a package deal, don't you know," he said.

"You are a generous and wise man, Jordon. Now, on to the second topic, which is what do you think of our new psychiatrist, Jordon?"

"Can I be candid with you, Jim?" he asked.

I nodded in the affirmative.

"I think she's squirrelier than a bat in a hamster cage! She silently stared at me for the first 10 minutes or so. Then she asked me why I was in her office. Jim, she had my file right in front of her on her desk. I told her that Dr. Gray wanted a real psychiatrist to review his conclusion and prescription. And you know what she said? She said, and I quote, "I want you to leave now." That's all there was to it. After that, what could I do but just get up and leave. I don't want to hurt your feelings or anything, but my guess is that you and Dr. Gray might not have the right person for this job."

"The truth is not going to be a wound to my feelings, or Dr. Gray's for that matter, Jordon, And, to be perfectly honest, I trust your judgment. You see, the problem is, Dr. Gray is so desperately in need of help, that he put Dr. Puhak on the payroll before checking out her references. We might have to help him back up on this decision, Jordon. And I thank you from the bottom of my heart for your willingness to act as the test canary. I promise you, I would have come running in there if I had heard you screaming!" I said.

"I am sure you would, and it is the least I can do for you guys. This is the steadiest and happiest I have been in several years, and I owe it all to you. If I was a hugger, I would give you a big hug, but this is me, and I would rather take you downstairs and show you what I have for you in the truck. Let's go. What do you say?" And he was already out of his seat and headed out the consultation room door before I could spit out an answer.

In his wake I followed down the stairs.

On his way through the waiting room, he gave his gentlemanly good-byes to Betty and Diane. Then with long, confident strides, out into the parking lot he went. The Dodge Ram was packed to the gunnels, a tightly tied tarp over a mountain of personal goods. When we reached the truck, Jordon guided me around to the passenger side door and opened it. Ringo was sitting on the floorboards, happy to see me if his tail wagging was any indication. Sitting on the passenger side of the bench seat, wrapped and restrained in the seat belt, sat a state of the art 19 inch black and white television set. "Open your trunk. It's yours," he said.

"I can't..." I tried to explain, but he cut me off.

"OK, then give me your car keys so I can put it in there. I've got no room for it, as you can plainly see. If I don't get rid of it, where is Ringo going to ride? He'll take my leg off at the knee if I make him ride all the way to Long Beach on the floor. If it won't fit in your trunk, I would gladly drop it by your house," he said. "Which rig is yours?"

"It's that little blue Toyota Corolla, but..." he again cut me off.

"Home delivery it is then. Give me the address and tell your lovely wife, I'll be there momentarily," he said, as he shook my hand, closed the passenger side door and headed around to the operator's side of the Ram. "Once we arrive at our intended destination, I'll send you a card to let you know we made it."

Closed for Repairs
12

Early Friday morning, I saddled up the county car and headed up Interstate 5. I was eager to meet Dr. Wiltse in his office at the appointed hour. Instead of paying attention to the radio, or focusing on the tune playing in my brain, I found myself entranced by all of the little side roads, hamlets, and pioneer farms. Some of the barns were swaybacked by time and gravity. Many an abandoned, dilapidated homestead was ensnared or half buried in blackberry vines. If this was going to be my territory, I wanted to get to know it intimately. Here and there, where the land was being intensively farmed, the fertility of the turned soil was obvious even to a greenhorn like me. Many of the decaying and abandoned homesteads appeared to have been replaced by manufactured modular homes. But sprinkled along the way were some upscale farmhouses with the latest model tractors and implements operating or parked nearby. In my mind's eye, I was trying to visualize a school board meeting on these machines out in one of these fields.

After leaving the Interstate, my route looped onto Old Highway 99, the cutoff to Yoncalla, and the southern approach to Drain and Curtin. After a few tight curves and one nice straight away on this old two lane road, I soon passed through Yoncalla. Off to my left were several well maintained and architecturally Spartan structures identified by sign to be the Yoncalla Unified School District. In the brief controlled speed zone, there were a few small businesses, and some homes, but it was clear to me that these school buildings were the heart and soul of this micro village. It was the focal point of their pride and identity, the linchpin of their sense of community. The athletic field was groomed, green and ready for action. Local businesses displayed their support and patronage with signs wired to the outfield fences. Both the fences and the brightly colored signs had a gloss that said "brand new." In a matter of seconds, even honoring the reduced speed limit, Yoncalla was receding from me in the rear view mirror as I made my way to Drain and Dr. Wiltse's office.

The steam was rising from the mill operation, commingling with smoke from the wigwam slash burner, and the sweet smell of fresh Douglas fir sawdust carried in the moist air over Drain. As I followed my hand-scribbled instruction on how to find the good doctor's office, on the first pass I glided slowly right past it, as I realized that the numbers on the buildings were now larger than the one for which I was searching. Backing up slowly, I spotted what I seemed to match my notes. It was a completely under whelming, gray shake sided single story building with only a small wooden sign to set it apart from the 1940's era residences flanking it. There wasn't the slightest hint of the energy, community influence and the skill lurking inside.

The welcome was as warm and genuine as I could possibly have hoped for. I was immediately surprised by the compact and efficient nature of the small town power structure. With a gracious smile, Cecilia ushered me into Dr. Wiltse's private office where not one but three people rose to greet us as Cecilia and I entered that room. Standing beside his desk was a tall, sturdy gentleman with a firm handshake and the same commanding yet inviting voice that I had heard on the phone. He introduced himself and made quick work of introducing the superintendent and the elementary school principal of the Drain School District.

Superintendent Benjamin Camel may have been in his early 60's and holding up pretty well under the pressures and responsibilities he carried, or he might have been in his late 40's with the ravages of his job taking an enormous toll on his health and appearance. He greeted me as one might a new recruit to the battlefield in which our side had insufficient weaponry and manpower. His navy blue pinstriped suit was probably the right size, but it had that slept in look. Or perhaps he had supervised recess a few too many times in it. Dorothy Madden was a full head taller than her boss, and seemed not the least bit shop worn. In her red blazer, gray slacks and sharp white blouse, she looked ready for anything that the school day was about to throw at her.

"I hope you don't mind jumping in the deep end," Bill Wiltse said. "Since the impetus to bring you here came from Dorothy and Ben, it seemed like a capital idea to invite them over this morning."

I tried to cover my shock with the best handshake and smile I could muster, and after swallowing a couple of times, I began to find my voice and a small amount of composure.

"I am honored to meet you both, and to be introduced in this way. This would never happen in Chicago. The introductions alone could easily take up two months. I think team building here is going to commence much faster, thank you Dr. Wiltse," I said. Within minutes, I could tell that this community held him in the highest respect and admiration and that his endorsement of me was a golden key that would open all the essential doors to the successful provision of services. Dorothy and Ben explained their dilemma, which in short was how to build a bridge between the hard drinking logger/mill hand subculture and the school deportment expectations of the first and second grade classrooms.

"Don't get me wrong," said Dorothy. "We have many terrific and intact families, the majority I would dare to say, but in a classroom of 25 to 30 children, five or six who have no grasp of personal boundaries, verbal problem-solving, and task sequencing can convert the whole place into a disaster zone. Students wandering around, students unable to take direction or instruction, students grabbing and hitting other students and taking the property of others, this is rough experience for our teachers in the lower grades. The law says when children reach a certain age; they come to school, ready or not. And, to be honest, delaying school entry to any of these children would undoubtedly be a huge mistake. We simply have to find a way to give them a boost so that they can succeed in school, and so that we can survive them."

Holding my letter in his hand, Ben said, "Dorothy and I were astounded by how closely the suggestions in your missive mirror our own visioning process. We weren't able to free her from her classroom on such short notice this morning, but we have a first grade teacher with great people skills who has ambitions of getting her school counselor's credential. Molly Merritt is her name."

"And my thought is that once a week, I could run Molly's classroom for a couple of hours so that you and Molly could select the children, get parental consent and then orchestrate your group. I've already sailed this past Molly, and she is ecstatic about this whole concept. How does that sound?" Dorothy seamlessly followed her superintendent's lead.

"I thought it might take us a couple of months put our heads together, get acquainted and field a team. This is just fantastic. Molly and I can meet next week, and immediately go to work on group composition and parent notification. Do you envision a mix of first and second graders, pulled from different classes... maybe seven to 10 children... maybe 60 to 90 minutes duration?" I asked, leaning slightly in Dorothy's direction.

"Yes, definitely a first and second grade mix pulled from different classes. Beyond those prerequisites, you and Molly can tell us what particulars make the best package," Dorothy said. "We only have four more months in the academic year. The way Ben and I look at it, we've got to jump on it as time is a precious commodity in this situation."

They were clearly charged up and after listening to them for this brief while, I was enthusiastic as well. Before Ben and Dorothy dismissed themselves, I was able to glean from them some times when I could most likely reach Molly by phone during the school day. After their departure, Dr. Wiltse said, "Sorry about surprising you with a room full of locals. It just happened as I stopped by Cathy's Café to pick up a cup of coffee. I ran into Ben and let it slip that you were coming up for a quick get acquainted session this morning. He didn't ask me if he could come. He just lit up with delight and asked what time he could come over. I didn't have the heart to tell him we weren't ready for him. By the way, I thought you did a capital job of handling the awkwardness of the situation."

"Thank you. It was a little like baptism at the deep end of the pool, but it would appear as if a great deal was accomplished in a flash. They were definitely primed for this opportunity. Never in my most manic dreams have I ever experienced the like of it," I said. "It blows my stereotype of the sleepy little country town all to smithereens."

"The truth is, it was your letter that kicked them into high gear. Ben told me that he never expected a response to his letter, much less a real live hot body. Now he damn sure doesn't want to miss a single minute of this opportunity. Anyway, that's the way I read it. Which reminds me, I want to put my design on some of your time also. I have depressed patients, psychotic patients, children of psychotic patients, alcoholic patients, and children and spouses of alcoholics, none of whom are going to drive all the way to Roseburg for an appointment. This room we are sitting in, I use it very seldom and need it even less. If the school groups take up half of your north county day, I could easily take up the other half, if you let me!" he said.

"I am beginning to see that. I haven't felt this wanted since I brought a box of donuts to a Boy Scout troop meeting. If I am going to come up here, I might as well settle in and make a day of it."

That was all the authorization Dr. Wiltse needed to launch into a description of the first three cases he intended to refer to me. There was a strapping young logger named John Melvin who had lost both legs in a cable accident about a year ago. While it was now certain that he would survive his injuries in a physical sense, John had not left his home in the eight months since he left the hospital. Dr. Wiltse was quick to point out that John was about my age, but his build was twice as sturdy. "Profoundly depressed, a definite high suicide risk, and nothing I have done for him has made the slightest amount of difference. He has not been willing to go to the prosthesis clinic for a fitting and he refuses to see a home health physical therapist. I am hoping that he will let you visit him at home for an initial contact. And then there is Alice..."

At that moment, there was a modest rap on the door, and Dr. Wiltse came around his desk to open it. Cecilia said, "Sorry to bother you gentlemen, but the Superintendent of Yoncalla is on the phone and would like to know if Mr. Henson could stop by his office on his way back to Roseburg."

My eyes moved from Cecilia's to Dr. Wiltse's, and I found him staring at the ceiling, looking as though he had been caught in the cookie jar once again. "Yes, Jim, he was in the Café also. He might have overheard me talking with Ben, but I didn't put him up to this. Honestly, I didn't."

"Cecilia, please tell him I can stop by after lunch for a few minutes, between one 30 and two, if that works for him. I can pick up his answer from you when Dr. Wiltse and I are done here. And thanks," I said. After the door closed, I said to Dr. Wiltse, "If you keep this up, I won't have time to find out about Alice!" And, to myself I was making note of Dr. Gray's wisdom for what seemed like the hundredth time in just a few short weeks.

"Oh yes, I want to introduce you to Alice as soon as possible. Chances are Dr. Gray and Hugh are at least acquainted with her by name. She is somewhere between 35 and 50 years old... no, I've got it here somewhere... here it is. She is a... I can't believe this, but it must be true. She's a 32-year-old paranoid schizophrenic woman who regularly cycles in and out of the State Hospital in Salem on an involuntary commitment. And she has a 16-year-old son that she dearly loves who has been raising himself and trying to take care of his mother pretty much all of his walking life. Mike is his name, and a walking miracle he is. He is kind, bright, clean, athletic and fairly well liked in his peer group, I think. When you see the inside of their house, you will begin to grasp what a miracle this is. There is a very complex set of dynamics between them... kind of a love hate thing on Mike's part. But, he is fiercely protective of his mother, and if we fail to help Alice reach a more stable mental status, Mike will continue to be symbiotically attached to Alice. He is unlikely to achieve anything like normal emancipation. For her part, Alice stays on her meds and gets along moderately well in the hospital setting. When she comes home, she refuses to go to your clinic for aftercare and medication follow up. Soon she drops her medication altogether. Within days or months, she cycles back to Salem."

He seemed to sink more deeply into his chair under the weight of his concern for these patients, and he became silent momentarily. I sensed that he hadn't completed his sharing about Alice and Mike. Soon, after a pregnant breath, he began again. "I will do my best to schedule Alice for an in office appointment here so that you can make a start on your work with her. When she is coping adequately, I am a welcome friend. When she is off her medication, as she is now, all bets are off. In her paranoia, I am the devil to be avoided. In the latter case, I will get you connected to Mike first, if that makes sense to you."

"We should be flexible, and go for the window they leave open," I agreed.

"That business taken care of, let's head down to the café for a spot of lunch and send you down the road to Yoncalla," he said.

"The infamous Cathy's Café it is then. I might just as welcome the rest of the way out of the closet," I said.

At Cathy's, the windows were steamy on the inside, and wonderful smells of home style cooking came wafting out the open door as Dr. Wiltse and I passed through it. It was immediate olfactory overload. Scents of freshly baked cinnamon rolls, fruit pies and tarts were dancing in the air alongside homemade chicken and dumplings and hearty beef stew served with melt in your mouth biscuits. Turning to the good doctor, I said in all seriousness, "If I hadn't just rented a little house in Roseburg, I think we could be happy right here." To myself I was thinking, those nurses who were laughing at me a few days back in the department staff meeting must not have found this place.

Cathy herself came out to greet us, and she and Dr. Wiltse soon had me informally introduced to all the regulars in the tightly packed diner. There were no printed menus, just a handsomely lettered chalkboard that announced Friday's specials, which included fresh caught grilled sea bass. Cathy explained that if they cut down a tree in the woods near Drain, they were determined to make lumber out of it, not waste it on paper. It was a tough call, but I settled on the beef stew and biscuit, with a tall cold glass of milk to wash it down. And then, just to test the springs on the county pool car, I managed to handle a refill on the milk with a piece of apple pie. Cathy threw in the a la mode for no extra charge, but I was not allowed anywhere near the ticket at meal's end. Minute by minute, this satellite gig was shaping up to be a bonanza.

Dr. Wiltse was mercifully non-judgmental regarding my self-inflicted agony as we strolled back to his medical clinic. Once again, my gastronomic ambition and my size 32-waist trousers were at war. It was only after the fact that I noticed that he had modestly consumed a sensible soup and salad combo. Back at the clinic, we wrapped up the unfinished business in short order. I expressed my gratitude for the meal and excellent mentoring. Soon after that, I prepared to point the county Chevy in a southerly direction, after agreeing to schedule my new referrals just as soon as some coordination of school and clinic activity could be arranged. Cecilia expertly negotiated arrival plans for my Yoncalla visit. One pressing question remained to be asked. "What advance information can you share with me about the Yoncalla situation?"

"Prepare to have fun down there," he said. "Arthur Patterson, the superintendent, is a quiet but solid citizen nearing retirement after a long tour of duty. And, if it hadn't been for the G.I. bill, he would most likely have been a saw filer like his father. Give the man credit where credit is due. When his schools began to fill up with inner city foster kids, he was the first one to raise the flag of concern... that these new young people would bring along with them all the problems of the families and cities from which they had come. Alcohol, drugs, gang credentials and a hostile view of authority figures, just to name a few. When a couple of these young gang bangers repainted his car, hung and burned him in effigy from the goal post, Arthur became very imaginative in his effort to find help. His letter to the County Commissioners was, I believe, a complete shot in the dark. That his letter ended up on Dr. Gray's desk probably never occurred to him as a possibility. In short, your letter might as well have been a thunderbolt from an ancient Greek god. He will undoubtedly hand you off to one of his underlings, but I think you can bank on having 110 percent of his support."

"Do you think he grasps my need to have a strong companion chosen from his staff?" I asked.

"I would bet big money, if I had any, that he has already reviewed his troops and recruited his most able deputy," was his reply.

After a pleasant send off, I was soon cruising the short distance between timber town and agro village. And having driven by earlier, I knew there was no way to miss my turnoff. Mr. Patterson was apparently awaiting my arrival, as I had barely killed the engine on the county Chevy when a tall, distinguished looking silver-haired gentleman stepped out of the main building on campus and made his approach toward me. I closed up the Chevy and made it to the sidewalk at the moment of his greeting.

"Welcome, welcome," he said, as if one welcome was insufficient to the situation. He offered his hand in friendship. His firm and callused grip was a tip off that his interests ran beyond education. "I am very pleased that you could make time to see us on your way home."

"This entire day has been blessed with one good meeting after another. Since I am on a roll, I intend to stay on a roll! Whatever this magic is, I don't want to lose my momentum," I replied.

"Your being here is our blessing. Come on in. I have people whose acquaintance I want you to make."

True to his word, we had barely cleared the entrance when we two came face to face with a vigorous, rosy-cheeked woman, possibly in her late forties or early fifties. "First, I want you to meet the most important person in this place. Jim Henson, please meet our business manager, Anne Powell. Without her patience and skill, my tenure here would have been brutish and short. Impossible actually."

A quick blush covered her face and ran down her neck. "Mr. Patterson exaggerates, but I appreciate his opinion. It is very nice to meet you. From what I know about our current foster care student status, you are most apt to be the next person placed upon one of his pedestals."

"Or be run out of town as the next goat!" I cautioned.

"I don't think there is much chance of that. Come on. Follow me down to the teachers' break room. I want you to meet your new group co-leader. His name is Karl Douglas, and he is half-time instructor and half–time dean of students. He doubles as counselor, disciplinarian... lots of hats. I know we shouldn't put such a load on him, but our budget is tight and he hasn't said "uncle" yet. After that, I want you to meet our high school principal, Larry Mack, who has taken refuge in my office."

It was an odd choice of words, I thought, but I couldn't quite figure out how to frame a response.

As the good superintendent took big strides down the corridor, I had to hustle to stay up with him. My mind soon left that station, and I began taking in the sights, sounds and smells of this much used but well maintained building. "Something smells good in here," I made known my olfactory research.

"Chicken pot pie day. You missed it. They are beginning to clean up now. But there is always some kind of dessert on the table in the break room," he said.

"Oh please no. Thank you. Doc Wiltse treated me to lunch at Cathy's Café. Fool that I am, I had to add pie on top of the beef stew." "A la mode, I expect," he rightly concluded. I gave him a guilty nod. "Does it show?" I asked, as we arrived at the break room door.

Before opening the door, he turned toward me, winked, and said, "Us tall guys know how to hide it." Then he made a handsome and precise military about face, and proceeded into the faculty break room. On a scale of 1 to 10, this room would score 1.5 in the ambiance dimension. A couple of rectangle, Formica-topped folding tables surrounded by numerous government-issue-looking folding chairs occupied the center of the room. A smaller table at the far end of the room featured a coffee pot, various snack and dessert items and a mimeograph machine beside a stack of paper. No curtains, no overstuffed chairs, this was a low on comfort working kind of place.

As we entered, the two occupants rose in unison to greet us. One was a very fit, athletic, very curly haired young woman wearing gym attire and a corded whistle around her neck. Sallie something was her name. The introduction and her exit from the room were so swift that I didn't catch her whole name. The second body belonged to Karl Douglas. Not quite as fit as Sallie something, but not out of shape either, he had a relaxed aura of charm about him. I was guessing him to be in a range of not more than five years my senior, but I could also sense that he was packing at least a decade more experience and ambition than I felt I could call my own.

After the briefest of introductions, and a parting shot to meet him at his office before I left the building, Super Patterson made his exit, leaving Karl and me to our own devices. "It's been a very long school year, and it is almost precisely half shot," Karl began. "But I think, with you on the team, we could have a better second half. It'll be like a basketball game, bring in a fresh pair of legs off the bench somewhere early in the third quarter. Let's take it to 'em," he said, while passing to me an imaginary ball.

"What are we up against?" I said, catching it on the fly and heading down court.

"They are massively anti-authority oppositional, and several are wannabe sociopathic little snots.

"A core of adolescent foster kids, and a couple of local hangers on, they want to keep this school in a state of continual ruckus. I say wannabe because I don't really think, for the most part, that they are hardcore gang bangers. But in this little country school, it's like they are working over-time to prove that they are hardcore, the real thing," he said.

"What leverage do we have?" I asked.

"Good question. I like the way you think. For what it's worth, the ones I most want to target are wards of the court. The starting five will either be in our group or be gone. I've already extracted that guarantee from their caseworker at Children's Services Division. I am still working on parental consent for the local three that have been sucked into their orbit. By Tuesday, I think we will be ready to rock and roll. If this early afternoon slot works for you, I've located a vacant classroom that we could expropriate for our purpose. It can be ours whatever your north county day turns out to be," he said.

"Coordination will be the challenge. Drain has some ambitious plans, and Dr. Wiltse has laid claim to a piece of my north county day. I see no reason why I can't begin my day on the northern end and spend the day working my way back home. Also, I am leaning toward a Monday or Friday preference for no particular reason that comes to mind. What do you think?"

"Any day but Friday would be my suggestion. Anything we accomplish on Friday will have been forgotten by Monday. And secondly, Friday is pep assembly and game day, which tends to wind the kids up tighter than a 13 day clock. My vote would go to Monday or Tuesday," Karl said.

"OK, Monday or Tuesday it is, assuming no veto from my boss, or the Drain contingent. Your points against Friday make perfectly good sense to me. Are you honestly suggesting that we could be under way by a week from Monday or Tuesday?" I asked.

"That's exactly what I had in mind. Heck, all we need here are three parent permission slips and a couple of beers to work on our game plan. That we could polish off with time to spare. Next Friday around 4:00 o'clock, I could take you on an unabridged tour of Yoncalla. By 4:10, we could end up at my place for planning and refreshments. What do say?"

"This whole day has blown my mind. As I was daydreaming up the freeway, I imagined a leisurely, slow-paced entry. Friendly say, but like the pokey little pony. Instead, it has been embracing and bracing... filled with energy! Thank you. Let me check in at home and massage my schedule, then call you before noon on Monday. If that won't put you off too much," I said.

"No. That's fine. While this may all seem quick to you, we've been in this jam looking for a way out since the end of September. It feels miraculous that we are actually going to get to take a shot at this mess. It doesn't feel like a minute too soon. You know what I mean?"

And I did. We both stood up, shook hands in a manner no longer of just "welcome," but much more of a sense of contract, of agreement to forge ahead into the as yet barely sketched future. After that, Karl took me back out into the hall and properly directed me toward Super Patterson's office.

Once I located the school office, I found a receiving desk with a cheerful student behind it. I wondered to myself whether she was generally a positive spirit, or happy to be out of some particular class. She didn't introduce herself, but expertly guided me through the maze, past the business office, counseling office, and principal's office, to the door of the superintendent. She politely rapped on the door, and announced my arrival. Super Patterson quickly thanked and dismissed the student aide, swept me into the room and closed the door.

Sitting behind Super Patterson's desk was a tall, slender, deflated man who was perhaps approaching 40, or a very shop worn 30 something. "Jim, I would like you to meet our principal, Larry Mack. Larry, this is Jim Henson. Jim, when Larry went home for lunch today, as is his custom, no lunch was awaiting him. However, Jody, his wife, had left him a note on the kitchen table, anchored to the spot by a can of Nalley's chili.

Well, it's your story, Larry. You tell him." Super Patterson encouraged. "Larry has been hoping to spend a few minutes with you in private since ... since he wandered back from his noon break. Speaking of privacy, I believe this would be the proper moment to leave you fellows. Jim, I plan to be shuffling paper or working on the budget with Anne Powell for the next hour or so. After you and Larry finish up your conversation, please interrupt me. I would like a one minute summary of your session with Karl."

He gave me a quick pat on the shoulder on his was out the door, and as he passed by, I had a fleeting thought that I had just been promoted to the rank of prison chaplain. "Sure," I said, but I wanted to say, "Perhaps I will, if you promise to provide no more surprises."

After the door clicked shut, Larry looked up at me and said, "Please have a seat. Thanks for coming." As if I had made this trip to north county on this very day for the benefit of his nascent crisis. "I am sorry to impose on you like this. I'm feeling terribly embarrassed … not how I thought we would get acquainted, but I am a total mess. I would be eternally grateful if you could spare a few moments with me."

Now I was beginning to feel a slight twinge of compassion for this man. And I began to feel that my presence in this room was by invitation, not conscription. "OK, tell me what's going on," I said as I let my weight come to rest in one of Super Patterson's two oak captain's chairs.

"Jody took our two kids out of school this morning, packed up some of their things, and drove up to her parents place in Portland. Eleven years we have been married. We've had words before, but never anything like this."

"What did her note say," I asked.

"It was short… something like, "This isn't working. I have to get away for a while. I will call you on Sunday afternoon."

"Larry, I've seen worse notes than that. She says her getaway is possibly temporary, and that some communication will happen at a certain date and time. But you have to identify and fix that which is not working… at least what's not working for her. Hopefully, you already know what she's talking about, because I certainly don't."

"We never talk, she says. We never have time just for the two of us, she says. Our house is always jam packed with our neighbors and their problems, she says. We have this big family room with a pool table, ping pong, foosball table, darts and a bar with a keg refrigerator on the west end. I think it's fun. But Jody was an only child and could be delighted by herself in an overstuffed chair by the Franklin stove, curled up with a book for hours on end," he said.

"Do you want her back?" I asked.

"Oh, for sure I do," he said. "Can't function without her. She's a terrific mom, keeps us organized and manages our finances. I would just unravel without her."

"In that case, home has to be a space that meets her needs too. Put a sign out at the front of your driveway that says, 'Closed for Repairs/ Family Members Only.' Then take time to find some middle ground. Think of her position as a compliment. Though it's hard for me to figure out why, she actually wants be alone with you, and perhaps with you and your children," I said.

"That really sums it up. So it's not yet the end of my world, maybe. And, there is some action I can take...whew. This job may have to go though," he said.

"Why do you say that? I don't remember anything like that in my five cent prescription," I replied.

"Because my life is kids and parents all day long, and sports or school board at least half of the evenings, I'm not much of a husband or father. When I get home, I seek out mindless activity like shooting pool and drinking beer... expecting to be waited on."

"So you are saying that you are very lucky that Jody and your own kids are only gone for a long weekend to get a break from Prince Charming," I said.

"I haven't decided if I like you or not, but you are damn good at whatever it is that you do. Thanks for holding up the mirror."

"You are most welcome. Now, I need to saddle up and head back to the Burg. This day has been bountiful beyond all of my imaginings; however if I don't get back fairly soon, I too will need a counselor. And, I think your boss committed me to see him before I make my getaway. We will have other chances to get acquainted. And on some of those days, you will be doing celebration instead of grief," I said.

"I hope you're right. I think I'll head home and start making a yard sign. Hey, maybe I could become a sign maker."

"Those sign makers have shitty health insurance, Larry," I said, as he came around the table to shake my hand and guide us both out the door. His handshake was stout, and his general color indicated that his blood had resumed its proper circulation. At that moment, Super Patterson was headed our way, so I decided to see if I could hit two birds with one flying rock. When all three of us converged in front of the business office I said, "Gentleman, Karl and I have made phenomenal progress toward the establishment of an eight student therapy group. Actually, he did most of the work before I set foot in this building. By a week from Monday or Tuesday, it is our intention to be under way. We are a bit wobbly about which day because of my need to coordinate my Roseburg, Yoncalla and Drain schedules. Karl has lined up space. I hope these plans meet your approval," I said.

For a second, the two of them focused on each other. Then Super Patterson gave me a jovial pat on the back and said, "Congratulations. If anybody can rein in these juvenile interlopers, it will be you and Karl. Karl, you see, has ... how shall I say ... a significant residual of untamed adolescent daredevil left in him. And, he sees more hope in them than most of the rest of us do. It's great to have you here."

I acknowledged the warmth of their welcome as they escorted me out the door and to the waiting county Chevy. As I buckled up, cranked her up and slipped into reverse, I caught a glimpse of Larry, loping off toward what I imagined to be his sign shop.

Georgia and Naomi

13

The ride home from north county was uneventful. It seemed like a short trip, as the events of my extraordinary day played through my weary brain. Slowly, the beef stew and biscuit with the pie and ice-cream on the top began to slide downstream, and my distress from gluttony had passed. By the time I dropped off the county car and arrived home, it was approaching 6:00 PM. And, as insane as it might sound, I began to think of food again. A figure of speech from my family of origin came to mind: "We aren't rich, but we sure do eat like it."

Aaron was in a happy mood, and after nursing, soon zonked out. I shared with Annis Rae my impressions of Yoncalla and Drain, and the new cast of characters on stage that first full day. I just couldn't get over how primed for action they all had been. What I forgot about entirely was Dr. Puhak. On Thursday, I could hardly think of anything else. My crap detector mechanism was so high over my head that I had even conspired with Jordon Johnson to scope her out. She had fallen out of my conscious mind like a crashed plane off the radar screen only to come back to haunt me at 2:00 AM.

There in my dream state was Gary. The kindest, most gentle member of our staff, was on his back fighting for his life in the hallway in front of his consultation room. Straddling him and strangling him with gigantic, powerful hands was Dr. Puhak. And I am powerlessly observing from the far end of the hall, remembering that I had mentioned my suspicions and Jordon's observations to no one. I think I must have screamed as I heard a desperate rattle come out of Gary's throat, because I am sweating and suddenly sitting up, wide awake!

"What's the matter honey?" my sweetheart sleepily asked.

"I was having a really scary dream, a nightmare I guess. Poor Gary was getting choked to death by Dr. Puhak ... right in front of his consult room at the clinic. And, it's all my fault. She's got these great big powerful hands..."

"So how is it your fault?" she asked, now wide-awake.

"Well, you see, I've had this premonition that she's nuts. And I even sent Jordon Johnson into her office to get a second opinion, and he basically confirmed my worst fear on Thursday afternoon, but I haven't gotten around to telling anybody yet. All day yesterday, I was having such a great time, it slipped my mind completely. And now, maybe Gary's dead!"

"No he's not, silly. It was just a dream. You can call Hugh in the morning," she said.

I had to admit that she was most likely right. I was probably riding off on a guilty conscience. And my heart rate was beginning to return to the 60 beat per minute range once more. "OK," I said. And I was soon back in la la land, making obnoxious snoring sounds.

On Saturday morning, I waited until close to the hour of social decency to call Hugh and Fran's house. With those five daughters in the household, I was pretty certain that I would hear nothing more than a busy signal. Evidently, none of them was big on early, because the call went right through, and Fran answered on the third ring. After exchanging courteous pleasantries, I asked if I could speak with Hugh. He hadn't come out of the shower yet, but when he did, she said she would have him return my call.

While it seemed like an eternity, in fact it was probably less than 30 minutes until the phone rang. Waiting time can be incredibly slow, and doing time can be amazingly fast. Is this what Einstein's theory of relativity was all about? "Hello," I said.

"Good morning, Jim. What's up?" he asked in his before coffee voice.

"This may sound kind of weird, and please tell me if I'm out of bounds here, but my gut feeling and unconscious alarm has been going off since the middle of last week. Contact and communication with Dr. Puhak has been... how can I say it politely? It's been strange. So I sent in one of my clients to a medication review, and that went... not well. Then, to cap it off, I dreamt last night that the good doctor strangled Gary in the hall outside his office! So, maybe it all adds up to nothing, but..."

"Too bad you missed out on yesterday," Hugh cut in on my rambling. "I went up to see about her dictation. You know, she had seen eight or 10 patients so far over the course of the week, and the admin team hasn't seen a word of dictation come out of her office. I thought perhaps she could use a little tutorial on the Dictaphone. Her door was closed, so I knocked. No Answer. I turned up the volume on my second knock, but that netted me the same result. While I was pretty damn sure she was in there and did not have a patient, I was feeling at a loss as to what my next move should be. What I decided to do was come back down stairs, get out her resume and start making some calls to the references and her last employer. All three of the references were spurious leads, going nowhere. When I called Pueblo State Hospital in Colorado, the personnel director said that her records were sealed, that he could not discuss her situation without her written authorization."

"These are not good signs," I said softly.

"You're telling me!" he said with certitude. "My next stop was to Dr. Gray's office." Good move, I'm thinking. "I wanted to bring him into the loop and get his take and suggestions on our situation. That old fox said to me he thought Dr. P would come out of her own volition at 5:00 PM, and we could talk to her then."

"What made him think that?" I asked.

"Because, he told me, that's how institutionalized people behave. They go with the routine of the institution. 5:00 is when this institution closes for the day," he said.

"Was he correct?" I asked.

"The two of us were standing by her door in the hall. At 5:00 sharp, her door opened, just like a damn glockenspiel. Dr. Gray politely told her that her services would no longer be needed. And she said, 'I know.' Then we stepped aside, she went down the hall, down the stairs and out the door to her car."

"What are the odds that she will show up at 8:00 on Monday morning?" I asked.

"Dr. Gray called the hotel where she had been staying. They told him that she had already checked out. I think it's a chapter closed."

Relieved that Gary wasn't dead, I said some trite thing like, "All's well that ends well." Before I hung up the phone, I shared vaguely that I too had had a fabulous day in Drain and Yoncalla, promising a full briefing next week.

The rest of the weekend flew by as we tried to get resettled on Follett Street. We hadn't shipped that much stuff out from Chicago, and I was beginning to think what we had shipped was probably the wrong stuff. For example, that beautiful old oak dining room table and chairs, the one with the extra leaves hidden inside of it, we had given it away. I missed it. It was a Salvation Army thrift store find, but it had character. Annis Rae had wanted to keep it, but I had foolishly talked her out of her position, saying we needed to keep our moving van cost as low as possible. In retrospect, she was so in love with and focused on our baby boy that she let herself be talked into numerous things that would later to come back and bite us both.

As I looked over my schedule on Monday morning, I could see that Betty or Diane had found a spot for a new client. Naomi was her name. It dawned on me that I enjoyed all of my established clients, but it was the new ones that peaked my curiosity the most. The unknown that had yet to be revealed, there was always something special about that. Like those coastal pines, all gnarled and leaning away from the surf, you just know that there are undoubtedly some interesting stories behind these shapes and formations.

Once upstairs in my consultation room, Naomi sat primly on the front edge of her chair, large brown leather purse on her lap, and both hands on the purse. And, as she slowly and unconsciously patted her purse, like she was trying to comfort it, the tears made trails down both cheeks. In her mid to late forties, her obvious emotional pain added 10 years to her appearance. With Naomi, there was none of the usual light, general get acquainted exchange. She was fully loaded with grief and intended to make every single minute count.

"Fifteen years ago today, I married Vern, my one and only husband. At the time, he had been divorced and single parenting two little girls. Georgia was 11, and Deirdre was six. Vern told me that the girls' mother had just upped and left one day, decided she was a lesbian, and moved to Idaho with her friend, companion, whatever. From the date of her leaving, the girls had virtually no contact with their mother, though I never stopped trying to promote it. Between her leaving and our meeting, about two and a half years, Vern's mother and sister pitched in quite a lot in an effort to keep some semblance of organization, but those two, with Vern's tacit support, would always override my suggestions for contact between the girls and their birth mother. To be honest, the girls' mother never made much of an effort to maintain a connection to her daughters. Mr. Henson, I was young and may not have known all that I should have known about how to be a mother to these two girls, but I always did my best." At this point, Naomi shook slightly as she sobbed and the tears continued to flow. She accepted a tissue in one hand and held on to the purse tightly with the other.

"Vern wasn't home much in the first five or six years of our marriage. I think he was what you might refer to as a compulsive worker. Vern's mother and sister have swung back and forth, alternately labeling me 'the wicked step-mother,' or 'the idiot.' And perhaps I am the idiot for staying all of these years in a loveless marriage and making every effort to parent my girls. Those two women did everything in their power to poison the relationship between us, Mr. Henson. And Vern did nothing to stop them."

"Naomi, I think they put three strikes on you before you even came up to the plate for your at bat," I said. "You and Vern did not function as a parent team. He would not protect you or back you up, much less work with you. And then, the girls have this mystery woman out there somewhere. If I were one of the girls, I would be mad as hell at an abandoning mom and an absent dad. And the only person left to take out their anger on was...guess who."

"Deirdre, my youngest, and I are very close. Amazingly close, considering the amount of poison in the pot, but that brings me to why I came here. I love both girls, and I have always tried my best to be available to them and be the mother they would never otherwise have," she said, patting her wet cheeks with the tissue I'd given to her. After tucking the tissue into her coat pocket, she gently lifted her purse to an upright position and pulled open the main compartment of it. Next, she deftly extracted a puffy number 10 envelope, and then set on the floor the purse that she had so carefully protected for the entire session.

Her tears continued to flow, but now she paid them no attention. "Last week I received this letter from Georgia. She's 26-years-old now and recently disengaged from a fellow that she has lived with since she graduated from college. Mr. Henson, there are eight pages here with writing on both sides." I could see the yellow legal writing pad sheets poking out of the envelope. "There are eight pages, 16 sides worth, of anger, resentment and hatred directed at me. And page after page is packed with the venom, word for word of what the girls heard from their grandmother and Vern's sister. All kinds of alleged cruelty and mean spiritedness on my part. It breaks my heart," she said.

"I want you to consider giving your heart the protection it

deserves," I said. "I have a suspicion that this letter may contain lots of factual errors. Would I be correct in that assumption?" I asked.

"Yes, that's true," she said, as the tear trails were gradually becoming salt tracks.

"And, would you say that Vern was most probably a child neglecting workaholic before you met him, even if you liked his courtship behavior?" I continued.

"Yes, that's also true," she allowed.

"Do you think that you caused your mother-in-law and sister-in-law to be mean, toxic people?" I asked.

"Oh, I really don't think so. Vern's mother became bitter and vengeful when her husband left her for a younger woman, and she felt forced into working full time and single parenting Vern and his sister from the time they were small children. Perhaps she was unhappy before that, but I don't know for sure. Beckie ... it's funny that I didn't notice when Vern and I were dating ... she has been seething possibly her whole life. Father abandonment issues, do you think?"

"It would only be a guess. But it might be a good guess. My point is that you only need to take your own inventory. It makes no sense to take responsibility for all the manure from one end of the field to the other. Would you like to sort the piles and acknowledge only your own?" I asked.

"What do you have in mind?" she asked.

"One suggestion might be to photocopy all 16 pages, that way we don't miss anything on the back of each page. I am going to give you two new envelopes. I am going to write your name on one and Georgia's name on the other one. OK? My suggestion would be for you to cut that letter into pieces, keeping only what belongs to you in the Naomi envelope. All the rest goes in the Georgia envelope. That's for starters. What do you think of this idea?"

"I can do that. No, I want to do that!" she said with emphasis on "want."

"OK, hold tight. I'll go make the copies," I said. And, in gig time, I was out and back, copies in hand. "There you go," I said as I handed her the pile.

She seemed to be having a grand delight, whacking away at those pages, and when she had all the pieces neatly tucked into one envelope or the other, she asked, "What should I do now?"

"What would you like to do?" I asked.

Though the silence was brief, I could hear her mental gears whirring. "I'm going to keep what I know to be mine. And, I am going to mail the rest back to Georgia with a little note that says, 'I am keeping the parts of your letter that I recognize to be true. You will have to decide what to do with the remainder. Love, Mom.'" And, for the first time in the session, Naomi sat back in her chair and let out a long slow breath.

"How do you feel now?" I asked.

"Better than I have for a week. No! Better than longer than that! Can I come back and work on what I want to do about Vern... I mean about my non-relationship with Vern?"

"It's your call," I said.

Take Another Shot
14

In the early afternoon, I caught sight of Dr. Gray in the hallway making conversation with Roger, one of the sanitarians. I didn't want to interrupt whatever it was that they were working on, and so I was about to turn and head downstairs by another route when he must have finished up or in any case looked up and spotted me. "Jim," he hailed me. "May I have a word with you?"

"Of course," I said, frozen in my tracks, having no idea what was coming.

It's a well-known fact that you can't outrun an adult bear and it would be pure folly to try. I saw in a book about hiking the trails of Glacier National Park the recommendation to take along slower companions. My point is, for an older, large adult male, Dr. Gray is amazingly quick. And he closed the distance between us in just a few long strides. "I wanted to thank you and Hugh for protecting my back side on my psychiatry fiasco. Hugh spilled the beans on your creative and enterprising research project involving Jordon Johnson. It never would have occurred to me to do an inside job on her."

Feeling pretty embarrassed by my choice of tactics, I could sense the heat rising in my face. "I probably owe someone an apology for that stunt. The only thing I can say in my defense is that my gut instinct was making too much noise to ignore. And Jordon, I thought, was sturdy enough to act as a decoy."

"No, no...don't apologize. Your instinct or intuition, whatever it was, was right on target. I shouldn't have been so eager to pounce on the first psychiatry prospect to stray into our neighborhood. I was, in hindsight, blinded by what looked like an opportunity to get some help," he said.

"Well, it's a relief to me that I'm not on your stink list."

"Far from it. And by the way, Dr. Wiltse tells me that you and he had a pretty exciting day up in Drain. To hear him tell it, your work up there is rapidly taking shape. I really think you are going to like it up there," he said.

Acknowledging to myself once more the nature of the fish bowl in which I am swimming, I told Dr. Gray that if anything the Yoncalla half of the project was moving faster that the Drain half. "I've never seen anything come together quite like this," I said.

"I'm happy for you. Say, before I let you go, I thought that you would be interested in knowing that I have my eye on another psychiatrist for our program. And this one, I know for a fact, is the real deal. He's been working for Multnomah County Mental Health for years, but he is coming up to compulsory retirement age up there and I hear he is looking for something else to do. He and his second wife, a psychiatric nurse I believe, went all over the state twisting the arms of County Commissioners to allocate money to develop county mental health clinics. Those two are largely responsible for what we have in place around the state today. I'm going to take another shot at this thing and see what it would take to entice Dr. Waterford to come down here."

To myself I'm thinking that there might not be any such a thing as "compulsory retirement age" in the civil service ranks of county employees. That might be age discrimination, I thought, but what I said was, "If he brings his wife down here with him, could we end up getting two for the price of one?"

"No, I don't think he and Minnie are still married," he said.

"Oh, well good luck on your recruitment efforts then," I said, before we parted company.

Later in the day, Hugh and I did find time to discuss the Drain/

Yoncalla satellite progress. "Dr. Wiltse appears to be the pounding heart of health and education up there, and he has so much good karma that buckets full of it were spilling over on me," I said. "People trust him implicitly, and his presentation of me to those educators had the effect of anointing me as his agent. I've never felt greater welcome anywhere."

"When June rolls 'round, I hope you still feel this good about the whole experience," spoke the mature voice of reason. "Have you settled on which day of the week you plan to work up there," he asked.

"Nothing is firm. Karl Douglas, the teacher/counselor at Yoncalla High and I are exploring the possibility of Monday or Tuesday, but I have yet to meet or even talk to the teacher assigned to work with me in Drain. Your opinion would influence me as well. What do you think?"

"One Monday per month our professional staff has lunch with Forest Miner. He's the psychiatrist from the Veterans Hospital I mentioned to you, I think. It's pretty informal as psychiatric consultations go, but it does mean something to Dr. Gray that we have this opportunity to review problematic cases with a psychiatrist. Also, most of the holidays fall on a Monday, so you would have more misses if you settled on Mondays," he said.

"Both good points," I said. "It's kind of funny, I think, that when I started to discuss which would be the best day with Karl, I was thinking Monday or Friday might be the best...just off the top of my head, but Tuesday does have more going for it. When I talk to my teacher contact in Drain this afternoon, I'll pitch Tuesdays and see what she says. Changing the subject for a moment, did you know that Dr. Gray is moving forward on another prospect for staff psychiatrist?"

"No, I haven't seen him today. What's he up to now?" Hugh asked.

"Up in Multnomah County, there's a psychiatrist named Waterford... John, I think it is. Dr. Gray says he's about to take retirement from Multnomah and might be open to recruitment for our position. Do you know him?" I asked.

"I've met the man, but I have never seen him practicing the discipline of psychiatry. I have always thought of him as a public relations kind of guy, very lively and humorous. He may have memorized every joke on Earth. I've never heard him tell the same one twice. Unlike Dr. P, he definitely has the proper credentials. He and his second wife, Minnie, deserve more of the credit for the establishment of the county mental health system than anyone else. However, if memory serves me, while Dr. Waterford entertained and schmoozed the County Commissioners for money, Minnie had the brains and the organizational savvy to get the clinics up and running. One thing I can guarantee, if Dr. Waterford comes down here, he won't be a catatonic mute! Guess we'll cross that bridge if we come to it," he concluded.

"Both you and Dr. Gray referred to Minnie as Dr. Waterford's second wife. How many wives has he had?" I couldn't keep my curious mind from asking.

"I don't rightly know, but it is for sure a number over the total of yours and mine combined," He said after a moment's calculation. And with that topic plumbed as far as it could go, we mutually decided to get on with the next responsibilities of the day.

Hard of Knowing
15

"Jim," Diane said as I was passing through the admin area, "I just got off the phone with Dr. Lee. He's an internist, I think. He has a patient named Lyle Carpenter who he says is some kind of miracle. During World War II, Lyle was a young Navy fighter pilot in the South Pacific ... flying off the deck of an aircraft carrier, lots of missions, never a scratch on him or the plane. One tough costumer is how Dr. Lee describes him. After his discharge from the Navy, he came back to the valley and opened a crop duster service, aerial application of pesticides on field crops mostly. Twenty years plus without a mishap in the sky or on the ground until last June... that's when he hit a power line where he didn't expect to find one. I remember newspaper articles about Lyle. Nobody expected him to live.

"The surgeons at Mercy Hospital said it was like trying to put a jigsaw puzzle together in the O.R. But now, let's see, about nine months after the crash, Lyle is a walking, talking miracle. Dr. Lee says that from a medical perspective, Lyle is ready to be released from medical care, ready to return to work. And SAIF, you know the workers accident and disability insurance outfit, wants to declare him healthy and cut off his disability income. But, Dr. Lee says that it's high time for someone to help Lyle with the emotional trauma part of his injury. He's referring his patient to a workers compensation attorney also. Would you like to take him on?"

"Hurray for Dr. Lee, a doctor who knows when and how to make a mental health referral. Maybe you should assign him to Denny or Gary, someone with more experience with injured workers and lawyers," I said. "I've never had a case like it."

"Denny, Gary and Hugh are all booked out for about three weeks. Dr. Lee is hoping we can tackle his referral within the next week. Lyle is freaked out about the cutoff letter he received from SAIF on top of his post trauma emotional freight."

"OK, I will take on Lyle as long as I can arrange for ongoing consultation, as needed, from Gary or Hugh," I said. "Assuming one of them will take me on, go ahead and find a spot on my schedule for him."

At home that night, I mentioned to Annis Rae that I was soon going to be over my head with a recovering disability case. "A seasoned pilot about my dad's age who nearly died in a crash this past Spring, he has made a miraculous physical recovery, enough so that SAIF wants to call him recovered, which means they plan to stop making payments to him since there is no longer any bleeding. I think these workers compensation insurance companies equate mental health with witch doctoring. Or, perhaps it's just anything to end their financial liability for the injured. His doctor says he's nowhere near emotionally ready to go back to his old job. I think this guy is extremely fortunate to have this doctor going to bat for him. It's his doctor that referred him to us and also to some legal help," I said.

"Do you know anything about treating such a person?" she asked.

"Not yet, but I only took the case with the understanding of guaranteed back up from Hugh or Gary. They have both spent copious time with Vocational Rehabilitation referrals. I'm hoping to learn some new tricks," I replied. "The part that is potentially bothersome to me is the possibility of getting caught between two or more attorneys firing shots at each other."

"You might need a flak vest!"

After dinner was over and the pots and dishes were washed and sitting in the drying rack, Annis Rae commenced to give Aaron a pre-bed snack. I began cruising the newspaper for diversion. The headline read "Big Illinois Valley Pot Bust." Nothing new there, I thought. On to the sports page, the banner announced "Indians Dominate Cavemen." If this was a title from the American Journal of Anthropology, this would be interesting! Then, it was on to the classified ads, even though we have no money and I don't think we are looking for anything. Scanning down the column to "Miscellaneous," an item caught my eye. "Gurdies for sale, $25.00 each."

"Honey, what's a gurdy?" I asked.

"I don't know. To gird means to surround, I think... you know, like in girdle. What's the context?" she said.

"The context is 'miscellaneous.' Does that help?"

"No silly, that doesn't help!" she said.

"There's a phone number here and an address in Winston. I'm going to give them a call and find out what's what. Maybe I'll learn something new tonight."

"Go get'em, Tiger," she said, but she had a dubious look on her face.

After a few short rings, I heard the voice of a mature woman of undetermined age answering my call. "Hello," she said.

"Yes, I am inquiring about your advertisement in today's newspaper. Are these good girdies that you are selling?"

"They are excellent. We have many happy and repeat customers," she said.

"I see," I said, but of course, I didn't. "And is $25.00 a good price for a gurdy?" I asked.

"Oh my yes, it is. We make them here in our own shop, don't you see. So there is no salesman or store mark up on what we build," she said.

"That's wonderful," I said. "Can you tell me what I might do with one or two, if I bought some?"

"You're not a deep sea fisherman are you," she put it out there as a matter of clear and objective fact.

"No, ma'am, I am not. But I am very curious. My wife guessed that since the word 'gurd' is in gurdy, that maybe it was something that surrounds something... like a girdle or gurdle. Would she be right?"

By this time, the poor woman dealing with the idiot on the phone was laughing so hard that I became afraid she might fall out of her chair and hurt herself. After she calmed herself down a couple of notches, she said, "A gurdy is a type of winch that returns the nets to the deck of the boat. So in a way, your wife is correct. When the nets return to the boat, the gurdy surrounds or contains them. You don't want to buy one, do you?"

"That, I am afraid, will have to wait until I can buy a sea-going fishing boat and learn to operate it. But thanks for your time and patience," I said. After I returned the phone receiver to its cradle, Annis Rae implied that we don't really need Jordon Johnson's television set. "Our taste in entertainment runs to the simple and interactive type, like the Cutco knife salesman in-home demonstration, or the Kirby guy that shampooed one third of the carpet in the living room and showed us that frightening picture of a bed mite taken with an electron microscope," she said.

"T'is a gift to be simple. I think it says so in the Bible," I said. "Or maybe it's just an old Quaker song."

It dawned on me that I could probably really benefit from a conversation with Dr. Lee, the referring physician in the matter my new crop duster pilot client. Never having had a client like Lyle, I was definitely going to need all the help I could get. Early in the week, I was able to reach Dr. Lee by phone. "I might not be the best person on our staff to pick up counseling responsibility for your patient, but being the new kid in the neighborhood, I am the one most available," I said. "Gary, Hugh and Denny are at least three to four weeks away from taking on any new cases."

"Yes, and this is one that needs to be addressed sooner than later. I appreciate the fact that anyone over there is able to take on Mr. Carpenter now. Let me give you a bit of a run down on the course of treatment thus far, and why we need your help." And I am thinking thank you, thank you. Guess who needs whose help. "Mr. Carpenter is the original Humpty Dumpty who had a great fall. Concussion, coma, separated shoulder, broken ribs, broken arm, hip fracture, broken legs, many lacerations requiring one hundred fifty seven stitches, the list goes on and on. But the miraculous thing about his case was how little internal damage he sustained. Some bruising of the lungs and spleen, beyond that he incurred little or no organ damage. Of course it goes without saying he lost a lot of blood, which by itself could have killed him had there not been a swift and skilled EMT response; the king's horses and king's men, which would be the ER docs and the orthopedic surgery team. Together they fashioned a recovery that not one of us alone could have imagined, and he has done a superb job of healing. Now, approximately one-year post trauma, he continues to have symptoms that do not seem to have an identifiable medical cause. Frequent bouts of nausea, reports of chronic fatigue and weakness seem to be the core constellation of symptoms. By week number three, he was out of intensive care. At the end of month number three, he was discharged from the hospital to outpatient rehab follow up for range of motion work and the like," he said.

"Would you venture a diagnosis, as you see him now," I asked.

"There could be some residual brain injury from the head injury, concussion and coma, but neurology doesn't think so. They brought in a neuropsychologist from Eugene who ran Mr. Carpenter through two days' worth of tests and couldn't find anything that would explain the symptom set. Pardon the pun, but he passed those tests with flying colors."

I like this doctor! He has great gallows humor. "Which leads you to what conclusion, not that I am going to hold you to it," I said.

"I am thinking neurasthenia. I don't think Mr. Carpenter is malingering, or faking anything. My guess is, and don't forget I am not the mental health guy, that these symptoms are his body and mind's way of coping with all that has happened to him and all that is yet to come, for that matter."

"Including, but not limited to going back to work," I said.

"You got it." He said. He thanked me for tackling this case and wished me the best of luck. I wondered if he knew how over my head I felt. I thanked him for his candid and helpful overview of Lyle's status and assured him that I would keep him posted on progress or lack of it and that I might be back with a new crop of questions. Again, I am in the deep end of the pool with no water wings.

Later that day, I cornered Hugh in the hall outside his consultation room and begged for a few minutes of his time, which he generously gave. In the sanctity of his office, I shared with him Dr. Lee's summary. "Either in session or after session, I'm pretty sure I am going to need to consult with you on this one," I said. He was kind and obliging, but gave me a brief encouraging pep talk.

When the day arrived for my first interview with Lyle, I was surprised to see a cane resting across his knees as he sat in the waiting room, anticipating our session. Though I am pretty sure I was the most nervous of the two of us, I spotted the cane as a metaphor representing a search for stability of any kind...physical, mental, or financial.

After introductions, we headed upstairs to my consultation room and got settled into our respective chairs. "How are you feeling today, Mr. Carpenter?" I asked.

"The same way I felt yesterday and the day before that. You can call me Lyle," he said.

"All right, but I need you to help me a bit more, because I wasn't with you yesterday or the day before that. How do you feel today," I asked.

"Didn't my doctor send my chart over here? I mean, do I have to start over from the very beginning with you?" he asked, with an air of irritation in his words.

"Your doctor's office hasn't sent any records over here, but your doctor gave me a very thoughtful summary on the phone. He gave me an overview that included a description of your accident, your injuries and miraculous survival and recovery. I could tell that he has a lot of admiration for you," I said.

"Yeah, well he might have admiration, but he hasn't done much to solve my medical problems for the last six months," he said gruffly. "I've not made much headway for that long."

"How would you describe your current medical problems?" I asked.

"I thought you said that you talked to Dr. Lee. Didn't he tell you anything," he said, sounding more and more agitated.

"Mr. Carpenter, Lyle, I am trying to find out what you think and feel. I want to get to know you, not just what someone else has to say about you.

"Oh for Christ's sake, I'm sick damn it. That's all there is too it. Are you going to be able to help me or not, 'cause if you're not I might as well be on my way," He said, while leaning forward on his chair like he was about to take flight.

Now, I thought to myself, would be a darn good time to call in some help. I am about to lose this one to the street. In a silent prayer I say, Let Hugh be there. Let him pick up the phone. "Lyle, with your permission, I would really like to see if my boss is in his office and willing to give us the benefit of his deep experience in occupational injury recovery work. Would you give me your permission to do that?"

"Well, we sure as hell aren't getting anywhere, are we," was his terse rejoinder.

I took his response as permission to call in the cavalry, and as I contacted Hugh and requested that he join us, Lyle eased back off the edge of his chair giving every indication that he was prepared to stay a bit longer to see how things would pan out. Hugh bounded up the stairs rather quickly, and after his introduction, for a few moments he acted as observer in our midst. My questions were going nowhere, bouncing off Lyle as before Hugh's arrival.

Then, after making a guttural throat clearing sound, Hugh asked Lyle if he was hard of hearing. Lyle said he was not. Then Hugh asked, "Why is Mr. Henson speaking so loudly?"

"It's only a guess, mind you, but I think it's his weak and frustrated attempt to get through to me... to make a point of some kind. But you could ask him if you like."

Hugh took in Lyle's answer, but ignored Lyle's suggestion. "So if you're not deaf, what are the symptoms of your ongoing illness," he asked, with point blank eye contact.

Looking at the two of them, I observed that they were much closer in age that Lyle and I, and I felt like the kid in the room. After the briefest of hesitations, Lyle began to answer. "I feel weak and tired all the time. Off and on, maybe 10 or 12 times a day I feel like I'm about to throw up. That's the way it's been for over six months. And it isn't getting any better."

"Is there a food or a smell or a thought or a sound associated with your off and on nausea?" Hugh asked.

Hugh's question was met with silence, and I thought for a moment that he had run into the same brick wall I had pressed up against. Soon large tears began to stream down Lyle's cheeks, and his mountainous shoulders began to shake as his chin rested on his heaving chest. It seemed as if time was suspended in the quivering quiet space. Hugh patiently waited for Lyle, and I knew enough to keep my mouth shut. At the level of a whisper, but spoken with great clarity, Lyle's words began to form. "Every time I hear a plane," he said. "My whole life has been airplanes, over 30 years, nothing but airplanes. And now I want to throw up whenever I hear one." Another wave of tears punctuated by ragged breathe gasps followed this declaration. "What the hell am I going to do now?" Lyle's question seemed to hang in the air like words in a cartoon bubble for close to an eternity.

With great compassion and certainty, Hugh's answer broke the silence in the room. "You can do any damn thing you want, Lyle. Any damn thing you like."

Almost imperceptibly, he nodded his weary, worn and wet face, signaling affirmation.

Lyle pulled a handkerchief out of his back pocket to wipe off his face, sending his comb flying across the room. He either didn't notice or didn't care. "I'd like to come back and work on this mess again, if I could," he said.

"Would you like us to continue as a threesome?" Hugh asked, making what I thought was a vain effort to keep me connected to the case.

What happened next, given what I thought had just transpired, caught me by total surprise.

"Naw, I think I could work with the kid just fine. If we get stalled someplace, we can always give you a call," he said. Perhaps I was learning something, to keep my mouth shut and not put too much stock in my assumptions about what might be in someone else's head.

More Shooting
16

Molly Merritt, one of Drain Elementary School's first grade teachers, was everything her principal said she would be and so much more. She was flexible in mind, body and spirit. Tuesdays, she said, would be fine. 60 to ninety minutes in the morning, beginning at 9:30, would be terrific. We settled on a 60-minute interval for the group itself, and 30 minutes to debrief the session or strategize for the week to come. In the time it took me to review my plans with Hugh, and finalize Tuesday with all the players, Molly and her peers had already selected 10 first and second graders, and acquired parental consent on eight of the 10. "It's a bit of a shame given the needs of the kids in question, but we may never get parent consent on those last two," she said. She had the clearest of blue eyes, which her students were sure provided her with x-ray vision, the kind that can see straight through a lie or a desktop. "If we don't have approval from those two parents by the time we are ready to begin, we can move forward with the group we have. They can be the control group, the ones who needed but didn't get any help. Oh, I all most forgot to tell you. As far as the teachers are concerned, we have already succeeded by giving them an hour per week of peace and tranquility!"

She was slender and athletic, about my age, possessing both order and playfulness in one package. Within minutes of meeting, I could tell that we had identified a common goal and that the will and the energy to succeed were present. Bringing boundaries to feelings, thoughts and behaviors in children who were out of control in one or all three of the aforementioned areas, which was our ambitious goal.

Together, week by week, we would invent games that would be both fun and instructive at the same time, games that would allow the 10 or 12 of us to practice one or more of these three life skills. Feelings could be explosive, stuffed, or shared in a respectful manner. Thoughts could be creative, rigid or criminal! Behavior could be helpful, mean, cooperative or self-indulgent. We were determined to have fun with this process of inventing and enacting games that focused on self-respect or self-control in one of those three areas.

More excited than I had seen him since the Puhak debacle in which he had hired a patient from Pueblo State Hospital instead of a psychiatrist, Dr. Gray brought his smile into the family service clinic, capturing an audience with Hugh, Denny, Diane and me in the waiting room. Holding up the fingers on his right hand, with the thumb and forefinger close together, he announced, "I am this close to closing the deal on a new psychiatrist. The last little piece is housing. I have a call out to Dr. Valenti because I heard this morning that his new home in his vineyard is within days of completion. The modular unit he has been living in out there will be empty, and it sits on a gorgeous site surrounded by acre upon acre of wine varietals."

"Is the new psychiatrist a wino?" Denny asked.

"God, I sure hope not," Dr. Gray replied. "The last thing I need right now is strike number two."

"Dr. Waterford, and I am assuming that we are still talking about Dr. Waterford, does have a bit of a reputation as a party animal. But then at 65 or 70, whatever he is now, perhaps he has moderated his self-abuse to some lesser degree," Hugh chimed in.

"I don't want any negativity or doubt raining down on my parade! You'll see. It's going to work out this time. I think we are going to catch a break on this one. No one in this State has more experience in community psychiatry than John. Multnomah County's loss is going to be our gain," spoke Dr. Gray in a voice that sounded somewhat less certain than the words would imply.

"I hope you are right. All of us will be the beneficiaries if it works out," Hugh said, trying to remove any adversarial air in the room. After the staff meeting, Hugh pulled me into his office, closed the door and sat down like a sack of bricks. "Legend has it that the boozing isn't really the most problematic aspect that comes with the Dr. W. package. What got him fired was his hand up inside the skirt of the Multnomah county assistant counsel."

"Ouch, that's pretty bold!" I said. "Young woman attorney I take it."

"Yes, it was not a Scottish Rite's bagpiper. And I am telling you this because I have just appointed you to the chairmanship of our just formed vigilance committee."

With great success, in but a few days, Dr. Gray negotiated a housing deal between Dr. Valenti and Dr. Waterford. Before hearing from Dr. Gray, Dr. Valenti's only plan for the modular unit was to sell it and have it hauled away. Collecting a thousand dollars a month for it from an apparently upstanding member of the medical community for an unspecified period of time sounded like a posh deal. Just how many bottles of wine from the estate went with the bargain, outsiders would never know.

On that glorious morning, Dr. Waterford's first day on the job, the sunshine was shimmering brightly through the colored windows on the east side of the clinic building. It was one of the perks of working in a building that had formerly been the Nazarene Church. The other perk was working in a Sunday school classroom size consultation room. Betty and Diane were already in place, organizing schedules and parceling out transcription assignments. Card-carrying Sierra Club member Denny had just wandered downstairs to pick up his daily ration of client files. Hugh was seated at his desk in his downstairs office with his door open. The stage was all set for Dr. Waterford's grand entrance. Through the door, into the waiting room he came with the head of a mountain goat under one arm and the head of an elk, complete with a humongous rack of antlers, under the other arm.

"Hi, everyone," he called out to all and no one in particular, "I'm Dr. John."

Trying to match Dr. Waterford in tone and style, Denny Martin was the first to reply. Holding out his hand before he realized what he was seeing, he said, "Hi, I'm Dr. Denny." Then, observing that Dr. John's hands and arms were both totally encumbered with dead animals, Denny took a step back and dropped his extended hand of welcome. "Where do you think you're going with those heads of beasts?" he asked.

Correctly anticipating an imminent collision between his Sierra Club psychologist and his brand new, rifle-building, just retired psychiatrist from Multnomah County, Hugh came flying out of his office hoping to head off a looming disaster. "Hello and welcome aboard, Dr. Waterford," he said, while valiantly trying to position his body between the two doctors. Perhaps he momentarily forgot the fact that it is the stuff in the middle of Oreo cookies that gets eaten first.

"Yes, hello and where do you think you're going with those wild animal heads?" Denny repeated.

"Beautiful aren't they. I'm a Boone and Crockett trophy hunter," he announced proudly while looking around at the available wall space and giving the women a winsome boyish smile. "These would look wonderful right here in the waiting room, don't you think." And, not pausing for a response, he continued, "I've got a couple more beauties for my office waiting in my truck out there." He pointed in the direction of the parking lot.

The veins on Denny's neck were pulsing with his raging heart. "It's a sacrilege and desecration to go into the forest and kill off these magnificent animals," he said. And he was on a roll that Hugh could not rein in. "No way in hell are you going to put these heads up over the waiting room chairs ... over my dead body."

Keeping that youthful smile in place as if he weren't General Custer facing tribes on a Dakota field, Dr. John launched into his obviously practiced position. With amazingly calm deportment, Dr. John continued with his presentation as if there wasn't a steaming bald-headed blusterer standing toe to toe with him. Actually, Denny stood at least a head taller than Dr. John, but the latter exhibited not a shred of the appearance of intimidation. "You are not the only one to misunderstand the Boone and Crocket ethos. Once each year, the Department of Fish and Game conduct a very special limited tag hunt, issuing a permit for one or two very special individual animals of a given species. For example, this mountain goat here came from Steens Mountain in eastern Oregon. It was chosen for the hunt because it is a very old mountain goat that was not expected to make it through another rugged high mountain winter. If it dies in a mid-winter storm out on some desolate rock outcropping, no one would ever again have a chance to enjoy this magnificent creature. Many hundreds of hunters pay to participate for a chance to hunt this one individual animal, but only one permit or tag is issued. Some hunters have paid into this lottery for decades without ever winning the tag. In other words, we are paying to sustain the organization which protects our wildlife and seldom get a chance to shoot," he concluded.

Hugh appeared to be impressed by this high-minded presentation. "Well there you go," he said.

"Not so fast," said Denny, who was in no mood to just roll over and accept Dr. John's position. "If I follow and accept the logic of your position, are you saying that we should have a lottery and shoot our most accomplished senior citizens?"

"OK, OK, as the boss of this place, I am going to make an executive decision. I find both arguments very elegant and persuasive. Dr. John, I want you to have as many heads in your consultation room as you like. Dr. Denny, in honor or your sense of taste and decorum, we shall have a head free waiting room. Welcome aboard, Dr. John," Hugh said.

Science and Dream Work
17

In the local high schools each year, science classes engage in a unique sort of competition that has always attracted my interest. The contest presents itself to be an engineering challenge where in each student or group of students study, design and construct a bridge made of tooth picks and glue. The contestants meet at the local community college where the design merits are compared and judged, and then, one by one, each bridge faces the ultimate test. One by one, each bridge is placed inside a set of abutments and then subjected to an increasingly severe test of strength. Unit upon fractional unit of weight is hung from the structure until it finally succumbs to collapse. The designated winner is the bridge that carries the most weight before caving in to the stress load.

While it is certainly not advisable to do so, my observation tells me that many people put themselves through a simulation of this kind of stress test every day. Only the few and the fortunate have the serenity prayer memorized and anchored into their decision making process.

Both Hugh and I had the good fortune of attending Jim Heenan's workshop on Gestalt dream work. The road trip to Salem's Holiday Inn was well worth the effort. Gestalt, by the way, is not the sound of a sneeze. It's a branch of psychology that explores all aspects of human sensory awareness for patterns and for the totality of experience. It tends to focus on present sensation and phenomena. The way Jim Heenan applies gestalt theory to dream work allows the phenomena of the machinations of the unconscious mind to be explored in the context of a therapy session.

Are you following me so far? I hope not to misrepresent Jim's practice by reducing it to a paragraph or less, but he views the dream state as the unconscious mind trying to solve, by the process of metaphor, problems which cannot be resolved by the conscious, rational mind. Have you ever gone to bed in a state of confusion and after a good night's sleep, found that the next morning you had your answer? What happened during your sleep that brought about this resolution? Wouldn't it be great to harness the power of the conscious mind and the unconscious mind in the counseling process to achieve therapeutic results!

"Let's encourage the people in our adult therapy group to do dream journaling a la Heenan. I really think he's onto something. The idea that all parts of the dream, being created by the self, are parts of the self... no matter how disguised they may be by the metaphor... that makes sense to me," Hugh said.

"I like the 'night janitor of the soul' idea. You know, how the dream tries to clean up the mess left by the unresolved problems of the awake and conscious part of the life. If I understand what you are suggesting, we would encourage every group member to keep a spiral notebook on the nightstand beside his or her bed. And, within the first five minutes of waking up, we would encourage them to use Heenan's dream journal scheme to record their dream memories. Then we would have them bring their journals to the group session. Is that what you're thinking?" I asked.

"Exactly. They take notes on each distinct dream memory just like it's the script for a play. They would list and describe each character and each object. Then they would make a notation of the setting... place, surroundings and past, present or future tense. Finally, they would take note of the mood that they are experiencing during or after the dream. What am I leaving out?" He sounded enthusiastic about the prospects for this activity.

"Well, if I remember correctly, Heenan thought it was OK for a person to make note of a theme or a plot, if one seemed obvious," I said. "We could make up a little paragraph handout with these ideas on it."

"Yes, that's right. How do you feel about you and me keeping our own dream journals?" he asked.

"I've already got one started. I like getting to know this skill from the inside out. But since our therapy group is for the clients, I recommend that we look at our own dream journals during consultation or supervision time. After all, we don't want the clients to be overwhelmed with our pathology, do we?"

"Point taken!" he said.

Both Hugh and I were filled with vibrant energy as we began to sort through possible candidates for our group and shape our vision of the group therapy process. Each person had to be a volunteer and subscribe to the rule of group confidentiality: what is said in the group stays in the group. Each person would have an opportunity to do his or her own personal work in the presence of the other group members, which meant that trust building was a must. Questions and feedback from other group members to a given group member would be allowed on a consent basis. In other words, when one member completed a piece of personal work, other members might ask a question or make a comment on that piece of work only if the working group member was open to these. As therapists, we admired many of the qualities of a 12-step group, qualities like anonymity and the spirit of a commitment to a healing community. So while we initially sought a three-month or 12 consecutive week minimum, group members could remain longer if they wished and new members would be added from time to time in order to maintain a good working number. One of the major positive qualities of AA, we thought, was the therapeutic benefit of having a mix of experienced and new group members over the life of the group.

On the first day of this new adult group, the composition included four women who ranged from 22 to 51 years of age, and two men who were 24 and 55 years old respectively. "Possibly two to one is the ratio of courageous women to courageous men," Hugh speculated.

"You are a bloody optimist where the male gender is concerned!" I said. And we both enjoyed the laughter.

Most of the first group session was consumed by a relaxed and fairly unstructured get acquainted process. Hugh and I talked a little about dream work and suggested that each member of the new group acquire a spiral student notebook to keep track of their dreams.

Jerry, our 24-year-old guy, was strongly pressured to join the group by his parole officer. He was on the very raggedy edge for qualifying as a volunteer. His fear of his PO was such that he literally begged Hugh to let him join the group. Jerry was admittedly immature. Impulsivity and poor decision-making were obvious concerns, which became much enhanced by binge consumption of alcohol, but he vowed solemnly that he would attend every group session for the next 12 weeks. For him to be that methodical or consistent about anything for 12 weeks would be a major accomplishment, even if all he did was fill a chair.

Eldon was a genuine worn out 55-year-old cowboy, and had the hat, boots, horse and belt buckle to prove it. Though we never saw Eldon's horse, the stuff on his boots left little doubt of its existence. Bulls and mustangs had dropped him on his head and stomped on him so many times that it was a monumental challenge for him to climb the stairs to the second floor conference room where group would meet. He was far too macho to complain, but it was agonizing just to watch him make the ascent. His depression was largely the result of all the losses he experienced as a result of his multiple disabilities. In his younger days, he might have had a lot in common with Jerry. In his present age and condition, he was one of the most gentle and kind people I have ever met. It was from Eldon that I learned the expression "If I had known I was gonna live this long, I'd a taken better care of myself!"

At 51, June was a pleasant, moderately over weight, ever smiling depressed woman. The smile, she said, was a disguise meant to keep people out of her personal business. When she decided to give counseling a chance, it was a therapy group she went looking for because she had heard that some counselors were crazy. She was confident that she could hide out in a group if the need arose or communicate with the sane clients.

Some mental health professionals might have pegged Laurie, age 39, with a bi-polar disorder label. She was the kind of person that all the soccer moms turned to when it was necessary to organize a fundraiser or navigate the logistics of putting on a 10-team tournament. The church to which she belonged might have folded were it not for her constant willingness to do whatever the day required. Outgoing, and highly verbal, there wasn't an ounce of fat on her slender, always moving frame. The only exception to her full-speed-a-head program was the occasional depressive episode during which she couldn't get out of bed.

Susan had four children under the age of 10 before husband emptied out their joint checking account and left town with his secretary, a childless woman 10 years her junior. Her turn was coming, he kept reassuring her. She said she was in group to rebuild her self-confidence and reacquire her adult social skills. For the past 10-years she had majored in domestic engineering and kid speak. Every shirt she owned had stains on it from having been spit up on multiple times by each successive child. She supplemented the family income by cleaning houses. At 31, she was desperately trying to figure out how to upgrade her education so that her month would not out run her paycheck. Her personal goal was to acquire a two-year business degree from Umpqua Community College, but she lacked the money to enroll and expressed grave concern that her old beater of a Ford Galaxy would die in the campus parking lot, leaving her stranded and unable to get back home.

And, last but not least, Naomi opted into the group as a place to figure out what to do with her non-marriage, and subsequently the next phase of her life. Living with Vern, she decided, was just a long-standing bad habit. The shake up with her older stepdaughter Georgia had served to remind her that her girls were now independent adult woman. For better or worse, her reason for sticking with a loveless partner had long since been fulfilled.

Waving her spiral notebook over her head like a child volunteering to be an ice-cream tester, Laurie got our second group session launched with abundance of enthusiasm. "I've got my recurring nightmare right here in the first three pages!" she said. "And you're going to cure me of all my mental pathology today!" She exclaimed as she scanned from Hugh to me and back again.

I'm thinking, "Oh, shit. What kind of a monstrous expectation did we create?"

But Hugh just waded right into the stream of conversation with much apparent confidence. "That's terrific, Laurie. Tell us what you've written there."

"This is the dream that I have over and over again. I invariably wake up screaming and sweating. My husband is talking about sleeping on the living room sofa to preserve his sleep and safety. It always goes something like this. I see myself sleeping in my bed, in my home. Then I see myself sitting on the side of my bed in my nightgown. Next, I am walking zombie-like, out of my bedroom, down the hall, through the living room and out the front door. I'm not entirely sure at this point if I am awake or sleepwalking, but then, I can sort of see what's in front of me, so I'd have to say that I am somewhat awake. Once out the front door, which by the way I do not remember opening, I proceed down the sidewalk toward the curb where a huge truck is parked. Other than huge, I am a bit sketchy on the details about the truck. It could be like one of those Euclid highway construction-type dump trucks, or the largest garbage truck you've ever seen. Then a peculiar thing happens. The passenger door swings open. All by itself, the door swings wide open. I don't know why, but I feel compelled to climb up the steps and plop myself down in the passenger seat."

Laurie took a deep breath, during which all of us silently and eagerly waited for her to resume. "As soon as I am fully in the truck, the door closes ... all by itself. I feel a small panic rising in my throat as I begin scanning the interior of the truck. Looking at the door from the inside for the first time, I notice that there are no door handles. I'm in for the ride, wherever that may be. I don't remember a motor sound, but the gigantic truck is soon slowly moving down the street ... my street, I think. People, some I recognize and some I don't, come out to the curbs in front of their houses carrying all kinds of garbage and trash, armloads of stuff. All of which they pitch into the bed of the Euclid. It seems like everybody has a huge load to pitch in, and it doesn't take too long before the truck is swaying with a ponderous load of crap. I can't actually see the load, but can see what is going in and I can somehow feel its weight.

"No sooner than I sense the magnitude of the load, I am aware that the truck is on a downhill grade beginning to pick up speed. My panic growing, I notice that there is no one in the driver's seat and even if there were, no clutch or brake pedals graced the floor. Steeper and steeper becomes the incline. Faster and faster goes the truck. I think to myself, thank God it's the middle of the night and the street is otherwise deserted. Up ahead, I can see a T-intersection ... a stop sign and just beyond that a wooden barricade that I am barreling toward. That's when I brace myself and scream bloody murder, anticipating the inevitable crash," she said as she exhaled and slid deeper into her chair.

For a moment, the room was silent. Perhaps everyone in the room was as profoundly stunned by the power and force of the dream as I was. All were in reverent awe of what Laurie had revealed. Hugh broke through the quietness with a question directed to Laurie. "What is the most powerful part of the dream for you, Laurie?" he asked.

The truck, it's that damn truck!" she replied.

"And how are you like that damn truck?" he asked.

After the slightest hesitation, Laurie began, "I am everything like that truck! As the truck, I lure Laurie in and take her for the same ride over and over. She's such a sucker. As the truck I haul her around, load her up and offer her no escape ... no handles, knobs or brakes. Sickness or death, a crash of some kind has been my only recourse. My God! What am I doing to myself?"

"That sounds like a very important prayer you've just made. What do you think God's answer will be?" I asked.

For a second, Laurie had a puzzled look on her face. "Yes, yes, I think it is a prayer. To begin with, it was a question, but now I think it is a prayer. I believe that God would say, 'Laurie, if you compulsively say "yes" to everyone, the joy will be sucked out of your life. The life will be sucked out of you. And you are stealing from others the opportunity to make a contribution. Get some handles and brakes for your truck, for crying out loud! Better yet, sell the Euclid and get a pickup, a wheelbarrow or a grocery cart!"

With a big smile on his face, Hugh said "And the people all said... "

And everyone, even Eldon, responded, "Amen!"

Fridays
18

As the morning began, one could be lulled into thinking it was just another day, but in the mental health business, Fridays are usually special. They are similar to 4:45 PM on any day, except magnified five times. If a person is going to have a crisis, they intuitively know that it is best to have it at the most inconvenient possible time. It isn't really a crisis unless the therapist is packing up to leave the building for the weekend, preferably a three day weekend ... the kind with Monday tacked on for good measure.

"We handled a lot of difficult and severe cases back when I worked at the State Hospital," Dr. Waterford began to say for no apparent reason, but with his winsome boyish smile, he managed to attract a small audience in the waiting room. "For instance, there was this cowboy named Jake who hailed from out in Eastern Oregon. From time to time, he claimed to have violent headaches and events that looked something like grand mal seizures. He would roll around on the ground, cursing and thrashing about until he was exhausted, lying there on the ground in a sweaty pile.

"He came to the State Hospital only after the most thorough of neurological examinations and various medication trials. Jake had a brief career riding broncos on the rodeo circuit. It was Jake's contention or hallucination that he was possessed by a wild stallion, one that lived inside him and that would episodically go on a rampage, throwing him all over the place. We tried everything we could think of to cure him and the interval between episodes was so random that sometimes we thought we had found the right drug or procedure. Then he would have another of his 'seizures' and we would have to start all over again. We tried all of the Antipsychotic medications. We tried electroshock therapy. We tried it all. Months went by. One day, Dr. Brooks came up with the idea of psycho pseudo surgery. The old hospital still had a surgical set up on the ground floor from its previous use as a tuberculosis sanitarium, and Dr. Brooks pointed out that this operating room even had a window with a view of the field on the north side of the building.

"His idea was to put Jake under a light general anesthesia, make a superficial incision across the area where Jake believed the horse to be located in his body. We would symbolically remove the horse, suture the incision closed. After the anesthetic began to wear off, we would bring the horse up to the window so that Jake could see that the procedure had been a complete success. I suggested that we spread a bit of horse manure on the operating room floor so as to add to the realism, but I was over ruled by the others for alleged hygienic reasons.

"We informed Jake of our plan, discussed all the risks and possible benefits. Jake was most enthusiastic as he believed that we were finally listening to him and had come up with a promising solution for his affliction.

"On the day of the surgery, we were all scrubbed and gowned. Before we gassed Jake, he drew for us a mark on his abdomen, which specified the exact point from which we should remove the horse. The procedure was completed flawlessly and Dr. Brooks did a beautiful job with the closure. On cue, as Jake came out of the sedation, one of our maintenance men held the reins of a magnificent white horse in the field, just outside the window. When Jake began to feel the return of his strength and consciousness, he rose up on his elbow and looked out the window.

"He's a beauty, isn't he?" Jake exclaimed. "But there has been some kind of mistake here. The white horse never caused me no trouble. It's that damn black one what causes me all my troubles."

Betty and Diane laughed and slapped their thighs. Gary rolled his eyes. Hugh gave me a wink before disappearing into his office. Denny groaned and walked away mumbling something to himself. I'm not sure I caught it precisely, but it sounded like... "And he's the one making the big bucks." I personally enjoyed the entire scene, including the story and the assorted responses. Before I could refocus on the day ahead, Betty recovered sufficiently from her spasms of laughter to signal to me that she wanted my attention.

"A woman who lives out in Tenmile area called this morning. Says her neighbor, a 30's something single mother of four, had been talking about killing herself ... maybe drowning herself and her children. Says the oldest is about six, but there is a set of twins in there somewhere. The caller asked what she could do, so I told her to find another neighbor to watch the children and then to bring the mother in here to you to see," Betty said, now very concerned and sober in appearance.

"Thanks," I said facetiously.

"You're very welcome," she said, as if I had fully and positively disclosed my sentiments in a simple statement of gratitude. "It will take a bit of time for her to get this rescue organized out there and then its quite a drive from out there. I asked her to call before she hit the road, but I doubt that she will get here before 4:00 PM."

"About quarter to five, I'd guess," I mumbled to myself.

"What did you say?" she asked.

"Oh nothing, I was just talking to myself. I've heard of Tenmile. Wasn't there an article in the newspaper last week, something about a new stop sign or parking meter?"

"Yes, that would be Tenmile. The owner of the General Store, the only store actually, is going to put in a parking meter because he said that he was unhappy about locals driving all the way to Roseburg to shop when he has everything they need right there in his store. Says that he has everything that Roseburg has except a parking meter, so he's putting in one of those," she said with a chuckle.

"Where is Tenmile?" I asked.

"I'd guess it to be about halfway to Coquille, which is the southern route to the coast. You know, just go south on the Interstate to Winston and turn right."

"And what is that part of the county noted for?" I asked.

"Poverty, I think. Seems to me the cows are so skinny, their hides hang on bones. If you tried to milk them, you'd probably end up with a bucket of dust," she said without a speck of humor in her voice.

"You think this mother of four could be in a pretty desperate situation, don't you?" I asked.

"I think you can be near certain of it. I think she's lucky to have a neighbor who cares."

"OK then, she's mine. Call me when we have an approximate time of arrival," I said.

"You can count on it," she said. "And if I hear anything more about the situation, I'll bring that to you also."

It was mid-afternoon when the call came in on the intercom from Betty. "The Tenmile woman and her suicidal neighbor are on their way now and will be here shortly after 4:00."

"OK," I replied. "It'll be at 4:45," I mumbled to myself. This is the very situation I thought perhaps that I could have prevented by hiding out in Drain or Yoncalla on Fridays. "What about the kids?"

"A friend of the neighbor has that handled, so they are safe," she said. And, after a brief exchange of shallow pleasantries, we severed the connection and I began to tackle the pile of dictation stacked up and waiting in front of me.

At exactly 4:45 PM, the intercom buzzed again. Betty notified me that the crisis had arrived. Judy Nevelle was her name. Her neighbor made the introduction in the waiting room and assured me that she would remain in the waiting room until Judy's appointment was over. "I'll just read this book I brought along to keep me entertained," she said. Betty assisted Judy with the clinic application.

Though Betty indicated that she would soon be leaving and was about to lock the outside door for the weekend, a portion of my distress had vanished the moment the neighbor committed herself to not just drop off Judy and dash. My assessing and hopefully not judging mind began scanning the situation before the initial very limp handshake. Judy was extremely slender. One could say possibly anorexic in severity. Betty's description of the domestic livestock out in Tenmile fleetingly came to mind, but Judy was small boned and resembled no livestock of any kind. Her head was down cast even at the moment of introductory handshake, and my sense of her was of not only depression but extreme shyness as well.

Once we were seated in my consultation room, I was painfully aware of how quiet the whole building had become. There wasn't going to be any backup from Hugh or Gary on this one. For them, the weekend was under way. I could say it was quiet as a church in the midst of silent prayer because it was an old church building, and I was passionately praying that Judy and I could find a way to navigate around her suicidal preparation.

Dressed in a simple cotton shift with a faded floral pattern, her focus appeared to be on her hands, which were folded in her lap with the fingers entwined. I had no idea how to make a connection with this somber young woman. "Now that you are here, are you glad that you came?" I asked quietly.

"No, I just want to lie down and die, but Barbara wouldn't let me," she said.

I liked the passive sound of her death wish. Nothing of a violent type, she mentioned no weapons or drug overdoses. There was no hint of the drowning scenario mentioned earlier in the day. "What seems to be at the heart of your unhappiness?" I asked.

"I'm tired of care giving, tired of being hungry, tired of being lonely ... and tired of being tired," she said.

"It sounds like this tiredness has been accumulating for a long time, like you have had many bad days over a period of months or years even," I said.

"That would be true. I was 10 years old when momma died. I was pretty small, but I was the oldest. That put me in charge at home. I began care giving and exhaustion on a regular basis back to then," she said, looking up for the first time.

I could now see the dark circles under her eyes as she made visual contact at this moment. "So what you really need is some help and some serious rest, but maybe not death," I suggested. "At least maybe not death today. Maybe not death this weekend. What do you think?"

"Maybe not death today or this weekend, if I had some help with the children and some rest," she said with a bit of relief mixed with despondency.

"If Barbara could round up some help for you and the children for the weekend, would you promise me that you will be in my office alive and well for an appointment on Monday?" I asked.

"What other choice do I have?" she answered in a "no choice" victim tone.

"Or I would have to make arrangements for you to get your rest and safety at Douglas Community Hospital for the weekend," I said, hoping it sounded more like a second option than like a bald threat.

It was a visit with Barbara that Judy chose as well as acceptance of the pledge to return for an appointment on Monday. Barbara quickly called her friend who had taken Judy's children for the day and asked her if she could manage to keep them through the weekend and possibly until after Judy's clinic appointment on Monday. From a distance of 10 or 15 feet, I could overhear Barbara's end of the telephone conversation she was having with her neighbor. Barbara's friend had left her holding the phone for a few moments while the friend checked with her husband. Soon Barbara had her answer. Her friend not only gained spousal approval, her teenage daughters volunteered to be part of the play and care team. Barbara offered her home and support to Judy for the weekend respite.

Within a few minutes, the women were out the door and I was

ever so grateful to Barbara and her friend that my weekend was under way.

Once home, I couldn't believe my eyes. Aaron was alternately walking and falling on his well-padded behind. There was a giggle and grin that accompanied his intermittent triumph and relapse. The contrast between what I was now experiencing at home and the view of family life and parenting given to me by the last client of the week couldn't have been more at odds. At the heart of the difference between the one and the other resides a loving and supportive partner and co-parent. A single woman who intentionally impregnates herself with her brother-in-law's semen using a turkey baster, that's my definition of insanity!

When Judy and Barbara drove out of the clinic parking lot on Friday evening, I must have had a lot of confidence in Barbara as a nurturer. My mental delegation to her was so complete, I never gave that situation another thought until I arrived at work Monday morning and began to gear up for the oncoming day. It was shaping up to be a beautiful day in the neighborhood. A gentle breeze had overnight blown out the fog, smog and drizzle that so often mucks up the valley sky in February. The combination of morning sun and moisture on the ground gave the appearance of diamonds scattered everywhere. I could feel my spirits rising with the barometer. With the daily ration of files in my hand, I bounced up the clinic stairs like a young pronghorn.

The sound of the intercom brought me crashing down to earth. "Could you please come down here?" Betty said in a near whisper. "I need your help. There is one very irate woman in the waiting room who is asking for you."

Some screaming was unavoidably wafting up the stairs and down the hall. "Lucky me, I will be right down," I replied.

Standing in the middle of an otherwise empty waiting room stood a loud, animated, red-faced Judy with her hands on her hips and the veins on her neck sticking out. I briefly scanned the area for Barbara, expecting the two women would be arriving together. Not sighting her, I somehow knew I was alone on this one. "Good morning Judy, it's good to see you."

"Don't you good morning me. You best be figuring out how to help me get my kids back."

"That shouldn't be all that difficult to arrange," I said. "Let's get out of this waiting room goldfish bowl. We can get some privacy upstairs, and you can tell me all about your restful weekend." Then I turned and headed back up the stairs.

She must have decided that she had my attention, or she wanted my ear more that she wanted Betty and Diane for an audience, because she piped down and follow me up the staircase.

Once seated, I said, "You don't look depressed or suicidal. As a matter of fact, you look down right energized. Tell me about your weekend."

"Those women ... I'm going to have them arrested ... put in jail for kidnapping!" she said, beginning to rebuild the fire she had started down stairs.

Hoping to avoid another conflagration, I cut in. "Judy you chose to receive the help of those two women."

"Maybe so but I had no idea what those two Christian women were going to do to me and my children," she said, emphasizing "Christian" and "do to me."

"What did they do?" I asked.

"That Christian friend of Barbara's, she came over to Barbara's house, picked up my children, and I haven't seen them since ... and I don't know where she lives. And I want them back now!"

"If memory serves me, the deal you made here was that when you came in for your appointment today, we would decide together if you were sufficiently rested and ready to resume your parenting duties. I assumed that Barbara would bring you to your appointment this morning. By the way, where is she?" I asked.

"I ... couldn't take it anymore. I ran away from her house last night when she wasn't looking. When we got to her house Friday night, no sooner than the kids were whisked off to God knows where by her friend, Barbara offered me food and a glass of milk, turned down the covers and tucked me into bed ... I mean, tucked me in like I was a little kid ... turned out the light and shut the door ... up on the second floor. So, it wasn't as if I could just up and jump out the window! Food and rest and food and rest ... the woman wouldn't let me do anything! I thought I would go mad. Don't you see, I had to run away!"

"I think she took you at your word. You said that you were exhausted, totally despairing and suicidal ... couldn't possibly do another thing. That woman, Barbara, gave you total care, and your children are exactly where she said they would be. It was perfect ... like in heaven!" I said.

"Well, I guess I'm not ready to go to heaven yet. And I'm ready to have my kids back," she said quietly.

Mom and children were soon reunited. Barbara was in the waiting room when we came down the stairs, genuinely relieved that her runaway was safe at the clinic. As I reflect on this scene, I suppose it is another example of the old story "Be careful what you wish for." I am also acutely aware of the fact that Barbara and her friend had effected a cure in a manner in which a therapist or counselor never could, and I was immensely grateful to them even if Judy was not.

Screwed If I Do
19

Amazing to me and I am certain absolutely astonishing to Hugh, Jerry the parolee arrived early for adult group. And he sprinted up the stairs ahead of everyone on his way to the conference room. "All right Jerry, what's up with you? You have never been early for an appointment with me. Why are you so eager for group to get under way today?"

"It's my parole officer ... says I am on very thin ice. Friday when I saw him, he said that if I looked cross-eyed or even farted one more time he was goin' to haul my butt back to jail. I told him that I made it to group last week and that should count for something. He said I better be the first one here and the first one to go to work on my insanity or he'd throw me back in the can tomorrow."

"Jerry," Hugh said, "I thought your parole officer was hovering over you about your criminality, not your insanity. What is he referring to as your insanity?"

"I'm not sure for sure. But he told me that before my next meeting with him, I am required to see Woody Allen's movie "Take the Money and Run." He says I am way too impulsive and cracked in the head to ever make it as a criminal. Like last week, I went into a tavern out on the Diamond Lake highway, the one near Susan Creek campground.

"I saw this girl sitting at the bar. She had nice looking legs coming out of a miniskirt. She was sitting there by herself and I thought she was, you know, kind of hot looking. So, I wandered over there to introduce myself. She told me to get lost ... that her boyfriend was in the bathroom and would be back out any minute ... that she didn't want to see me get beat up. That right there just shows how much she cares about me, don't you think? And, I was thinking, what's he got that I don't have? It turns out he's six or eight inches taller and out weighs me by 50 or 100 pounds. He has the same stuff, but a lot more of it. When he came back to the bar, he grabbed me by the neck and a leg and pitched me out into the parking lot, head first.

"Turns out my cousin knows this fox. Knows where she lives too. So, I took a drive out that way to see if she was home. Couldn't really tell from the road ... the living room blinds were shut. So, I walked around her house a couple of times, but everything was closed up tight. So, I got back in my car and was just about to leave when two cop cars pulled in behind me. They told me to get out of the car, put my hands on the hood, the whole deal. And I said, what's this all about?"

"Jerry, Jerry," said Hugh. "I don't even know where to begin."

"Do you mind if I have a go at him? I mean if it's OK with Jerry," Eldon said.

Jerry nodded in the affirmative and Hugh said, "Be my guest."

"You see, son, you haven't yet figured out right from wrong, good from evil. It seems like you are without a compass, no basis from which to make a moral or even a safe decision. You're just being pushed along by whims and hormones. I mean, that stuff you just spewed out there; do you know which part of it is insane and which part of it makes sense?" Eldon asked in a very gentle tone.

"No, I guess not," Jerry confirmed.

"You see, that's the first thing you gotta be able to differentiate. You gotta be able to tell the difference between nutty and sane. Maybe we can help you with it until you can do it for yourself. See, I've got an idea how we can do that for ya. Out in my truck, I got a fairly clean piece a rope maybe 10 or 12 feet long. Because I like you, I'm gunna tie a nice hangman's noose knot on one end of the rope. Now ya see, you can slip that hangman's noose over your head and hand the opposite end of the rope to one of the other group members here, someone who can already tell the difference between criminal, crazy and sane. Whenever that person hears crazy or criminal come out of your mouth, you will authorize them to give a little tug on the noose. Then you have to identify the crazy part, and speak your piece again. After you can hear and catch your own crazy, criminal ideas, you can take charge of your own rope."

"Oh for crying out loud, Eldon, I don't think we can do that in group," Hugh said.

"I want to try it. It might work. If I can't figure out why my life is so messed up, I'm going to jail for sure," Jerry said.

"OK Jerry, if that's what you want. It will be just a gentle reminder tug ... and you can say, 'I want to stop this,' any time you wish. But remember that what people say and do in group is entirely confidential. I've never heard about a therapy group doing something like this," Hugh said with some uneasiness in his throat.

Jerry turned back to Eldon and said, "You're not fit to be running up and down those steps. Give me your truck keys and tell me where the rope is. I can zoom down there and be back faster than you can reach the second story landing."

"Right there Jerry ... that was an empathetic thought," I said. "You actually appear to care about Eldon's wellbeing," I said.

"Is that a good thing?" Jerry asked.

"That's good, Jerry," Eldon said as he handed a wad of keys on a ring to Jerry. "Rope's behind the seat on the passenger's side. That long silver-looking key with the round head and hole will get you into the rig."

Jerry took the handoff of keys from Eldon, and was out the door in a flash like he was being timed. After the group room door closed, Eldon tilted his head in my direction and said, "Do you think I'll ever see my truck again?"

"It certainly was a heroic act of trust on your part, Eldon. However, I believe there is a parole officer who will intercede on your behalf if necessary!" I said.

Momentarily, Jerry returned with a big smile on his face, keys in one hand and the rope in the other. He gently handed both to Eldon, who soon stowed the keys in his right front jean pocket, fashioned a hanging tree worthy noose and made a gift of it back to Jerry. Jerry slipped the noose over his head and handed the tail of the rope to a very sane and moral Naomi before he quietly sat back down in his chair.

For a few seconds, all in the room were quiet. Then, after clearing his throat, Hugh spoke up. "Who else has some personal work to do while we are together today?"

It was Susan, our young mother of four who broke the silence. "I have a confession to make," she said.

"Break out the priestly collars," Hugh said dryly.

"What is your confession, Susan?" I asked.

"Some of you know that my husband left me, that I have four children all under 10-years of age and that I have two crappy jobs without benefits. I have some ambition. I want to go back to school, but I am afraid that my old beater of a car won't start if I get it to run as far as Umpqua Community College. What I haven't admitted is how lonely I feel in this not-so-merry-go-round life of two by four, which brings me to my confession. I have this friend; well actually, she is one of the people I clean house for. Her name is Lea Ann. She's about my age, perhaps a bit younger. She's a single gal who has no children. We really don't have much in common. I think she may look down on me, because I have so little money and I think she can tell how lonely I am. Every so often, maybe twice a month, she will hire a babysitter for my brood and insist that we go out to the Fireside lounge for some dancing and a drink or two. She calls it my blues therapy. I tell her that it's not just the childcare I can't afford; I don't have money for the band cover charge or the drink or two or the gas to get us there. She tells me that she will cover the cover, and she will drive. I won't need any money for the drink either, she says. After she has shot down all of my excuses, what can I do besides go?"

All of the group members sat quietly, rightly assuming that her question is a purely rhetorical one.

"So, not long after we arrive at the Fireside some tall, wide-shouldered, narrow-hipped fellow in a button-down shirt and Dockers ... not a bad looking guy ... buys me a drink and asks me to dance with him. I tell him that's why I came to this place. A couple more drinks and several more dances, soon an hour and a half or two have gone by and I'm ready to go home. That's when I discover that my friend Lea Ann has disappeared. I mean, she's not in the powder room, not in the parking lot ... she's G-O-N-E. Checking around, I find out that she drove off someplace with the guy she's been dancing with most of the night. 'Not a problem,' says Dockers. He'll give me a ride home. What am I going to do? I am eight or 10 miles from home and do not have as much as cab fare in my pocketbook. Dockers takes me home all right, by way of the Travelodge. What with the alcohol and my indebtedness to him for the ride, what could I do? But by the time I got home, I felt like a cheap wh ... I felt like a wh ... I felt like a tramp," she said, as the tears began to course down her reddened cheeks.

The chivalrous Jerry rose up to the full height of his sitting position and declared, "who is this doctor who violated your ... you know, took advantage of you? I'll knock him upside the head!"

Susan ignored him and Naomi gave a serious yank on the noose. His face blushed as he turned from Susan to face Naomi.

Hugh started to respond to Susan, but in the same instant Eldon politely asked Susan if he could ask her a question. Before Hugh or I could intercede, Susan gave him a soft but definite "yes."

"I think you are a hardworking, intelligent, beautiful woman," he began. "And anyone in your position, with all those jobs and kids and not to mention a disappearing scoundrel of an ex-husband and all, is bound to get lonely some times. But don't you think you could figure out a way to get to and from the Fireside lounge without getting screwed?"

Susan seemed to perk up, straightening her shoulders and lifting her gaze in order to look directly into Eldon's eyes. "You're probably right, Eldon. I could drive my own beater, buy my own drink or not go at all," she said, with some degree of resolve. "That's exactly what I will do. I will get home with my dignity intact."

Hugh looked relieved and appreciative. "You amaze me, Eldon. If you keep this up, we will have to talk to Dr. Gray about putting you on the payroll," he said.

"And then Susan, you have one more item on you agenda," I said.

"I'm sorry. What would that be?" asked Susan.

"That old beater of a car that could fail to start on the Umpqua CC campus, leaving you stranded. So, you can't quite muster the courage to enroll for classes. I don't want Eldon to have to be the lone problem solver here. See what you think of this suggestion," I said. "I'm going to suggest that you drive out to the campus on whatever day and whatever time you think might be the most fearful time of the class day to be stranded out there. Once you are there, park and turn off your engine. Whether it will restart or not is inconsequential. Get out of the car, put up the hood and stand there for seven minutes with your head resting on your hand like this," I said, striking the damsel in distress pose. "Do you think you could do it?" I asked.

"Eldon wants me to become more self-reliant, and you seem to be encouraging me to test out my worst case scenario ... my barrier to enrolling. These two things are sort of like homework, aren't they?"

"If you choose to tackle them, yes they are," I said.

"Tackle them I will ... within the next two weeks. I can't promise to have them both done between now and next group," she said.

Before we all filed out of the group room, Jerry couldn't contain himself any longer. One last time he asked Susan, "what was that doctor's name?" Naomi gave one more stout pull on the rope and handed her part of the rope back to Jerry.

"I think you better keep this and bring it back with you next week," she said.

"OK," he said obediently.

The next group session, Jerry again was the first arrival and the first up the stairs ... rope in hand. Eldon was last up the stairs. Bless his soul; he didn't want to inconvenience anyone with his slow and halting ascent. When everyone was seated, Jerry donned his noose and asked Naomi if she would resume custody of the sane and moral reminder end of the rope. "It would an honor," she said.

Hugh restated the rules regarding the rope. "Jerry, we fell down on our follow through regarding the rope tugging last week. So, I want to go over your responsibility again. Let's say that if your personal work is the focus of the group when you receive the rope tug, you will be required to figure out what part of your thought is criminal, unsafe or not sane right then, before you continue any further. If someone else's personal work is the focus of the group like Susan's was when you received a couple of tugs last week, you will be asked to assess your thoughts as soon as the other person's work is completed. Do you understand me?"

"Yes, I think I've got it," Jerry answered meekly. "Like I shouldn't have been thinking about getting revenge on that doctor that was taking advantage of Susan, right?"

"Damn, Jerry, I think that rope just might be working!" Hugh said.

"Just out of curiosity, Jerry, how did you happen to select Naomi to be your noose handler?" I asked.

"I don't know, I think I would trust any one of you to keep me thinking straight, but Naomi seems so honest and kind. She always has that kind accepting nature, and yet I don't think she would let me get away with anything. You know what I mean?"

"Thank you Jerry," Naomi replied.

A peaceful quiet captured the room for several moments, and we all seemed content to let it rap around us. Hugh broke the silence. "June," he said invitingly, "you have managed to keep your anonymity here in the group better than anyone. Would you like to share something about yourself?"

"I wouldn't know where to begin. I know that I am not familiar with sharing anything about myself ... it was a dangerous thing to do in the intimidating family I was born into and the one into which I married. My dad and my husband ... one was and one is a belligerent drunk. They were not interested in hearing from or about me, and I did the best I could to be invisible. I didn't know I was marrying my dad's twin. The rescue and courtship days were wonderful, both of them."

"Does the smile indicate that you are a happy person, June?" I asked.

"Yes, it could," she said.

"But I thought you indicated that you gunny-sacked a lot of resentment during all those years of loveless, spouseless marriage?" Hugh questioned.

"Yes, I certainly did," she said.

"Wait just a darn minute," Hugh chimed in, "You said 'yes' to being happy and 'yes' to being resentful. How can you agree with both of those at the same time?"

"No, I said my smile could mean I am happy. 'Yes' in this case simply means I heard you. It doesn't mean I agree with you. I am just agreeing with the premise that a smile could mean that I am happy," she said.

"June, is it possible that you might be a professional conflict avoider?" I asked.

"I think you hit the nail on the head. I think 'yes' came to mean 'I hear you' because Ed, when he was home, was always looking for a fight. And I refused to give it to him," she said.

"Is there anything else that you want to say about this 'yes' business now?" I asked.

"No, nothing else. But I think it is a helpful discovery," she concluded.

"OK then, moving right along. Eldon you have managed to be a terrific resource to all of us. Do you have something that you want to work on today?" I asked.

"No, I can hardly wait to find out what if anything Susan did with her homework," he countered.

With that, everyone turned and looked expectantly at Susan. "I said it might take a couple of weeks to complete it," she began, "but once I got into it, I couldn't let go of it until it was all done. First of all, with respect to my old Ford Fairlane, I decided that I was most afraid of getting stranded after a night class. And, since I work on my two crappy jobs during the daytime, it seems a very likely scenario to go and get stranded at night. So I got out to campus a little before nine and positioned myself as close to an overhead light in the parking lot as possible. At exactly one minute past nine, I got out, put up the hood and assumed the pose. You'll never guess what happened. Within a couple of minutes, I was surrounded by about a dozen people ... some of them men around my own age! And did you know they have an industrial arts program that can actually fix up my old beater while I am in math or English class? I love that car!" she said, with blushing cheeks. "It's a pity it started up right away."

"You're going to enroll then?" asked Valerie.

"Absolutely, as soon as I can scratch up tuition for the first class," Susan responded.

"That's wonderful, but what about the second half of your homework?" Hugh asked.

"Well, that's sort of a different story. I called Lea Ann on Friday and asked her to meet me at the Fireside. When she said she'd come pick me up, I told her I had a few errands to run before so it would be best if I met her there. I just knew she would offer me a ride, so I kind of prepared myself with an answer for that. I was thinking of you the whole time, Eldon. I got there without a hitch, and I bought my own drink. After a few dances, I was feeling pretty confident ... but I didn't want to tempt fate too much. I looked all over for Lea Ann to tell her I was leaving. She seemed to have pulled the same trick as last time, because she was MIA again. As I saddled up to ride out of there for home, I felt like a virgin princess. As I rolled along, that theme song from Rocky was playing in my mind. You know, dah dah dah, dah dah dah," she sang. "That's about the time I noticed the flashing lights come on behind me. I pulled over, of course. And this State Trooper came up to my window. I felt like a bug waiting to be squished as I rolled down the window. While he repositioned the hat on his head and pulled the flashlight off his belt, do you know what I said? Right out of my mouth came the words 'screwed if I do, and screwed if I don't!' 'Madame?' he said. So, I blabbed out my whole sad tale to him. He explained that I was doing 50 miles per hour in a 35 miles per hour zone. I was so relieved when he wrote me a warning instead of a citation."

"I'll bet money that you could do the entire sequence without even getting pulled over," Eldon said dryly. "Want to go double or nothing?"

Of Laws and Limits
20

"There were these two women, both well past eighty," began Dr. Waterford with Hugh, Gary and Diane as his audience in the staff room. Whenever Dr. John goes showboating, I've noticed that Denny makes himself very scarce. "Every New Year's Eve they would meet at La Jolla Cove for a midnight swim. The air was cool and the water was somewhat breathtaking, but a tradition isn't a tradition unless it's kept. Into the surf they plunged, where they splashed and swam furiously for about 10 minutes before wading ashore to towel down. Though they had goose bumps and chattering teeth, they were smiling from ear to ear, having braved the ocean and survived the experience one more time. 'Wasn't that fabulous!' the one old gal gushed. 'Oh my, I'll say it was,' responded the other. 'The only thing that could make it better right now would be a cigarette to top it off.'

"'No problem at all,' said the first old gal, and she reached into the left breast cup of her swim suit, pulling out a condom closed at the top with a wire twisty like the ones you see in the produce section of the grocery store. Inside the condom were two cigarettes and one strike-anywhere-match. She struck the match on a dry stone, lit one cigarette and handed it to her friend before lighting her own.

'Now that's what I call fabulous,' said the second old gal as she exhaled, making smoke rings as she did. 'I must remember to get some of those condoms for myself next time I'm in the pharmacy!'

"Sure enough, as she goes into the pharmacy to replenish her supply of calcium and baby aspirin, she remembered her desire to acquire a condom, but she was somewhat confused by all the choices, so she approached the pharmacist. 'Could you help me select a condom,' she asked the pharmacist. Somewhat bemused by the octogenarian's request, he asked her to be more specific about her requirements. 'It has to be big enough for a camel,' she replied."

Hugh smiled and clapped at this performance. Gary wasn't sure how to respond, but Diane whooped with laughter. I missed the telling of this joke, but caught the responses to it as I passed by the staff room door on my way to the parking lot.

As I headed north on Interstate 5, I was mentally reviewing my good fortune. With Dr. Wiltse's help, I had been introduced to some of the most skilled and interesting people in the Drain/Yoncalla vicinity. Responding to the expressed mental health needs of these two communities was on a fast track because of his insights and contacts and the unwarranted faith he had placed in me. He had been singing my praises before we had even met.

Molly Merritt, energetic and skilled elementary teacher, proved to be an excellent organizer and co-leader of our blended first and second grader therapy group. She single-handedly selected the children, charmed the parents into giving their consent for the children to participate, and arranged the time and space for our meeting. All I had to do was show up. Jointly, it was our job to figure out how to convince these youngsters that rules, boundaries, structure and cooperation were good things. As the school year was heading from winter to early spring, we didn't have plenty of time to accomplish these ambitious goals.

The day of the first group meeting in Drain brought forth the most propitious storm. Early spring in this part of the State is notorious for volatile weather ... could be anything from sun to rain to a wet snowstorm. Today, just as we took our self-assigned places in a circle on the floor on pillows provided by Molly, the thunder cracked right over head, a large tree limb crashed to the ground outside within five feet of the swings in the play area. Then the power went off. After a couple more strikes nearby, the sky opened up and hail began to pour down, covering the ground to a depth of at least an inch and a half. The hailstones ranged from the size of marbles to size of jawbreakers. All of us just scrunched together in the semi-darkness as closely as possible in fear and mutual support as this awesome storm beat down all around us ... outside.

"Who wants to go outside right now?" asked Molly, in a voice that could be heard over the pounding din on the roof.

To be honest, her question frightened and startled me because I come from the school that says, "don't ask a question unless you are willing to live with the possible answers." And in this case, given the group that we were sitting with, it seemed to me within the realm of possibility that one or more of these little guys would want to run out and meet the storm head on. Fortunately, that was not the case today.

"Not me," said one. "Not me either," said another, and I was relieved when this quickly became the unanimous response to Molly's question.

"You mean to say," said Molly, "that it is a good thing to have a roof over our heads, even though we can't see the sky?"

Now I could see where Molly was going. She was taking the providence of this moment to address the heart of our mutually agreed upon task ... the beauty, value and necessity of limits and boundaries! "Miss Merritt, without that roof, that big limb might have hit us," said one wise little person.

"I think that lightning could cook us," said another sage.

"Hail is really cold, and it stings when it hits you," said yet another.

"I'm glad we have walls too," said a little girl whose name I have not yet memorized," because I don't want to freeze."

And that is how the group began, with everyone confirming in hundreds of ways how limits and boundaries are good for us and protect us. Now all we had to figure out was how to sell the ideas of sequence, order and cooperation before summer break!

Afternoon skies cleared, and the hail was soon replaced by moist, steaming roads and fields. The elementary school kids had me all charged up. My mind was churning with happy and mild mannered thoughts as I made my way to Yoncalla High School for the gang-banger-wannabe therapy group. When am I ever going to learn that getting high on one experience is usually soon followed by another that will bring me right back down to *terra firma*.

Larry, Yoncalla's Principal, was the first to see and greet me as I made my way down hall ... which today smelled of deep dish lasagna and garlic bread. "How's the family," I asked, right after, "hello."

"All are present and accounted for, thank you very much, but my sign is still up and I plan to keep it that way until after graduation day ... or maybe beyond. Nice sign like that, be a shame to take it down prematurely," he said.

Larry was referring to the "closed to repairs" sign that I had suggested for his driveway, so that he and his family could slow down the number and frequency of visitors and thereby get reacquainted with each other.

"I am glad you are enjoying that sign. Where's my main man Karl?" I asked.

"In the staff room, loading up on ammunition for your group I would imagine," he said.

"I will assume that ammunition is in the form of coffee and cookies until I see otherwise with my own eyes," I replied as I continued down the hall.

"Welcome partner," Karl said. "We are going to be one hombre short on the group roster today. It seems that Warren closed the car door before removing his hand this morning, so he made a quick trip to Dr. Wiltse's office. But, other than that, we are good to go."

As Karl and I plus seven not-so-happy-to-be-here teens filed into the classroom in which he had set up 10 chairs in a circle, the atmosphere was anything but jolly. Some faces were empty, while others seethed quietly behind hostile masks. There was none of that jubilant animation which characterized my morning at the elementary school. I had my doubts about whether Karl and I could find a way around the hot and defiant walls setting up all around us.

There was a brief attempt to create some sort of introductions process, but all we could hear were a few grunts and groans and an occasional word. The passive/aggressive stink was thicker than the atmosphere in a fart factory. Then Karl hit the central nerve of each group member dead center. "You understand, don't you, that you are all volunteers. Not one of you has to be a member of this group."

One of the guys, Witty was his street name, spoke up. "That isn't what my Caseworker told me. He said 'you attend this jive group or we gonna pull you outta that high school. You'll be back in Metro Juvenile Hall in a flash.' That's what he said."

That right there was more than the total number of words spoken by group members up to this point. "That's right," Karl replied. "Each of you has a choice to make. You can volunteer to be in this jive group or you can be in some other jive high school." It was dead silent in the room for a minute, and Karl just left it that way. Then he continued. "You see, Mr. Henson and I want your Yoncalla High School experience to be beneficial to you and the school. And so far it isn't. So you get to choose."

What followed this candid offer was absolute magic. One after another, all of the new group members presented the contrast between their life situation in Yoncalla with what the alternative would look like elsewhere. All that pseudo-tough bravado posturing began to melt away. One by one, each one volunteered to be in the group! And we were underway.

Mouths of Babes
21

"Jane and I are hosting a bit of a house-warming party at the vineyard house on Saturday, and you are all invited. I am going to grill on the barbecue wild game animals as a special treat for us all, including Dr. Denny. Jane has libations covered. If you each would bring along a salad or dessert, the menu will be complete," Dr. John announces at the end of Monday's staff meeting.

"That sounds great," said Hugh. This was followed by considerable head nodding and audible affirmations.

"Can you be more specific about the various dead animals to be grilled?" Denny ventured in a playful manner.

"There will be a wonderful assortment, you can count on it. Also, for the vegans like Mary, I will even grill up some veggies," John replied in his gracious host voice. Mary is Denny's wife, and how he knew that Mary was a staunch vegetarian I will never know.

John's response seemed to satisfy Denny's questioning mind. The staff meeting adjourned, and we all began to disperse to our separate tasks and appointments.

The remainder of the day flew by as many days do, filled with inconsequential details and events that do not rise to the level of memorable.

First on my agenda, Tuesday morning was a brief stop at Dr. Wiltse's office. "Could you double back here after your teen group in Yoncalla ... say between 3:30 and 4:00? My patient, Alice, refuses to come to the office these days, but Mike says he's coming by after school and wants to introduce you to his mother. It could be a huge breakthrough to get all three of you connected. What do you think?"

"When you put it that way, how can I possibly refuse? Let me call Annis Rae to let her know I'll be late getting home. Anything else I should know?" I asked.

"There are a couple of things, number one of which is that the father of one of the kids in your group with Molly was killed in a train/car collision Saturday night. Alcohol was undoubtedly involved ... the car was awash in empty beer cans and smelled like a brewery. Dr. Gray is doing the autopsy today. The second thing, there is a retired Navy gentleman and his family who lives between here and Curtin, at the intersection of old Highway 99 and Smith River Road actually. He is a most unusual fellow, and on the up and up I believe. Retired Chief Pharmacist's Mate, and self-proclaimed Christian man, he brought in a shaggy, disoriented young man who had wandered out of the drug infested Smith River commune and ended up in Bill's front yard ... which is, coincidentally, precisely where Smith River Road ends.

"Bill is the name of the retired Navy fellow. Is that right?" I asked.

"That's right. The young patient's name is Sarge. And I need you help me decide how much of his problem is drug abreaction, how much is schizophrenia and how much is the residual of his Viet Nam tour of duty. So, if it's OK with you, I would like to send them down to your Roseburg clinic for some diagnostic work. I know I am already keeping you pretty busy when you are up here," Dr. Wiltse concluded.

"I'll be glad to catch this one in Roseburg. I just cured a depressed woman from Tenmile, so there is a hole in my schedule," I replied. "And thanks for the heads-up about my morning group. Whoa, look at the time. This is one group session I don't want to miss. I'll see you about 4:00. I've got to make that quick call home and hustle over to the school," I said.

Molly greeted me as soon as I entered her building. "I'm so glad to see you this morning. We have shock and grief on top of our intended group agenda," she said.

"So I hear. Dr. Wiltse gave me a preliminary heads up on the death of a parent over the weekend. Whose father did we lose?"

"Tyler Moss, the angriest, most oppositional, most likely truant of the bunch," she said.

"Is he in attendance today?" I asked.

"To my great surprise, he is here this morning. Yesterday he asked me if we were going to have group today as he left the building. So, I really do not know what to expect. We could be in for a rough ride. Fasten your seat belt!" she said.

Our gang of first and second graders began filing in quietly shortly after Molly and I arrived in the classroom turned group room. The atmosphere seemed at once somber and charged with wary expectation. Every person in the group and for that matter every soul in the entire school was keenly aware that "Fireball Tyler" had lost his dad in a mangle of metal up on the tracks. Every student and staff member was puzzled by Tyler's attendance and wondering when he was going to explode like a time delay hand grenade.

When we were all seated, the silence remained for a couple of what seemed to be reverent moments. Some of the little students were looking at their hands or looking down at slowly swinging feet. Katie, a first grader of short and thin stature, who had said nothing the previous week, spoke first into the silence. "I'm really sorry about your dad," she said to Tyler, who was also looking down but gave a slight nod of his head, indicating that he clearly knew the message was for him.

Slowly, one by one, each of us spoke a word or two of condolence. "He didn't know," Tyler began. "He didn't know that the stop sign at the train crossing was for him. He never had a group like ours. Nobody ever told him that limits and boundaries protect us. Mom used to tell him that he drank too much ... asked him to slow down or set a limit on his beer. He told her to shut up and mind her own business. He said a quota was for wimps. Miss Merritt, what is a quota?"

"It is like knowing when you have eaten or drunk only a healthy amount of something and being happy to stop with that amount," she said.

"Not like Halloween, when I ate all the candy I got in one night and threw up in the toilet," said Katie.

"My dad would drink 'til he ran out or passed out. We would kind of hope he would pass out, because then he don't hit mom or us. And he wouldn't try to drive to the grocery for more. Just before he passed out was always the worst, because we never knew what he would do."

Several other students had similar stories to tell. Mack, a first grader with the thickest, curliest head of black hair I have ever seen, chimed in. "My mom divorced my dad because he wouldn't stop boozing. He would swear and chase us sometimes. He has quite a few guns. He pointed one at Mom once, near the end of the time where we all lived together. Last week my aunt and uncle were in town for a visit. It was my dad's weekend to have us. They get along pretty good with my dad even though it is mom's sister and her husband. They picked us up at mom's house, and then after a fun afternoon at the Wildlife Safari, they were going to drop off my brother and me at dad's house. Well, when we got there, all the doors were locked and nobody answered the doorbell. We were about to leave when my brother Jerry said he thought he could get in through a window around back. He went in that way and that's when he found my dad passed out against the back door in the kitchen. Jerry says to my aunt and uncle, 'It's OK, you can go now if you want. This is normal. We'll be OK on our own.' I said that it wasn't normal. Dad usually passes out on the sofa in the living room. He has never passed out in front of the door before!"

"What happened after that?" Molly asked.

"My aunt said she didn't care whether it was the usual or not. Usual doesn't mean normal. (And normal doesn't necessarily mean healthy, I thought) They weren't going to leave us without a responsible adult. So, me and my uncle wrote a note and pinned it to the front of dad's shirt. It said, 'Sorry we missed you. Please call when you are ready to visit. We will all be back then.' Then we got to swim in the pool at the motel where my aunt and uncle were staying. But we went to Dad's the next day."

"That sounds like a very smart plan, Mack," I said.

"Yah, because my dad was really nice to everybody the next day," Mack responded.

"Tyler, did you eat candy until you threw up on Halloween," I asked.

"Nah, I still have most of it, but it's getting kinda gray and hard now. I think I'm gonna throw out the rest of it pretty soon," he said.

"I think you're pretty smart, Tyler. Throwing up in the toilet isn't that much fun," Katie said.

"We have many very smart kids in this group, Molly. I think they are going to have a lot to teach us," I said.

After sharing a sumptuous meal of Jell-O salad and mystery meat served up with a carton of milk and a chocolate chip cookie in the elementary school cafeteria, I bussed my tray and said my good-byes to Molly and a small cluster of kids who had cozied up next to us. As I slowly cruised down to Yoncalla for the afternoon group, my mind was awash with the wisdom of first and second graders. At least on this day, they were clear-eyed observer survivors.

Every week, the contrast between the elementary age group and the teen group was jarring. You would think I would get used to it after a while. The first and second graders were, for the most part, very accessible, forthright and obvious with their woundedness, pain and anger. Teens, on the other hand, tended to hide the wounds and the pain, adopting a strategy of attitude and anger. Self-disclosure was possible, but seldom easy or free. This afternoon proved to be no exception to this general trend of difference.

After everyone had taken a seat, everyone except Witty who was leaning against the south wall with his hands shoved deep into his jeans pockets, the group got under way. "Witty, if you are in the group, you're in the group. If you're not just say so, and we can make other arrangements. It's your choice," Karl said.

Witty didn't verbally respond, but after a brief few moments of contemplation or defiance, Witty took his place in the circle of chairs.

"Who has something they want to share with the group?" Karl invited.

There was a morgue-like quietness in the room. For certain, nobody was in a hurry to self-disclose anything significant. Somebody cut a noisy fart, and much laughter followed. "OK, that is a something. Now, how about sharing something of substance or importance?" I suggested after the snickering had subsided.

It was back to the chamber of the dead. Karl threw out some fresh meat to see if he could get anyone to take a bite. "I understand one of you lost a part-time job last week, and someone else was suspended for three days. Would either of you be willing to talk about it?" Karl asked.

I liked how Karl put two relevant and current topics on the floor without blowing the anonymity of anyone in particular. It was Witty, who hadn't lost a job or been recently suspended, who spoke up. "Like I bet neither of you two counselors ever got fired or suspended when you were in high school," he challenged.

"You would be wrong about me," Karl snapped back. "I had feelings of pure hatred for my physics teacher, a man who probably shouldn't have been a teacher. He seemed to delight in rewarding a few kiss-ass students and did his absolute best to humiliate or intimidate as many other students as possible. He was a small minded, mean spirited hulk of a man. I did my level best to steer clear of the man. The dean of students put him and his apple polishers in charge of senior announcements. You know, the things you send out to relatives and friends to announce that you are graduating. Are you sure you want to hear this?"

All heads nodded, and all eyes were on Karl. "OK then," he said. "I am sitting on my receipt for my announcements. It's tucked away in my wallet. Mr. Johansen decides to make up a list of idiots ... anyone he thought had ordered but not paid for announcements. His plan included dropping by senior level classes to read off the list of little idiots or "Dumb-Dumbs." Humiliation and intimidation, those were the top two main ingredients of his style of relating to students. I sat through a number of these readings. Mr. J. knew he could reach the maximum number of "dumb-dumbs" at senior choir. That was one of my favorite classes. Each time he fumbled through his list of names, mine was included. Little by little, I was loading up with steam, but I didn't say anything. When D-Day, that would be delivery day arrived, students took their receipts to a certain room at a specified time where his apple kissers were in charge of dispensing announcements. The apple guys said that even though I had a receipt, they couldn't deliver the goods ... because I was on the idiot list. Perfect, I thought to myself. I will come back during one of his most crowded classes and ask The Idiot for my announcements!" Karl paused here, and the only noise in the room was the low pinging sound of the heat register cooling off. He had everyone's absolute attention. When he resumed, he said, "It turns out his most populous class was at the same time as my third year of Spanish. So, I asked Mrs. Contreras if I could have a few minutes to take care of a problem I had with Mr. J. She asked for some specifics, and I gave them to her. Her exact response was, "I will grant you permission to leave my class for a few minutes, but I don't recommend it."

"I ignored her recommendation and I accepted her permission. Down the hall I went, bent on justice or revenge. You'll have to decide. I knocked on Mr. J's door. 'Who is it?' he asked. I opened the door, and stepped into his classroom. 'What do you want?' he asked.' I'm here to pick up my announcements because some idiot put my name on the idiots list. When I came with my receipt at the assigned place and hour, the idiot's idiots wouldn't allow me to take them. Do you think you could help me solve this problem?'"

"Mr. J. came flying around his desk. I had no idea he could move that quickly. His hands were drawn into fists, and his arms were up in striking position. I held my open hands up and said, 'you can hit me, but I don't recommend it!' I was trying to stay calm, but I could hear my heart beating loudly in my eardrums. He started to grab me, but my agility was better than his. Finally, he stopped moving forward and said, 'Let's go down to the Vice Principal's office.' I let him know that I thought that sounded like a lovely idea. Our V.P. was a reasonable man. It was an offer I was willing to accept."

"What happened when you got to the V.P. office?" Witty asked.

"He suspended me. He had to. He had to show some support for his teacher whose classroom I had entered. He said to go home. 'Come back tomorrow. I'll hear your story then.' So I left. The next day, he commended me for my sense of justice and suspended me for the rest of the week for not bringing the problem to him in the first place. I guess Mr. J.'s ulcer was acting up, because he didn't come back for a week."

"OK, I think I get it," Reggie grumbled. "It's normal for me to be angry at that grabby handed Hetzle kid for hitting on my girl. But it's probably going to get me suspended for stuffing him into his locker."

"I couldn't have said it better myself," Karl replied. "Other people's objectionable behavior does not justify our own objectionable behavior. When we respond, it's a good idea to mix in a little wisdom, consider the consequences of the choices we are making."

"Bet you never got fired from a job, though, like happened to me at Osborn's Grocery," Morgan chimed in.

"How old are you now, Morgan?" I asked.

"16," she replied.

"At precisely the age of 16, I received my one and only firing ... at least so far," I said. "But there were many important lessons learned that day. I'm going to ask you to tell me what you think they were or should have been. OK?"

Morgan nodded her curly blond head, and fixed her sparkling blue eyes on me. So I began to dive into the story. "It was another hot, boring day in the monotonous, noisy cannery. It's mid-August, which means pear-packing season. I needed the money for car insurance, gas, dates, movies and other essentials. My friend Cliff and I were working at the bottom of a two-story high monster machine called the grader. Pears went in at the top all random sizes, from small to huge. At the bottom, Cliff and I caught them in lug boxes after they had been sorted out by size by this monster. We stacked these lug boxes on pallets, and the Hyster driver would come in and pick up the full pallets. Then we would lay down another pallet and begin this process over and over until our shift was finished.

Are you bored yet? A chimpanzee might have found this job stimulating. Cliff and I did not. On the other side of the machine, doing the same monotonous job were two other chimps just like us. The only difference between their scene and ours was the fact that the exit from the warehouse was on our side of the machine. One activity kept us awake, alert and semi-sane. Every once in a while, large and mushy over ripe pear would come down the chute ... one that would surely disintegrate in mid-air if tossed up over the two-story monster. Constant vigilance was required, especially after making a magnificent score on the opposing team. We could hear all kinds of moaning and cursing over there after a particularly good score.

Little did any of us know that on this particular day Mr. Ruckhauser, the plant foreman, was giving a tour of the cannery to a major stockholder from San Francisco who was wearing an amazingly expensive three piece suit. Having just plastered the poor chimps on the dark side of the machine, Cliff and I could vision a potential problem as Mr. R. and the stockholder strolled into the warehouse. As a matter of fact, the closer to us they came, the more certain we became of an imminent disaster."

There was a general moan audible from the group at this point in the telling of the story.

"You guessed it. Just as Mr. R. began his introduction of Mr. San Francisco, the ill-informed gentlemen on the other side of the machine let fly with the biggest, rottenest, stickiest pear ever to come down the chute ... which pretty well coated the expensive suit and allowed considerable overspray to the cap and overalls of the plant foreman."

"Oh my God," gasped a wide-eyed Morgan.

"Having no choice but to show some semblance of authority, Mr. R. fired all four of us on the spot and then he apologetically led Mr. San Francisco out of the warehouse."

"I've got some ideas about lessons that apply to you and to my fiasco at the grocery," Morgan said. Others in the group mumbled that they had some also. "One that really strikes me hard is that just because you think some playful behavior is harmless doesn't mean it is. Just because you don't foresee my problem doesn't mean there aren't any," Morgan continued.

"It proves that you should never wear an expensive suit into a factory," Reggie added.

"That's true, Reggie, but let's try to keep our focus on what Morgan and I have learned from getting fired. What else?" I asked.

"If you accept the job and the pay that goes with it, you have to live by the rules of the employer," Witty volunteered.

"Amen to that. And there are books full of rules that go with the jobs of teaching and counseling. Take that buggy whip Mr. Metzger has up on his wall above his desk for instance. No matter how angry and upset he gets, it has to stay up on his wall," Karl said.

"I'm really glad to hear you say that, Mr. Douglas," Reggie said with a look of relief.

Ignoring Reggie, Morgan made another important observation. "From your story, it seems clear that you can also be held responsible for the behavior of the people around you. So you also have to consider the company you keep," she said.

"Interesting that you would mention associates, because there was another chapter to the above experience," I said. "Early the next morning, Cliff and I went to Mr. R.'s office to plead our case. How could he blame us for the bad behavior of the guys on the other side of the monster machine? We were just doing our job at the moment of impact."

"Boys, boys, I wasn't born yesterday," he said. "In fact, at one time or another, I have worked every job in this cannery. Believe me when I tell you that I know what goes on at the grader. Among the four of you, there are no innocents. But I will say this in your behalf, you two always show up on time, work hard, and come to work sober, unlike some of the winos that have worked here. So, tell you what I am going to do. I am going offer to you a couple of different jobs, where you will never be seen by guests and stockholders. How does that sound?"

"Oh, that would be swell," replied a hopeful Cliff. I just nodded, because the humorous look on Mr. R.'s face didn't have me feeling as hopeful as Cliff sounded.

"OK then, I need a couple of second story men on graveyard shift. Cliff, I want you to run the syrup kitchen. Jim, I want you to manage the can track. If you gentlemen would like those jobs, you are welcome to report back for duty tonight."

"Cliff was ecstatic that we had scored jobs. I just couldn't shake the feeling that Mr. R. was setting us up as he was patting us on the backs and chuckling to himself as we left his office. That night, we learned why those two jobs were vacant and why Mr. R. was smiling. To put it in theological terms, we had just been promoted from purgatory to the center of hell! At the top of the cannery, a high-ceilinged building with a tin roof, there are two platforms. The one on the left held the syrup kitchen, a huge cauldron of boiling sugar solution which was gravity fed down to the canning line below. It was a gas fired boiling pot. As you will recall from your science class, heat rises. And here at the top of the factory was a blast furnace under a tin roof ... the heat having no place to go. On the right platform was the can track, a few yards away from the syrup kitchen, but at the exact same elevation. Managing the can track was not a management position! It just required a person to keep the long line of empty cans flowing continuously to the production line downstairs. If anything, it was more mind numbing than working on the grader. And that is how Cliff and I finished off the summer," I said.

"What's Purgatory, Mr. Henson?" asked Reggie.

"My understanding of it is that it is a place in early Christian doctrine where dead people would go while they are waiting to find out if they are headed to heaven or hell. Their living relatives were supposed to pray for their souls and give money to the church to influence the outcome ... something like that," I said. "But what, if any, are the additional lessons from the second part of the story?"

"Persistence and being sober pay off sometimes ... sort of," ventured Tyler in a tentative voice.

"We are all going to hell, whether we keep our jobs or not? We just have to survive this purgatory that we are living in now?" Reggie was waxing philosophically.

"I think maybe we should stay in school so that we have a chance at a better job, not just some minimum wage robot action. You know, it's one thing to have a summer monkey job, but not a lifetime of summer monkey jobs," Megan contributed.

"Way to go, people. I think we have gotten about as much mileage out of this session as we could have hoped for. We'll see you next week," I said.

As the County's gray Chevy Malibu sedan is humming me back to Drain for my meeting with Mike and possibly his mother Alice, I am reviewing with amazement all the insights these kids possess. And I am wondering if any of this apparent wisdom will come to the front drawer of their brains when they need it. I would really like to be there if and when this happens.

Mike has arrived at Dr. Wiltse's office ahead of me, looking very athletic and sharp in his jeans, polo and letterman's jacket. "Mom's really looking forward to meeting you," he says.

"What the heck do you suppose Dr. Wiltse told her?" I puzzled aloud.

"I think he told her that you were the guy who could keep her out of the state hospital permanently," he said.

"That sounds like a really huge assignment to live up to, Mike. How many times has she been hospitalized so far?" I asked.

Mike tells me that he can remember about seven or eight times, but there could have been more. "Dr. Wiltse says she always makes a good recovery in the hospital, then comes back home and gradually falls off her medication, which leads to an almost certain relapse. Is that the way you see it, Mike?" I ask.

"It is exactly like that. If only science could come up with a one or even three shot vaccine for schizophrenia like they have measles or polio ... kind of a once and done medication, mom would be fine," said Mike.

"Amen to that. But in the meantime, you and I have to come up with an incentive plan for your mom that really grabs her and holds her on her medication." Then I asked Mike if he had any idea what the grabber incentive could be.

Mike said he would give it some serious thought, and get back to me. "Let's just walk over to our cabin from here. I don't want the County car to put her in a panic," he said.

It wasn't a long walk, three or four blocks tops. At one time, probably back in the 1920's and 1930's, Mike and his mother's cabin had been part of a thriving motor court on the main north/south highway between Roseburg and Eugene. The interstate highway and time had by-passed and abandoned these cottages long ago. Some had become derelict and been torn down. Some were derelict and boarded up, waiting to be torn down. One or two had caught fire by sleeping, smoking alcoholics, and been thereby reduced to ashes. None of the four remaining cabins had been freshly painted for over 20 years, so they had no distinct color beyond that of smoke stack gray. And they were all small, square and probably one bedroom. In their favor, the roofs and foundations looked sound, and they appeared to have indoor plumbing. It was what Alice and Mike could afford on her Social Security Disability income.

Before Mike knocked on the door to announce our arrival, he turned to face me and said, "I think I've got it ... the incentive. More than anything in the world, I think mom wants to see me graduate from high school. I don't think any other incentive would have more power to keep her on her medication."

"Well Mike, that's not permanent or forever, but it sure sounds like a great beginning. Who knows, if she can stay on her meds that long, she just might come to like being sane."

At which point the front door flew open, just missing Mike's chin, and Alice popped her curly, moppy head out, catching us like deer in the headlights and said, "Are you boys talking about me?"

Mike knew this look intimately and knew that the only acceptable answer was the truth. "Yes Mom," he said.

"Well OK then," she said. "Come on inside and I'll make us some tea." Mike and I followed her in.

It took a few moments for my eyes to adjust from the bright glare of the afternoon sun to the drapes pulled dungeon of the living room. As my pupils began to dilate, I began to make out piles of papers and magazines stacked to the ceiling on all sides of us. We were being led through a maze of dense and elaborate magnitude. It was living archeology. I had come to the dig site! How on earth does Mike manage to come out of this place each and every school day looking as put together and healthy as any other kid at the high school? I wondered.

Alice made every possible effort to be the best hostess she could be. She had obviously spent the better part of the day clearing a path and making a place for the three of us to sit down. And she found three cups and boiled the water. She moved the new teabag from cup to cup, but cordially handed me the first brewed cup. She was managing to have company and live within her budget.

While Alice was clearly roughed, tumbled and prematurely aged by her illness and the life that resulted from it, Mike was the prize and delight of her life. The incentive plan that Mike and I laid out before her made all the sense in the world. She thought she could do it, staying on her medication one day at a time ... "Just like an upside down AA program," she said.

I wasn't altogether sure what she meant by an "upside down AA" program, but she was quick to clarify. "You know, by plan, I will be a little bit chemically altered every day." It was, perhaps, a very apt description. Alice's craziness and love for Mike were both blazingly obvious.

Everyone Present and Accounted For
22

The vineyard in the season of spring is a veritable Garden of Eden, fresh with new possibilities. It was a place of verdant foliage and natural serenity. Oh yes, and then, just as in the first Eden, the people began to show up! This is the setting for Dr. John's festive staff barbecue and potluck, where things previously shot will now be grilled. But first, there will be some bottles of the fruit of the previous year's vine consumed with veggies, chips and dip along with little clusters of conversation.

Hugh, Betty, Annis Rae and I are out on the deck, basking in the warmth and beauty of the sunny vineyard. Dr. John was in the den holding an audience composed of Gary, Diane, and Betty's husband Herb, showing off his extensive gun collection, one rifle at a time. Always helpful and thoughtful, Fran was out in the kitchen with Jane, Dr. John's 3rd and present wife, getting acquainted and offering her services as the last of the guests were arriving and the party was commencing. I can see Dr. Denny and Mary, his vegan bride, approaching the scene as their dusty green Volvo wagon wends its way up the long gravel track to the vineyard house.

In the midst of show and tell about weapons and hunting exploits (including which rifle goes with which trophy on the wall), Dr. John cannot control his egoistic need to pull out his pride and joy, the rifle that he made.

"Look at this baby ... perfection in balance, accuracy and power. I took this one to the limited tag hunt for Rocky Mountain sheep on the eastern flank of Steens Mountain. Now that's some rugged country, almost vertical. I was crawling around those rattlesnake-infested boulders for five long days, camping at Page Springs at night. On the final day, I got my one and only chance, a clear shot at about two hundred and fifty yards at that brute hanging over the mantle there. Of course, when I took aim, he was on a rock cornice above me. One shot ... right through the heart ... instant death, he never knew what hit him," he said, with prideful boyish grin.

Diane gave him a little pat on the back and an admiring smile. Then John handed the rifle to Herb so that he could pay complete attention to his wineglass full of Umpqua Valley red.

As a seated Herb held the rifle gently on his lap, his right hand slowly stroked the hand rubbed cherry wood gunstock, he looked up at Dr. John and said, "Impressive piece. Very nice workmanship, John." And, as Dr. John set down his nearly empty glass, Herb returned the rifle to its maker/owner.

"I've done some camping and fishing up at Page Springs. There's no doubt that it's a beautiful place," Herb continued. "The Blitzen River, the gorge and the entire Malheur Refuge area is magnificent, but truthfully, I found Page Springs a bit spooky. As I was cutting across the thick, waist high grass to get to river's edge, those three inch flying grasshoppers taking off at my feet sounded just like rattlesnakes. You know, I couldn't decide whether to look down, run or wet my pants. There definitely were some hefty trout in that stream, though."

"I know that feeling," said Dr. John, while cradling the rifle in one hand and refreshing his wine glass from the bottle with the other. After he leisurely consumed half its contents and placing the glass carefully atop the bookcase, he grasped the beautifully crafted rifle in both hands, bringing the butt of the stock to his right shoulder. Slowly he panned the north wall through his sights, as if following big game in his imagination. When, in his reverie, his aim was dead on, he pulled the trigger.

Yes, the weapon was at least as loaded as Dr. John. The "kaboom!" was deafening and shook every wall in the lightly built modular home.

The surprise and the recoil bounced John into the bookcase, and after the wineglass hit the floor, but before our ears stopped ringing, an uneasy quiet hung over the house. To a person, our thoughts turned to the path of the bullet and who if anyone might no longer be standing. We all began to drift toward the sound of the explosion, to the trophy den where the rifle was still smoking and the smell of sulfur was pungent. And John for once was not talking or smiling. He couldn't think of a joke that went with this situation. And there on the north wall was a perfectly round hole ... going where? "The guest bathroom, that's where it's headed. Oh God," mumbled the badly lapsed Catholic shooter, "I pray no one is in there."

Hugh took the lead to the guest bathroom. The door was less than an inch ajar, so Hugh gave it a push, affording a full view to those gathered in the hall. The bullet passed through the wall into the inner layer of the heavily enameled sink. A large bulge appeared in the bowl of the sink, and the entire guest bath was shrapnelled with shards of enamel. The room was otherwise empty. The lapsed Catholic prayer had been answered. Moments passed, with the party in a state of suspended animation. One at a time, everybody made a pilgrimage to the guest bathroom to view the mangled sink. Some stared in shock and disbelief, and some reached out to touch the fractured bulge in the metal to establish confirmation of our great good fortune.

Genetic Predisposition to Predation
23

Monday morning, before the press of people in a schedule, I quietly slipped into Hugh's office, closing the door tightly behind me before lowering my body onto one of several beige fabric covered side chairs. "Morning," I said, as he looked up from the never-ending paperwork on his desk.

"Was that 'good morning' you meant to say?" he replied.

"I'm not yet willing to commit as to the prospective quality of the day one way or the other. What I do know is that I had a doozy of a nightmare last night that I feel strongly compelled to share as it takes place in this office. Not yours specifically, but this clinic. May I go on?"

"You have my attention now. Go for it," he said.

A big guy in a uniform that looks more like a military officer's uniform than a delivery guy outfit delivers a medium size cardboard box sealed with shipping tape. You and I and Gary look it over, trying to figure out who it's from and what the contents could be. There seems to be some rustling and possibly some hissing sounds coming from inside the box, which sends the hair up on the back of my neck, and you and Gray also appear to be feeling tentative about what to do with this package. Then Denny comes into the room, sees the box on the desk. He asks us, "What's in the box?" Gary tells him that we have no idea, that it was just delivered, and we haven't opened it yet, and in the dream Denny, without taking time to listen to the noises coming from inside the carton, clicks into helpful mode and says, "I'll get it for you." In no time at all, he has the tape pulled off and the first flap pulled open. Then he lets out a blood curdling scream and jumps back just as two snakes pop their heads up out of the box. I'm not sure, but I think they're cobras. I wake up screaming as these two vipers are working their way out of the box!"

"So the snakes are a metaphor for what?" Hugh asks.

"Evil, pure cunning evil, that's what I think," I said, without hesitation.

"What about the agent delivering the box? Do you sense evil lurking in him?" Hugh asks.

"I think he's just trying to do his job. His arrival doesn't set off any alarms in the observers," I said.

"What do you think the dream is suggesting, if anything?"

"Truly I can tell you, I have never had a dream like this one ... not even close. It may have to do with the fact that you ask me to be the designated observer of our new shrink, but I don't know for sure. In Freudian literature, aren't guns and snakes both supposed to be phallic symbols? Maybe the dream is just a response to the frightening gun incident out at the staff party in Dr. John's vineyard home, but somehow I don't think so, because I didn't feel any evil intent present at the staff party. Alcohol, Ego, and stupidity were present for sure, but no intentional plan of harm. Then, too, I don't get the business of two evils, you know, two snakes. Even if there exists some evil in John, and I am not saying there does, I don't know why the dream is pushing the notion of two evils. Maybe the answer is related to my indigestion ... the battle between the grilled elk and the grilled bear meat."

"I don't think this dream is about indigestion. Until further notice, I am going to accept it as a call to be extra observant ... even a bit vigilant. Thanks for sharing it with me. I think you are a pretty intuitive fellow, whether consciously or unconsciously. I think we are going to find out where this dream is pointing," Hugh concluded.

Glad to have the nightmare off my chest and feeling less crazy than before the telling, I felt ready to hit the day. "Thanks for listening," I said.

At the far eastern end of the second floor hallway, I could make out three figures having a conversation. No, there were three individuals, two of which were being entertained by the third. Dr. John was up, bright and chipper, as if he had been sober all weekend and hadn't blown up his bathroom sink. I slipped into my office before being spotted, but I left my door open plenty wide enough to hear Dr. John's booming and colorful voice. Yes, I was eavesdropping. His audience appeared to be Dr. Gray and Roger, the chief sanitarian.

"At their class reunion, these three classmates were gathered around the spiked punch bowl, and they began to speculate theologically, if you will, as to the nature of God. The well-dressed somewhat pompous looking fellow in the group said, 'I imagine God as a master physician. How else could you explain the creation of man and all of the elaborate workings of the body and mind?' The woman standing in this trio disagreed. She said, 'The true nature of God is that of an artist, because the complexity of creation is truly overshadowed by its magnificent beauty.' The two of them turned to the third member of the group, a bushy haired fellow with a plastic pocket protector and half a dozen pens stuffed into his shirt pocket. 'If the two of you were a bit more observant, you could not help but notice. The true nature of God is that of a civil engineer. How else can you explain the fact that man's primary recreation area is located in the midst of his sanitary waste facility?'"

Before I shut my door completely, I overheard a mixture of moans and chuckles, and I wondered quietly to myself if Dr. John would ever run out of jokes. Then I remembered something Hugh had said to me in passing. Dr. John and his second wife were largely responsible for the founding of Oregon's county mental health system ... if you could call it a system. The two of them circumnavigated the entire State for over a year. Dr. John entertained and cajoled each set of County Commissioners out of enough cash to match the State Mental Health

Division to create county mental health clinics. Ava, his second wife, had been an RN and a very competent administrator. She worked with county health officials like Dr. Gray and organized local mental health advisory boards, which brought these local programs into being. In short, he was a gypsy pickpocket, and she did all the rest of the work.

My workday went by pretty smoothly. A telephone message taken for me by Betty is the only item that really stood out. It was from Dr. Wiltse in Drain. "I have it on the highest authority that you really charmed Alice, Mike's mother," it said. I left a message with his receptionist. "Don't credit me, credit Mike."

With my jean jacket slung over my shoulder, making my way through the admin area toward the door to the infamous parking lot, Hugh spotted me as I stepped past his open door. "Just the person I want to see," his invisible sheepherder's staff was slipping around my neck.

Making a quick U-turn into his office, he asked me to close the door before I could sit down. I thought the request a little strange, since I seriously doubt anyone else was left in the building. But it soon became apparent that he wanted to take no chances that we would be overheard.

"You are better than a damn bomb-sniffing dog," he began. "Dr. Gray came down here just after the noon break to inform me that there were a few additional enticements in his agreement with Dr. John that he had previously 'forgotten' to share with me. It seems that Dr. John has a nephew attending Harvard Medical School who could use a summer internship in community psychiatry. His name is Vince, and he will be arriving to begin his three month summer internship in about 10 days!"

"The second snake," we both simultaneously mumbled.

Letters

24

Driving up to Drain the next day, I had the overwhelming sense of how little time was left in the school year for the students in our groups. It was the knowledge of the impending arrival of Dr. John's nephew that kicked me into this heightened awareness of the change in seasons that would inevitably turn my schedule upside down. I am now totally hooked on my day away from the office, and completely in love with my new north county friends and clients.

With the schools about to take a summer break, I am thinking that the Health Department and the Family Service Clinic will most likely pull me off the north county satellite duty, but then I had no idea that there were political undercurrents at work in my favor. I did not know that the people who brought me to this dance were already conspiring to keep me here right on through the summer. Letters had gone out to Dr. Gray and the County Commissioners from Dr. Wiltse and the two school superintendents attesting to the urgent needs of families and children in north county.

I was doing a terrific job, they said, but had only scratched the surface of the need. I had been embraced by the communities, they said. It would be an unqualified shame to interrupt the flow of this important work, they said. Had I known any of this lobbying was taking place, I might have felt an inflated sense of importance.

I certainly would have agreed with the "only scratched the surface of the need" part of the letters. At a minimum, I might have felt some reduction in my sense of urgency to accomplish something of value in the schools before the academic year's end.

Molly and the elementary school administration had evidently already decided that our little group of battered souls was an unqualified success. Each child seemed to be thriving in school, making healthier decisions and transitions from one activity to the next. The battle fatigue experienced by the first and second grade teachers was said to have been reduced. At the high school in Yoncalla, school administrators and teachers were again in charge of the building instead of the inner city foster kids. So said the letters!

From my vantage point, inside my head and looking out the windshield of this county car, there is a lot more unfinished business to address than any success to crow about. There is, I am certain, an epidemic of alcoholism in Drain. Poverty and domestic abuse follow in the wake of addiction. To a lesser degree, some of these same problems exist in Yoncalla, but the wholesale introduction of adolescent foster kids from the city into this neighborhood cast a long shadow over other problems and needs. The fact that our group is comprised of these adolescents, most of whom would otherwise be in some institutional setting, my primary feeling this morning is urgency, not one of boy wonder. So much to do, so little time ... that's where my mind was wandering as the County Chevy rolled to a stop in front of Dr. Wiltse's unpretentious office.

Without a moment's hesitation, Cecilia ushered me past a fully populated waiting room into Dr. Wiltse's office. "You are at the top of doctor's list. He said to bring you in here, away from the coughing and sneezing. It will be just a minute or two, I would guess."

Dr. Wiltse was all business when he found me seated in his office some moments later. "Did you have your car radio on this morning?"

"No, the conversation I was having with myself was too loud to hear anything else," I said.

"Two Yoncalla High students were killed in a collision with a white oak tree last night on Old 99. Old man Applewood gave his grandson a combination graduation/birthday present ... brand new 240Z. Of course the first thing the grandson had to do was to show his girlfriend how fast it would go and how well it could handle the corners."

"Come to think about it, I just drove by a curve on Old 99 where the gravel shoulder was all plowed up and a tree was sporting a brand new wound."

"That would be the spot all right. The Old Man has quite a bit of clout around here, and he wanted the visible signs of the tragedy removed immediately. That Z was virtually wrapped around that tree like the sweater on my older sister's Chihuahua. They had to cut the car off the tree with a welding torch. If the Old Man had been thinking a little more about the community and a little less about appearances, from my way of thinking he should have left it there on the tree for a while," he said.

"I know what you mean, but the pain of driving by it again and again ... maybe he thought that would be too much for the family to endure," I replied.

"You're right. Who am I to judge his motives? God only knows what I would do in a similar circumstance. Anyway, good luck with your afternoon group at the High School," he said in a sympathetic tone.

All morning long, I could think of little else. I know the elementary group came and went and so did the morning, but I couldn't tell you a thing about it. Thankfully, I had a most competent co-therapist who was alert and fully present.

When I arrived at Yoncalla High School, Karl was there to greet me. The school flags were at half-mast, and the mood in the corridors was lower than that. "I took the liberty of announcing to the faculty and student body that you and I would be available in the gym after group for anyone who wants to gather for a few moments of silence. There is going to be a memorial service here Saturday morning. The churches are too small to hold the expected crowd. There will be a provision of time there for anyone who wants to speak. Also, I put the word out that if someone needs a personal, private conversation with us, all they have to do is ask. Sorry about not checking with you first, but honestly I haven't had the time. Is this going to be OK with you?" Karl asked.

"I think you have done exceeding well, Karl. But before we dive into the afternoon, I have to let my wife know that the day has changed, and make sure I am not dropping the ball on anything important on the home front."

It was a somber and subdued small group. Even Reggie, the perpetual wisecracker, was in a thoughtful and self-revealing mood. "I've always thought that if I had a bundle of money, all of my problems would pretty much be over. A fast car or a super-fast motorcycle... That would be my first purchase. John Applewood had a large bundle, and his life is over. It just blows my whole program."

Pros and Cons
25

"He's here," Hugh said softly into my right ear, his hand clamped firmly on my shoulder.

"Who's here?" I replied in a confused stammer.

"Dr. John's nephew, Vince...he is here a week ahead of Dr. Gray's prediction."

"I guess we had the weekend to prepare and didn't even know it," I said. "Have you met him? And, if so, what's he like?"

"Oh yes, I've met him all right. He must still be on East Coast time, because he and John were the first ones in the building this morning. He seems very outgoing and personable, great smile and firm handshake, a couple of inches shorter than you, and equally fit, I would say. He seems genuinely delighted to be here. With his wavy hair and New England accent, he seems somewhat Kennedyesque, a 25 year old version. Shallow as it is, that's about the best I can do with the two minute introduction."

"So maybe the two snake dream thing has no connection to Dr. John and Vince... just one of those wild and wacky dreams that fell out of my own squirrel cage. In Jim Heenan's dream theory workshop, he really downplays any prognostic quality in dream work. He thinks that dreams are on the whole attempts by the unconscious mind to unscramble complex problems that the logical conscious mind cannot comprehend. He likens dreams to theater, and all of the characters, settings, and objects are symbolic representations of our own personal unresolved crap," I said.

"That may all be true of normal people, but in your case I am not going to rule out the paranormal. Keep your eyes and ears open. We may not be out of Alice's Wonderland yet," he said, as he released my shoulder and began to head off in the direction of his own office.

A few minutes later, as I settled into my office to review my case files and schedule of the day, I could hear Dr. John's voice in the hall through my partially open door. Then there came a polite but brisk knock at my door just before it eased open more completely.

"May we come in?" asked Dr. John, as he strolled in with a handsome young man about my age in his wake. "I'd like to introduce you to my nephew," he continued.

He didn't seem to notice that he hadn't given me the opportunity to answer his question and that I hadn't answered. Quick as a wink, I decided that it was an entitlement thing or a rhetorical thing. He is a doctor after all, and therefore doesn't need to be bothered with real questions and answers.

"Jim, this is my favorite nephew Vince. Vince, this Jim, the best psychiatric social worker in North Umpqua County," John said, with his best Huck Finn smile radiating at the corners of his up-turned mouth. "Vince is a medical student at Harvard Medical School, and he will be with us for a summer psychiatric internship."

"Your uncle, Dr. John here, is right in his description of me," I said. "Of course, it goes without saying that I am the only psychiatric social worker in North Umpqua County!" And all three of us emitted a socially correct laugh.

"I'm going to slip out of here and give you boys a chance to get acquainted without my interference," he said, assuming that I had plenty of time for the introduction as well as some acquaintanceship.

Not wanting to be rude to Dr. John's nephew or the client in the waiting room, I asked Vince to excuse me while I gave Diane or Betty the heads-up that I would be a bit late coming down to greet my first client of the day. "This is a jumping place this morning. Is it always this busy?" Vince asked.

"It pretty much is a jumping place. That's one of the reasons I especially enjoy my day a week in north county. It's a change of pace and a world apart from this clinic. This County is approximately one hundred 60 miles wide and more than a hundred miles north to south...bigger than several of your eastern states. And we're the sole mental health service for all that territory."

"That's what Uncle John tells me ... and tons of rivers, lakes, forests and trails to explore. I know I am going to love it here. I guess you must know by now what an avid hunter and fisherman I have for an uncle. It must be genetic, because I am so jazzed about getting out there and hooking the wily trout or steelhead," Vince bubbled.

What I wanted to say was, "Did you hear how your uncle got plastered, shot the sink and fragged his bathroom?" But, what I said was, "I guess you've come to the right place. This is a hunting/fishing/hiking paradise. I've got to chase you out now, but in the next few months we should have plenty of time to get well acquainted."

As I ushered Vince out of my office and headed down the stairs to connect with my client, I couldn't help but wonder if Vince had any interest in the psychiatric internship or if hunting, fishing and hiking would be the core ingredients of his summer experience.

During the week, Vince made himself scarce, but on Friday morning, I was surprised to find him sitting in my office when I arrived outside the open door. At first, I wasn't sure it was him because the cheerful face and upright posture were gone. His head was hanging down and to tell the truth, he looked dejected and forlorn. What I wanted to say was, "What the heck are you doing in there?" However, I thought that would sound way too harsh for a person who looked like he had already been put down. I decided to go neutral. "What's up, Vince?"

"Do you know that story about the two fellows who are starving while seated at the banquet table which is loaded with the most delectable food of the earth? Each one has a four foot long spoon permanently strapped to his right arm, and a four foot long fork similarly attached to his left arm, and therefore neither man can get any of the food to his own mouth?" Vince quietly intoned. "I am a starving man."

"That story sounds familiar. It's about cooperation, if memory serves me. They could feed each other from across the table with this long-handled flatware, but they could never feed themselves. Is that the gist of it?" I asked.

Vince sadly tipped his head in the affirmative, so I ventured in a bit further. "How does this story apply to you?" I was hesitant to ask how this tale might apply to us.

"Yesterday I went into Garden Valley Hardware and Sporting Goods to check into hunting and fishing licenses. When they told me I was an out of State applicant, and cost would be five times higher than for an instate resident, my heart sunk into my loafers. You know, I've been scraping by on student loans for so long my wallet takes up no space in my hip pocket. Honestly, I was hoping that you could help me out."

"Don't count on finding much besides lint in my wallet. Where tuition and fees are concerned, I expect the University of Chicago and Harvard have a lot in common, and I am just one year out with a wife, mortgage and baby," I replied, figuring these words would kill this conversation.

"Oh I totally understand how tight your resources might be," he said. "I would never ask you for money. If I need an advance before my first intern check arrives, I wouldn't hesitate to hit up Uncle John for a loan. No, no... I would never do that to you, Jim. What I was really hoping you could help me with, and I know this is a stretch... and please feel free to say no...could you please loan me your fishing license, just for this weekend. Then I think I can handle it from there."

I can't entirely explain the next words to come out of my mouth. Maybe I felt some sympathy for his story. Perhaps I was relieved that he wasn't hitting on me for money. It is possible that I am truly weak between the ears, but whatever the case might be, and not without some cognitive and visceral dissonance, I acquiesced to his request. He thanked me, shook my hand like a used car salesman closing the deal and was out the door before my buyer's remorse could kick in.

One thing I can always count on is an honest appraisal of my position and decision making from my loving wife. "You did what? That might rank right up there in the top 10 of the stupidest things you have done this year! Of course nothing is apt to top driving a car with a broken gas line to the carburetor ... at least we can hope nothing comes along to top that. We'd be dead," she said. "What's going to happen when the game warden checks his license and it doesn't match his driver's license?"

"Yeah, yeah, I know already. It's not like I can afford a fine or some jail time right about now. I feel terrible about it. My stomach has been complaining about my poor choice even before you diagnosed me, but he was so smooth ... like a gypsy pickpocket. When I let him know we are as broke as he is, I just thought that would be the end of it," I said.

"Well Mr. Psychiatric Social Worker, how are you going to recover your license and get some of your dignity back? You can't let some summer intern bamboozle you!"

I gave her a weak answer, something like "I'll think of something."

As much as Vince was unavoidable on Monday, He was absent or down right invisible during the remainder of the week. He allowed zero opportunity for confrontation and license retrieval. What I didn't know was how busy he was lining up other pigeons..., which would have explained his absence in my life.

"Where is your nephew?" I asked Dr. John.

"I don't know. Jane and I haven't seen much of him since he borrowed my pickup," he answered. And, I thought to myself, "at least he didn't lift your driver's license."

On Thursday I bared my stupidity to Hugh. "I do think he might be the second snake. He conned me out of my fishing license so fast, I had to check later to see whether or not my underwear was also missing."

"He's on a mission to go fishin', Jim. If it makes you feel any better, he has my tackle, creel and waders. Gary told me Vince talked him out of his fly rod and reel. You and I both know that Gary is more apt to loan out his wife than his Fenwick fly rod. Then there is Denny. He's the topper. Somehow he got Denny to commit to replacing his damaged canoe just so Vince can borrow it!"

"What a bunch of dupes we are. OK, I feel a little better now, but not much. I am the only dupe stupid enough to take a fine or go to jail for this smooth hustler," I sulked. "Maybe I can still catch up with him before he hits the stream with my license."

"I don't think so," Hugh said quietly. "He stopped by here at lunch time to announce that he was on his way to Steamboat and he'd check in with me on Monday to begin his summer internship. I think prayer is the one option you have left."

Suffice it to say, I didn't sleep well and prayed mightily all weekend long. In a strange way, my prayers were answered. Vince checked in with Hugh first thing Monday for his orientation and initial assignments. Then he bounded up the stairs to report on his "fabulous (four day) weekend." Mixed into his explication of adventure, he mentioned returning Hugh's now leaking waders. Gary's three-piece Fenwick was now a four-piecer. Over the weekend, 2000 additional miles appeared on Dr. John's truck. Denny was the lucky one because he hadn't yet had time to replace the boat he had destroyed on the North Umpqua. Then he turned a solemn face to me and made his report on how many fish he had caught, but somewhere along the trail or out on the river itself he had lost my fishing license. "I'm really sorry, Jim. I have turned Uncle John's truck upside down, and gone through Hugh's tackle box again and again. I'm so sorry it's gone. Is there any chance that you could get a replacement for it before Saturday? There are so many more places I have to try out in such a short time."

I wanted to say "thanks be to God that you lost it," but what I said was "I don't believe I will be able to replace it any time soon."

More relaxed than I had been for four days, I recounted all of these misadventures to my wife as we prepared for bed. "What makes you so sure that he was telling the truth when he said he lost your fishing license? Can you trust anything he has to say? Suppose he is saying that he lost it so he can keep it all summer long," she said with a seriously sober face.

"I guess I may never know for sure," I said. Worry was creeping back into my voice. "But he did seem genuinely sad that he lost it, and he seemed pretty determined to get another one. Tomorrow I'll go down to the Department of Fish and Wildlife to report it lost and get it replaced."

"And then leave the replacement license at home with me. I'll hide it in my sock drawer for you!" Annis said.

As the summer progressed, Vince, Nephew of Dr. John, continued to be Vince. But his persistent and consistent mooching and con job behavior turned out to be a back door blessing of sorts. All of us gradually began to wise up and toughen up. It was a personality type to which we perhaps had insufficient previous exposure, so we needed to have our cognitive antibodies stimulated.

Within the first month of the summer, Vince had pretty much gone through every possible staff member... including the night janitor. With our immune systems on full alert, Vince turned to the larger community to meet his various and self-serving needs.

From that point on, we just didn't see much of Vince. Toward the end of August, he slipped off back toward Harvard... pretty much an unnoticed departure.

Birth of Sunapee
26

Nature abhors a vacuum, I guess you've heard, and it certainly has been one of the truths by which my brief life has been directed. Never a dull moment, and no chance for boredom..., if something winds down, two or three things wind up. The Spring term at Yoncalla and Drain was coming to a close, but something new was about to begin.

When Dr. Wiltse referred a young veteran from Curtin, Oregon I hadn't the slightest inkling what life was about to dish up next. About my age or perhaps a few years older ... it was hard to tell from the condition the patient was in ... Sarg was the person that Dr. Wiltse sent down to see me with the explicit instructions to determine how much of the diagnosis was post traumatic-stress syndrome, how much might be post concussive brain injury, how much street drug brain injury, and how much schizophrenia. Sarg was a 1000 piece jigsaw puzzle dumped out on the floor and randomly tossed back into the box.

The complexity of this case was staggering, and it was my immediate impression that Sarg needed diagnostic assessments and treatment solutions miles beyond my training and skill level. What was Dr. Wiltse thinking, sending this man to me instead of to the intensive and secure care in the Veteran Hospital?

Accompanying Sarg on this clinic visit was a broad-shouldered, stocky man about 15 to 20 years my senior who, when he stood up to greet me, came about to my chin. With a very warm smile, a labor calloused hand extended toward me, and a decidedly New England accent, he introduced himself as Bill. "Dr. Wiltse sent us down here...

says you're the man to see. We can use some help with Sarg here. He came a wandering up to our place some days back, confused, didn't seem to know where he was or why. My wife Joyce and I live up on Old 99 adjacent to the intersection with Smith River Road. It's closer to Curtin than it is to Drain. Up Smith River Road about five miles is a seriously sideways commune ... lots of pot, mushrooms and the like. I was up on the roof tacking some of the shingles back down ... quite a windstorm we had the night before... as Sarg found his way to our front porch. He asked me if we had anything he could eat, and I ask him if he knew what this tool was that I held up in my hand like this. What was it Sarg?" Bill asked, after turning slightly in his direction.

With a crooked, broken tooth grin, Sarg replied, "It was a hammer."

"And what did I ask you?" Bill continued.

"You ... you asked me if I knew how to use it, and I said I did," said Sarg, who seemed most pleased with himself. "You invited me up on the roof ... said if I got up there with ya, I was most welcome to stay for lunch."

"That's right, and I was a little worried at first, because Sarg was pretty shaky. I was afraid he might fall off the roof, but he didn't. And he's been with us ever since, helping me to rebuild the fence, put together a chicken coup and run, things like that. But he knows he needs some help. Don't you Sarg?"

"Yes I do," he responded, after a brief delay, as if it took the message several seconds to reach his brain and come back out his mouth.

I was not sure what my next move should be. The usual and customary procedure would be to thank Bill for bringing Sarg while inviting Sarg to come with me upstairs where he and I could work on his assessment. However, something in my head was suggesting that the assessment would be insignificant compared to determining a post-assessment care and treatment plan. Without the help of this retired Navy Chief Pharmacist Mate from New Hampshire, I couldn't imagine what that plan might be. "Sarg," I said, "do you want to see me by yourself or do you want Bill to be with us while you and I try to figure out what kind of help you need?"

"Bill with us," he answered, with certainty and much less hesitation than on the previous questions.

Up the stairs all three of us went, me leading the way, still wondering where Dr. Wiltse was leading me. With the mini-status exam with which Hugh had armed me, I began to plod my way through the assessment with Sarg: questions about things similar and different, questions about place, date and time, questions about numbers, sequence and memory. All six ways to Sunday, Sarg was a mess! His drawing of a box from memory looked like a jumble of pick-up-sticks.

From this simplistic test, there is no possible way of answering the complex questions being raised by Dr. Wiltse. How much of this dysfunction was post-traumatic stress syndrome, how much traumatic brain injury, how much brain damage from PCP, mushrooms, pot or heroin? I doubt if there's a shrink in this State who could figure out the answer to these questions.

"Sarg, have you checked out the Veteran Hospital to see what resources they might have to offer you?" I asked.

"Yes, they gave me some pills, little pinkish ones that made me dizzy, shaky and stumbly. And they told me ... if I don't take these pills ... don't come back." The sadness in his eyes underscored the helplessness of his condition. It was absolutely clear to me that regardless of the multiple causes of this young man's condition, what he needed was supervision, structure, guidance and love. A chance, through work and accomplishment, to rebuild some self-respect and confidence in a caring place would be a superior environment.

I knew that it wasn't a fair question to ask, but I couldn't help myself. "How long is Sarg welcome to stay with you and Joyce?" This stranger who had wandered onto their property days or possibly weeks before looked like a discharged broken bundle of need.

"As long as he is sober and is willing to help out around the place, he's welcome to stay until he gets back on his feet," Bill said, looking straight at Sarg. "Joyce and our children like him better than I do," he said, flashing a smile at Sarg.

Listening to Bill's response floored me. It was said with the same ease and conviction as if his family had just adopted a tail-wagging collie. "Perhaps you could come out to our place and check on him from time to time," Bill suggested.

Since Bill and Joyce had just assumed the heavy lifting, how could I refuse such a small request? "OK, the next day I am up in North County, I will give you a call and stop by your place," I said. And, with my newly acquired sense of the importance of living in the present, I immediately wrote this into my calendar ... like an appointment, not an empty promise.

"You can't miss us," Bill said. "We're on the right side of Old 99 where Smith River Road intersects. It's not a thing of beauty. It's a bit of a wreck, actually, but the house is fairly large and inexpensive. Our landlord is the State Highway Department. Some day we will be handed an eviction notice, when they find the money to knock the house down and widen the road, which could be days or years down the line. Thank you for putting us in your book."

The next few weeks and months proved to be astonishingly challenging, yet magical. The Sunshine Commune up Smith River Road was tearing itself asunder with interpersonal conflict and street drug use. Abreactions to the homemade concoctions and pot became increasingly common. Interstate 5 and the byways that fed into it became lined with many lost hitch-hiking young souls as the Viet Nam conflict continued. Bill and Joyce continued to incorporate more and more of these lost young souls into their household. Soon they needed bigger kettles and pots. Then they needed a commercial range to prepare meals for the growing community. More bedding and beds were needed. Each week on my north county day, this home became an essential stop, as Dr. Wiltse and Bill required additional assessments and counseling help.

Trust but Verify

27

The truth is that most of us are good at something, but most of us have our foibles and limitations. Twentieth Century theologian Reinhold Niebuhr said it much better than I ever could. He wrote: "Original sin is that thing about man which makes him capable of conceiving of his own perfection and incapable of achieving it." This is the same Reinhold who is widely given credit for constructing the Serenity Prayer, known worldwide as the prayer of Alcoholics Anonymous. On another occasion he said, "Man's capacity for justice makes democracy possible; but man's capacity for injustice makes democracy necessary."

During the so-called "Cold War," the United States had a large number of nuclear tipped missiles pointed at the Soviet Union. They likewise reportedly had many missiles targeted for the United States. The governments of these two nations created a stalemate known as "mutually assured destruction" before entering into missile reduction treaty discussions under the banner of "Trust but Verify." The short of it is, we need to trust each other, but we are not always trustworthy.

My neighbor Dan was a biologist by training, and he works for the State Department of Fish and Game. He was also a very handy and enterprising chap. It turns out that his brother left the relative stability of a career as a teacher to establish a kayak and canoe manufacturing company. Through a process that will remain a mystery to me, Dan acquired a canoe mold from his brother's factory. Being a thoughtful and generous neighbor, he agreed to allow me and my other neighbor Ron to join him in the enterprise of building backyard fiberglass canoes. It turns out that building canoes is a pretty labor-intensive process. Furthermore, some skill is required. Experience is valuable to have. Nevertheless, if you can tolerate some failure, experience can be obtained. Suffice it to say, the first boat was a disaster. As Ralph Nader would say, it was "unsafe at any speed." The three of us built five boats in all, counting that first mess, before we were ready to close the business. Ron took boat number two. I have boat number three. Dan ended up with numbers four and five. By the time the last boat was popped out of the mold and trimmed out in walnut thwarts and gunnels tied down with brass fasteners; we were getting to be pretty decent craftsmen.

One thing I know for certain, my dad always tried to do the right thing, and he liked to be right about things. I believe perfection approximated his goal, and he chose a profession wherein this ambition to be correct and get it right was absolutely necessary. Early in his adult life, he undertook an apprenticeship that started him on the path to become a master optician. He practiced this demanding and precise craft for fifty years. Things in his world were either in focus or not. They were plumb, level, or not. Either people did the right thing, or they didn't. I'm not saying that he never made any mistakes. He made at least a couple of beauties, but these were accidental and he was very contrite about them. For example he and I held in common two secrets from my mother, one of which I believe is still operative to this day... some fifty five years later and 11 years now since his death.

The one that's out in the open and I feel free to share has to do with salmon fishing on charter boats. In many ways, dad was very progressive, as on civil rights and diversity issues. However, until he was nearly 60, he still believed that deep-sea sport fishing was man's business. Women should stay in camp while the men tried to catch Moby, the big fish. It isn't easy to keep women off the boat. We know now that the primary reason to keep the women off the boat is that they will embarrass the men by catching more if not bigger fish!

The way we managed to keep mom off the boat for 25 years was to tell her a lie. "Mom," we said, "There's no toilet on the boat. The guys just piss over the side ... downwind of course." One day at Winchester Bay, the family was sharing a "crack of dawn" breakfast in preparation for the big male bar crossing. But, Mom is missing. Where oh, where can she be? The rest of us had our hands around a steaming mug of coffee, trying to get our eyes cracked open wide enough to see the menu, when the cafe door flew opened with a bang ... and there all puffed up like a cat ready for a fight, stood Mom, straddling the door jam.

"There is too a toilet on that darn boat!" she declared, "and I booked passage on the charter!"

From that time forward, if there was any charter salmon fishing going on, Mom was on the darn boat catching more and bigger fish. But I digress, as I do sometimes! You see that it is a mixed blessing to have a dad as precise and virtuous as mine, and I am forever grateful that he was not entirely perfect. The thing is, he could spot imperfection from macro close up or at a distance of more than a mile.

So on the day before an expected visit with Mom and Dad, when I was rehearsing my inferiority, I said to Annis, "I wonder what Dad will notice this trip that I have neglected, screwed up or built crooked?"

"Oh, honey, he might not notice anything wrong. Be more positive," she said.

"Not notice anything? Hell will relocate to the North Pole before he fails to notice something amiss. Don't you remember when he and I built the woodshed at the cabin? It took us four hours to set and make sure all the supporting piers were absolutely level. The man notices every detail.

He will notice something. I'd like to see if I can guess what it will be... Hmmm, what could it be? Could be the bent nails in the deck project. Could be the leaning grape arbor? No, I've got it. It will be something about my new pumpkin colored canoe. I'm sure of it."

Saturday morning, after their car rolled up next to our curb, Mom came right in the house and Aaron gave her a happy sticky embrace. It was such a good one that she had to go to the sink to scrub it off. Dad was still outside, cruising the yard. In a few minutes, Dad joined us in the house. "Where did you get the new canoe?" he asked.

Annis and I glanced at each other, and I was thinking "Bingo!" I tried to hide and stifle a snicker behind my hand. I swallowed my glee and said, "I made it Dad. In fact that is number three of five that Dan and Ron and I built out of a Klickitat company mold."

"That's good," he said, "I think you have always wanted one. But hey, where are the seats?"

By now, I'm half laughing and half talking. "This design has thwarts not seats. You can either sit on them or on the bottom of the boat, using a boat cushion."

"Oh. OK. What's so funny?" he asked.

"Dad, you are the great observer, scrutinizer ... finder of the flaw. I had a little bet going with myself about what would catch your eye. And, by damn, I won the jackpot," I said.

So, it came to pass one day later that month my wife's lovely parents came to visit at our new home in Oregon. OK, perhaps they weren't lovely in all ways, but they were lovely in very many ways. For example, they loved children and they especially loved their first and only grandchild. I suppose it's possible that they remembered the exhaustion that can accompany the parenting of a small child, but I prefer to think that they wanted some unfiltered grandparent time for their own playful reasons. "Why don't you two get away someplace overnight ... let us have Aaron to ourselves," my mother-in-law said. It was half question and half request, and it sounded pretty good. My father-in-law Ray nodded his head in support and agreement with the scheme being hatched.

I was either cowardly quiet or gallantly deferring to the response I expected Annis to make. "If you are sure you really want to do something like that, I think we could arrange to disappear for a day or two. What do you think, Honey?" She asked me.

No prompting or encouragement was necessary. We are talking about having our first overnight date since Aaron was born. "Let's jump on it before they change their minds!" I said.

Later that day, I had occasion to be on the phone with Anne Powell, business manager for the Yoncalla School District. I just couldn't help but crow about my good fortune, having in-laws who volunteered to keep Aaron for an overnight or two. "Where do you think you will take Annis?" she asked.

"My mind is still swimming with the idea of having her all to myself again ... for a night or two. One part of my brain says take her to the coast. That is always a restful and romantic destination. Then another part of my brain says to go somewhere that we can try out our new pumpkin-colored canoe."

"My husband and I have a cabin at Yachats, cozy little place with a wonderful ocean view. Not like Salishan, it's a cottage. It's a bit north of Florence, which has many freshwater lakes perfect for paddling. Let me check with Frank, and I will get right back to you. I am almost certain our family doesn't have any immediate plans for it, and I think it would be a splendid getaway for you two. If I can reach him now, you will hear back from me within the next 10 minutes. OK?"

"Every day, I get more thankful for my opportunity to be acquainted with Yoncalla and Drain. You are terrific and I thank you for your generosity. If it works out, you can count on my long lasting gratitude," I said.

Ann's word was golden. It couldn't have been more than five minutes before Diane buzzed my intercom with the message of an incoming call. "The coast is clear. It's all yours. Oh, and because you are special, the weather forecast is calling for not only sun but also hardly any wind. This, as you might suspect, is an almost unheard of combination. Why don't you swing by here, stop by the school and pick up the key. Then you can head out through Elkton to Reedsport.

This way, I'll get to meet Annis. How does that sound?" she asked.

"I can't imagine how that plan could possibly be improved upon. Chances are she may also get the opportunity to meet Karl, Larry and the Super. Then she will know the cast of characters I'm always talking about," I said.

At the last minute, I purchased a multi-purpose roof rack that attached to the car gutter rails. After padding a couple of two by fours with carpet scraps and bolting the boards to the rack, we had an adequate canoe carrying system. The boat, trimming out at 16 feet, hung over both ends of the Toyota Corolla so far that red flags might be required on both ends. "If people can't see us coming down the road now, they'd have to be totally blind," I said.

"Unless we catch a 40 mile an hour cross wind turning the boat into a sail, it will serve nicely as a safety device!" she said.

Very soon, we packed up, kissed Aaron and his grandparents goodbye and headed up I-5 to the 138 junction. Annis was teary eyed and I had to keep stifling my ear-to-ear grin so as not to appear to be a complete non-empathetic jackass. If I am any example of the male gender, women have a completely different infant bonding thing going on than men. Or, is it that most men are considerably more infantile than women? I mean a chance to be alone with this beautiful woman verses staying home with that little snuggler on her lap ... no contest. "We'll be back home in a flash," I said, and "isn't it nice to make your parents happy. After all, Aaron is a big toddler now. He'll be fine," I said, but I was thinking, "Will the mother be fine?" I was shoveling on behalf of my bias as fast as I could.

For several miles, I don't think I made any headway, so I finally got smarter and shut up. She continued to sniffle and look out the side window until we reached the Rice Hill exit, the cutoff to Yoncalla. Somewhere in that 40-mile stretch, she had given herself permission to trust her parents, ditch her guilt trip and allow herself a day off. Hallelujah!

On euphoria Cloud-9, we rolled into the visitor's parking area in front of the administration building. I can't tell you a darn thing about our brief visit to Yoncalla High School, checking in with Ann or any of it. My mind was brimming full with the thought of having Annis all to myself. How radiantly beautiful she looked. I had wonderful visions streaming through my brain about the cabin, the coast and the boat, and then Annis some more. I can only assume that she was more present, cordial and engaging than I was, because we were warmly welcomed back upon our return.

As we cruised past Elkton, a town easily missed in a blink of the eye, we couldn't help but notice Arlene's Cafe surrounded as it was by more than 20 cars and trucks. "This place has a reputation far and wide for big portions of extra hearty breakfast," I said. "Should we try it out?"

"If you insist. I'm a little hungry," she replied.

Fat and happy, we hopped back into boat-topped car, soon reaching Reedsport.

It was so unusual as to be downright freaky, the coast was sunny, warm and windless! "It would appear that there is not even a whisper of wind. See, the tall grass isn't even twitching," I said, as we got our first good ocean sighting. "Why don't we zoom on up the coast a way before we settle back to the Yachats cabin? We may never see another day like this. It seemed only moments later we approached the high Alsea River Bay bridge.

The water in the bay was as smooth and calm as a bathtub before the toddler jumps in. I could see a marina and boat-launching ramp on the north side of the estuary. I was uncertain if it was a public access facility or part of the shiny new Pat Boone Resort. "What say we head down to that marina and swanky new resort? I'd like to check it out."

She nodded what I took to be her approval of this spontaneous self-inflicted detour. As we rounded the corner to the left and headed down the grade to the resort, it appeared that the boat launch and landing was indeed a public access situation, complete with parking, a restroom and fish cleaning table and sink. "This is beautiful," I said.

"If you say so, but in my mind's eye, I can imagine what this place might have looked like before all this concrete and asphalt, and it looked a lot better back then. A big swath of plant habitat and wildlife has been scrapped away to create this so called improvement," she replied.

"You're right about that," I agreed, not looking to engage her in some silly controversy that would most likely spoil the mood I was trying to protect if not foster. "Given the fact that there is not a cloud in the sky and not even a whiff of a breeze, I was kind of thinking about launching the canoe ... going for a short paddle. We could take the crab ring and a float out in the estuary and try our luck at crabbing. You know, set it out there and check it when we return from our paddle."

"That sounds like an idea," she said. Like her nod, I heard this statement as informed consent to proceed.

Together, we carefully lifted then lowered then righted the canoe in preparation for the launch. Annis held the boat in place, snug to the dock while I moved the car to the parking area and locked it. The sun warmed and illuminated this fantastic day. Never at the coast had I seen anything like it. As we pushed off and began to paddle toward the middle of the estuary, I was filled with delight and unwarranted confidence. Ever the great outdoorsman, I was paddling my new boat, with my beautiful bride holding down the bow. What could possibly be better than this? Curious harbor seals popped up here and there on the glassy surface of the surrounding water about us as if they had never before seen two people out in a canoe in the middle of Alsea Bay. It was about this time that I began to notice that the canoe was proceeding rather quickly and effortlessly up stream. As a matter of fact, we began to pick up a rather alarming rate of speed without paddling a single stroke. We may be doing 10, 12 or 15 knots. Before panic hit me, the thought passed through my brain that we could perhaps pull a water skier at this speed! Looking ahead, which is generally a good thing to do when being propelled forward at warp speed; I could see the Bay Bridge and its extraordinarily large concrete piers looming ahead. They were rapidly gaining size as the distance between us and them was shrinking.

It was then that I remembered that we had not yet deployed the crab net. No longer was I thinking about catching our dinner. I was only thinking of saving our bacon! "I'm going to pitch out the crab ring, hoping that it will act like a parachute and slow us down a bit," I said. Paddle hard on the starboard side, please." I am praying that we do not become one with the bridge pier.

"Would that be left or right?" she asked.

"The right, the right," I implored. In unison, we paddled furiously, as if our lives depended upon it ... and they did. Breathing from a deep place in the fully flexed abdomen, sweat pouring through the two shirts I was wearing, The Creator Sustainer decided to let us live on to another day. As we zoomed past the bridge pier with inches to spare, I could see no more life threatening obstacles ahead. Gradually, in stunned silence, we made our way back toward the shore upstream from the monstrous bridge.

Out of the depths of my memory flashed a thought. This is the same bridge that my uncle Art had helped to build years ago. Giant forms were constructed to hold the concrete that would become the piers. Wooden flumes, some more than a quarter of a mile long, were then built to direct the concrete into these forms. A man, uncle Art had said, had fallen into the flume and down into the bridge pier form. An entire truckload of aggregate had gone in on top of the man before they could get the flow shut off. That man became a permanent part of the bridge. I am grateful that we had just avoided becoming part of the bridge and that I would live to endure the shame of major miscalculation.

When at last we made our way to shore, pulled up the crab ring, and tied up the boat, Annis turned to face me. "When we put the canoe in the water, did you know which way the tide was going," she asked?

"It just looked flat, calm and serene to me," I said with a dazed and embarrassed look on my face.

"In the future," she said, "I think I am going to have to do my own checking!"

And that's what trust but verify is all about!

In spite of our near death experience, this trip to the beach and stay in the Powell's cottage was one of the most lovely two-day interludes I can recall. I remember being present when someone asked my 84 year old father how he managed to live so long. He answered," It's because of the accidents I survived, that would be my guess." That cottage was a wonderful mood setter. Soon my estuary tidal stupidity dropped from our conversation and conscious awareness moved to the pleasant present. The crashing waves in the distance, the crackle of the wood burning fireplace mingled with the scent and touch of love. It was one of those moments which, when shared with our daughter 20 years later, she described it as "Way too much information!"

Upon our return, it appeared as though our son and his grandparents had played to the point of mutual exhaustion. The house was whisper quiet and all three of them were enjoying a much-deserved nap.

The Birth of Sunapee Part II
28

It was exactly like the story about cooking the frog. They say if you toss the frog into boiling water, he will jump out. However, if you put him in a kettle of cool water and gradually raise the temperature, he is soon cooked. Being with Bill and Joyce was like that. First there was the office visit by Bill and Sarg. Then came the trips up Old 99, where the roof was getting tacked down, paint was being applied to the exterior and interior, fences were getting mended, chickens tended and a garden planted.

One by one, more hands were added as the crew of young lost souls arrived and accepted two house rules: be drug free, and be willing to help around the place.

Soon, too the cast of supporters was growing. After all, it was impossible not to see that Bill and Joyce were the ones continuing to do the heavy lifting, and that young people were getting clean and sober. Yes, they were getting on their feet and heading for recovery. Dr. Wiltse unfailingly met the medical needs of the household, at no charge and with a smile. One day, he told me that he hoped to have a chance someday to take his medical practice into the mission field. (I am sure he meant somewhere like Africa or Haiti.) To this statement I replied, "What the heck do you think you are doing now?"

Then there was Marty, of slight build and serious manner. He was a lot closer in age to Dr. Wiltse's than mine, and he just happened to own the Army/Navy Surplus store where magnificent bargains in big pots and pans could be found. Another frog in the cool water, Marty became curious. Why would a single family out in the middle of nowhere need such big pots and a commercial range and freezer? He had to go up to north county and take a look. Bill, not wanting Marty to just look, invited Marty up for lunch. Marty not only sold Bill the kettle, he joined us in it.

Far too deeply steeped in the rugged individualism of the "Live Free or Die" State of New Hampshire, Bill and Joyce stubbornly refused to ask for charity; however, many who observed Bill and Joyce serving the needs of these broken young adults, on a mission that was otherwise being ignored, stepped up to the plate. Beds appeared, along with the bedding and clothing, toothbrushes and towels. With all the "helping out around the place," it began to look pretty good. How Bill and Joyce's own children were fairing with all this family growth was hard to say, but I knew there was unstinting prayer inside and outside this undertaking.

"Look at what we got in the mail today," Bill said to me, handing off a number 10 envelope bearing the unmistakable green certified mail sticker. The return address read "State of Oregon, Department of Transportation."

"Is this what I think it is? Is this our eviction notice?" I could hear the tremble in my voice.

Bill is very observant and misses almost nothing. He heard my tremble and he moved forward to put his strong arm around me. Yes, he's consoling me, and he is the one about to be evicted. I am realizing that I am the one upset, and he is calm. "It's our 30 day notice. But don't worry, we will figure out something." This, I am coming to realize, is the difference between big faith and hardly any faith at all.

Returning back through Drain, on my way home, I felt compelled to stop by Dr. Wiltse's office to give him the sad and dire news. Cecilia shepherded me back to his office and let me know that she would send the good doctor in to see me as soon as she could. When he stuck his head through the gap in his partially open door, he asked, "What's up?"

"Bill and Joyce received a formal 30-day eviction notice from

ODOT today," I replied with worry written all over my face.

"That's wonderful! I have been expecting this for some time now," he said as he joyfully marched fully into his small office.

"What are you saying? I think it's terrible. The Department of Transportation is about to come in with a bulldozer and level everything... the house and all the improvements Bill and Joyce have worked so hard to create. For crying out loud, what is the matter with you people? They didn't seem the least bit upset either."

"Now is the moment, Jim. It's the one for which Marty, my pastor up in Cottage Grove, and quite a few others have been expecting and preparing. That old rattletrap of a house isn't worth anything... nonexistent insulation, bad wiring and plumbing. From the foundation to the roof rafters, it's a dilapidated mess, and we could never buy it even if it was worth the power to blow it up, because, as you so aptly pointed out, the State sees it as nothing more than a barrier to progress. No siree, it's no big loss. Now we will be free to move ahead. What we do now is form a board of directors and file with the IRS for a private non-profit corporation. Then we go looking for something a lot more suitable to the work Bill and Joyce are doing. We buy it, get it move in ready and bang, they're in business."

I felt my wrinkled brow loosen up as all of me was warming up to the vision lighting up my mind. "I can see it!" I said. I had no idea that there was a community organizer lurking under the good doctor's white coat. "If there is a place in this effort for me, let me know," I said.

"Oh, you're already on the board. I'll call Bill and Joyce. Then let's set a date to meet at Marty's house in Oakland. I think that is equally inconvenient for everyone... about midway between Cottage Grove and Roseburg. How does that sound?" he said.

As I drove home, hundreds of hurdles were crowding each other for space in my mind. Where would we ever find such a house? How could we come up with the money to purchase such a place if it could be found? It would have to have acreage and that would make it even more expensive. Could we get the County to give us a permit for such a place...a home, a residential alcohol and drug treatment facility in an exclusive agricultural zone? Nothing ever happens quickly in a government bureaucracy, everybody knows that, and we are sitting on the first day of a formal 30-day eviction notice!

Thankfully, my beautiful bride was home when I arrived there so that I could immediately begin to disgorge my exploding brain.

As it turns out, Marty doesn't just live in a simple box house. It's a beautiful, historically significant Victorian, with all the gingerbread trim that you'd expect, and meticulously restored to its former glory. Until this moment, I had never really paid any attention to the town of Oakland. Interstate-5 bypassed it years ago, and from that point on, it became pretty much invisible to the 70 mile-per-hour traffic in the distance. It was here, baited with coffee, tea and cookies, that Sunapee Farm began to take shape.

It was Bill himself who came up with the name. "There's a band of Indians in New Hampshire where I come from known as the Sunapee Tribe. And the word Sunapee refers to the concept of new beginnings. In many ways, I think it fits our circumstances and vision of mission. We are creating something new, something unusual that has little or no precedent. We have our doors open to drug and alcohol effected young adults who definitely need a fresh start. And I'm just an old New Hampshire Indian."

All heads nodded, and as I looked around the room, everyone seemed pleased with the title and the vision that came with it.

"There's an attorney who attends the Presbyterian Church in Cottage Grove ... he wasn't able to join us today, but he is very interested in what we are doing ... who says he can help us with the private non-profit incorporation process," Dr. Wiltse proposed. Several people, including me, looked relieved and delighted that someone else was willing to assume that task.

"If he passes your test of competence Doc, let's sign him up right now before he finds another tribe to run with," Bill said. "Also, while I am thinking about it, does anyone know the story of that large nearly finished unoccupied house that sits near the Loraine Road intersection with Old 99? That place has been sitting there in that condition for months. Yesterday my curiosity got the best of me. I got out of the car and walked all around. It's big... four, maybe five bedrooms and multiple bathrooms, oversized garage. It looks like a Mormon mansion. Out front, on the construction power pole, there is some kind of stop work order sign from the County Building or Sanitation Department."

My ears perked up when I heard the word county, because to this point in the conversation, I couldn't figure out what my contribution might be. "Which county is it in, Lane or Douglas?"

"Good question. Looks to me like the property straddles the county line, but I think the stop work order says Douglas on it," he replied.

"OK, I can check it out either way. If there is a property description or a name and phone number on that order, please give me a call as soon as you can. We should be able to track down what's going on there," I said. As the meeting drew to a close, I could feel loads of excitement in Marty's house. Everyone had volunteered to do something or many something's and my wife and I were both happy to be a part of this new beginning... this Sunapee.

The next day, Bill called with exuberance and information. "It's Douglas County and it's the Sanitation people who shut down this job. I guess you know the number, since Sanitation is part of the Health Department. There's a signature on the sign, but between the scribbling and the weathering of the notice, I can't make it out."

"No problem, Bill. Thanks for the detective work. I can take it from here and let you know what I find out," I said.

As I was about to break free from the clinic and hotfoot it down to the Health Department, the intercom buzzed again. "Another call for you. Your buddy Karl from Yoncalla is on the phone," said Diane. "What did you roll in to be so popular all the sudden?"

"Cute. For your information, Yoncalla, Drain and Curtin happen to be live and jiving places. You can expect a lot more calls from up there in the weeks to come, so get used to it.'

"We never had any calls from up there before you started that Tuesday satellite," she shot back in a manner that didn't sound complimentary.

"OK, I'll take the blame," I said, then punched the blinking incoming phone line button. "Karl, how the heck are you? I been missing you since the school year ended."

"I've been missing you too, which is part of the reason I called. Would you like to come up here and cut some firewood and drink some beer with me on Saturday morning?" he offered.

"In that order?" I asked.

"In any order you like. I'll bring enough for before, during and after so you can make up your mind as the time passes. The other item: last night the school board appointed the new YHS principal, me. What do you think about that?" he said with enthusiasm.

"Congratulations... maybe, but what about Larry Mack? Didn't that job swallow him whole and destroy his marriage? I'm not positive this promotion is a good thing, Karl."

"Larry is doing fine since he put up the "Closed for Repairs" sign in his driveway. He and Mary Beth have been kissing and making up daily until their lips are chapped. I'm not Larry and Maureen is no Mary Beth. We'll be fine. Maureen grew up about a mile walk from the nearest road ... up the Rogue beyond Agnes. She was barefoot most of the time, no electricity or indoor plumbing. Her mother pressed her dress with a kerosene-fired iron. They had candles and hurricane lights. Her dad was a raving, firewater-breathing drunk who fed his family on poached game. When she, with her long black hair flowing down her back, caught the school bus to Coquille, the other kids on the bus thought she was an Indian. No matter what happens in our marriage, she knows she has it a whole lot better now. I think we'll be fine."

"Whatever you think, I am going to keep an eye on you anyway. I distinctly remember Super Patterson telling me how you wouldn't say no to anything he asked you to do, and you hadn't yet broken down. There is a limit to that scenario, and it's not a pretty picture," I said.

"It's what I have to do to get ahead. Don't worry, my friend, it won't swallow me up," he concluded. Before the connection ended, he thanked me for caring, and I thanked him for letting me know about his promotion.

Before the phone or anything else could intervene, I gathered myself up and headed down the hall toward the health department. In the brief time that remained until my next appointment, I was determined to see what I could find out about the Mormon mansion on Old 99 near Loraine Road.

Up ahead, I can see that the hall is blocked by a small cluster of employees gathered around Dr. John. Diane, and two men from the vector control section of Public Health, whose faces were familiar, but whose names I did not know, were John's audience. As I approached, I could hear Dr. John saying, "These three priests from Minnesota, one elderly and two much younger, were standing together in the Minneapolis/St. Paul airport terminal. They were intending to check in for the flight to Pittsburg, where a liturgical convocation was about to commence. What had them stymied and flummoxed was a gorgeous and very bosomy young ticket agent who appeared to be missing several buttons off her blouse."

"Pardon me, do you mind if I slip past? I have a meeting down the hall," I entreated.

"Oh you'll love to hear this one," Dr. John replied, and he and the gathered group didn't budge and inch. "So, as I was saying, these three priests were very aroused and confused about how to approach this buxom beauty. The senior member of the team turned to the youngest member ... as they all stood in rigid rectitude ... and said,

'You could use this earthly experience to practice the art of staying spiritually balanced. You go up to that young ticket agent, check our bags, get our boarding passes, and don't forget to get some nickels and dimes. We will need them for the phones and bus fare. Doing as he was instructed, the youngest of the three priests stepped up to the now available agent, and he said, 'Would you please check these bags for us? We three priests have pickets to Tittsburg.' He immediately caught his error, blushed profusely, and backed away from the counter.

"'YOU,' the senior priest hissed to the second youngest priest, as he nodded toward the agent. Wary, lest he maketh the same mistake, the second priest spoke very slowly. 'Miss, would you please check our bags. Here are our tickets. We three priests are traveling to Pittsburg, and also, if you would be so kind, we would like several dollars' worth of change. Please make it nipples and dimes.' The second priest, recognizing his error immediately, radiated various shades of crimson and fuchsia and backed away from the counter.

"'Gentlemen,' the senior priest said, 'I will now demonstrate how a mature priest calmly handles such a situation...'"

Sensing that this tale was headed from the tasteless to the profane, I managed to push myself through this obstruction of peers and arrived in front of Dr. Gray's office with sounds of laughter and knee slapping in the background. The door was open, but as the chair beside his desk was already occupied, I hesitated to knock. He looked up almost immediately and said, "Yes Jim, what can I do for you?"

"Excuse me for interrupting, but could you direct me to the sanitarian in charge of north county inspections?"

"Restaurants or septic tanks?" he replied.

"It must be the latter, I would guess. There is a home construction site right on the county line with a stop work order on it. We have some people up there inquiring about it," I said.

"That would be Roger, the man seated across from me right now. Be my guest, inquire away."

"Well thank you. This must be what they call a serendipitous moment. Roger, could you tell me what you know about the home under construction close to the Loraine Road intersection on Old 99? Neighbors out that way say that it has been sitting in a state of near completion for months, and it has what I believe is your stop work order on it," I said. I felt it was unnecessary and not politically correct to point out that his signature was illegible. After all, it was his help that I needed.

"People that live that far from the county seat sometimes don't bother to get building permits and approvals. We call 'em boon dock builders. The owners of that place managed to get a construction loan from the Farm Home Administration of the Federal government, and put up a building without getting a building permit or any systems inspections. After the fact, the owners were forced to comply with wiring, plumbing and other building code issues, but they will never get clearance to move in because their lot isn't large enough to accommodate a drain field for a building of that size," Roger said.

"Wow. So what's going to happen to the place now?" I asked.

"It may just rot on the spot. The owners have defaulted on their loan, which means that the government owns the lot and the house, which has no market value, since no one will ever be allowed to live there."

"Boy, that has to be a big fat coyote on the fence to any future boon dock builders," I said.

"That's what we are hoping. That's all it's good for now," Roger concluded.

On my lunch break, I called Bill and Joyce to transmit the gloomy news. The ever cheerful Joyce answered the phone, and when she heard my voice, she asked if I was in the neighborhood and would be coming to lunch. After thanking her for the offer and telling her that I was sitting at my desk in Roseburg, I told her I had some bureaucratic news for Bill. Joyce handed the phone to Bill.

"Bad news, Bill. I talked to the sanitarian who wrote the stop work order. He says the owners acquired a Federal Farm Home Administration loan, and then proceeded to build without any permits or inspections. The place now will pass code except for the fact that the lot is too small to accommodate the necessary septic drain field. He says it will most likely rot on the spot, because it will never qualify for move-in approval. The owners have defaulted on their loan, and the whole stinking deal sits as a worthless liability on the government loan books." I said.

"That's fantastic news. Wonderful piece of speedy research on your part. I do not think, in all of Heaven's possibilities, you could possibly come up with better news," Bill replied.

"Didn't you hear me Bill? It's a non-starter. The county will never give that building move-in approval," I said.

"It is perfect in every possible way. I just went 'round to the elderly gentleman that owns the property behind that house. He's willing to sell us 31 acres directly behind the house for the price he paid for it 30 years ago, because he likes what we are doing, helping Vets and other young people. He'll carry the paper. Don't you see the beauty of it? The size of the lot is no longer of any consequence! The house is worthless, a loss sitting on the books of the Federal Government. We can help them and they can help us. I'll call Doc. He knows people who know people in the government. Then I'll call you back," he said. And he was gone just that fast.

Bad news, good news... I am beginning to believe I can't tell one from the other. Before the sun set in the West that night, Bill called me back to say that Dr. Wiltse knows someone who is on a first name basis with both Oregon Senators. He was sure that we would be hearing back from the Farm Home Loan people within a day or two.

"That's great Bill. By the way, what was that acreage worth 30 years ago?" I asked.

I could hear him clear his throat before he answered. After a few seconds of silence... letting the drama rise, he said, "How does $100 an acre sound? And Doc thinks we can pick up the house for the repossession cost of about 7000 dollars. I think Sunapee Farm has found a home."

Pessimist that I can be, I saw more hurdles to jump. At the same time, we were making progress at warp speed, and I too could see the birth of Sunapee Farm coming at us headfirst. I gave out a whistle, and said, "All that for a whisker over 10,000 dollars. Who would believe it? What do you suppose the land would fetch in today's dollars?"

"About a 100,000 or maybe a 110,000 dollars, but this is no time for crowing. That's how the rooster lost his head. But, I do believe it will all fall into place. For one thing, I don't think the Feds are going to want to transfer the loan, and if they don't, we will have to do some hurry up fund raising," he replied.

Strange Love
29

The President is Republican in 1971, and so are both members of Oregon's Senatorial Delegation. Would you believe, at the urging of those three, the Federal Farm Home Administration transferred the warrant deed of the Mormon mansion to the newly minted private non-profit corporation known as Sunapee Farm. It only took a few weeks, not years or decades. The FHA even agreed to be our mortgage company. Now, armed with a 31.3-acre lot, Douglas County had no problem with our drain field plan. We had a friend at the Health Department. In went the tank, gravel and PVC pipe and out came our move in permit.

Founded on faith and two rules, be clean and sober and always be willing to help out around the place, Sunapee Farm (on the backs of Bill, Joyce and their children) was up and running. The multi-car garage became the men's dormitory. We even obtained a permit for that! No more boon docking.

Women, fewer in number than men, shared the largest of the four bedrooms. A beautiful large vegetable garden went in not far from the creek, where it would be easy to irrigate with a small pump. Water rights came with the deep loam fertile land. The fact is everything on this place grew marvelously well including the weeds! The answer, Bill decided, was to buy some goats. And the goats had babies. Pretty soon, the kids were raising the kids and both kinds of kids were having fun. As the herd grew, Bill saw the need for a certified milking parlor.

It turns out quite a few infants of the human variety can't tolerate cow's milk when their mothers can't or choose not to breast feed. For some of these infants, the answer is goat's milk. So it wasn't long before Bill managed to land a contact to supply the hospital at

Reedsport with grade A goat's milk. There was always lots to do on the farm and always many hands to do what needed to be done.

Week in and week out as the summer progressed, the garden flourished and I would provide counseling as needed to the residents of the farm on my weekly visits. After an afternoon on the farm, I would invariably come back to the county car packed to the headliner with the bounty of the garden, and sometimes a log or two of venison salami. (Some permits might have been missing. I will never know for sure, because a New Hampshire Indian was in charge. We could say that it might have been goat salami, but we suspect that they were too valuable to meet that kind of an end.)

Being on the farm is the high point of my work week, counseling while sitting on a hay bale in the sun or in the barn loft with a view of the bustling recovering young souls. I love Bill and Joyce, their kids and the crew. In all of this delight, there is only one small problem. It's almost too small to mention if it weren't such a burden. You see, in my family there is one small child and two adults. What am I to do with a carload of garden produce every week? Don't get me wrong. I love farm fresh carrots, peas, corn, lettuce, Swiss chard, broccoli, spinach, radishes, snap beans ... no, not beets, rhubarb or parsnips, and all these lovely things are loaded into the car each week when I wasn't looking. It takes us all week to consume what we can and find other homes for the delicious and sizable remainder. We especially try to get some of it around to other supporters of the farm.

This warm sunny day, I am going to fool Bill and Joyce. Today I am going to roll the car windows to within an inch of the top and I am going to lock all the doors, because, as much as I love Bill and Joyce and all the things helping hands grow, I can't spend all this next week playing "Duck the Delivery Truck."

All day, I have successfully pursued this closed car strategy. Every once in a while, I have glanced over at the car to make sure nobody has found a way to sneak anything in there. Now I am about to pop quickly into the car and head for home before anyone wises up to my plan. Oh my god, here comes Bill with a huge red contractor's wheelbarrow, produce hanging over the rim. Oh shit, now he's parked it right in front of the car. There's no escape.

"I've got some beautiful melt in your mouth ears of sweet corn in here for you today. I would have had the boys load it for you, but the car's all locked up tighter than a jam jar," Bill says to me as I roll down the window of this sweaty heap that's been sitting all closed up in the afternoon sun.

It's time to face up... since there is now no possible way to sneak out! "Bill, I know it is the most beautiful pick of the crop, but I can't accept any harvest bounty today. As hard as I worked at eating and sharing what you gave us last week, we still have plenty, honest we do," I said.

Within a second or two, I was shocked to see tears streaming down Bill's face. This rough, tough, Chief Pharmacist Mate, this broad-chested, ever joyful son of a New Hampshire Indian, was in tears. "Joyce and I love you, and we can't imagine doing this work without you. We couldn't. And you don't take a dime for the help you give us." Tears still flowing shamelessly down his cheeks, he continued, "How do you expect us to repay you if you won't let us give to you what we can?"

I got out of the bake-oven hot car I had been sitting in (only moments before hoping to escape unnoticed), wet stuff gushing out my tear ducts. I couldn't stop it. I wrapped my arms around his considerable girth, his head resting on my skinny chest. "You have it upside down Bill," I began. "I am the one in debt to you. You and Joyce give me your love so openly and freely. You make me feel like a better person than I am, because you let me come up here and help. My time with you guys is the very best part of my work week, always. Beyond all measure, I am the one indebted to you. I am forever grateful for the friendship that we share. That's more than enough. The rest is sometimes over the top. We need to negotiate that."

"What we have is pretty special, isn't it?" he said.

"You've got that right," I replied. And we stayed in that pose until we were both ready to push off into the surrounding world. We were both filled up, and I went home with four ears of corn.

Kubota Love

30

When I pulled into Karl and Maureen's driveway, the first thing I noticed was the fresh bandage on the forehead of Danny their youngest child. I am guessing Danny to be about two and a half or three years old. Karl was out beside his wood-gathering beast, a dusty rusty oversized Ford pickup, loading the chainsaw, gas cans, ax, beer cooler and the like into the truck bed. "What happened to Danny?" I asked.

"He climbed up into the back of the truck. He loves to do that for some reason. Then he jumped out head first into the gravel ... second time this week. Dr. Wiltse says if we bring him in one more time for the same injury, he's going to report us for child abuse, neglect or something!" Changing the subject completely, he added, "Hope you don't mind... Larry Mack invited himself to go along with us on our tree cutting expedition. He will be bringing his truck too."

"That's fine with me. I like Larry, and we haven't had a chance to visit in ages. By the way, speaking of our friend, Dr. Wiltse, I mentioned to him that you and I were headed off to do some firewood cutting and you know what he said to me? He said he was glad that you and I had become good friends, but then he issued a stern warning. He advised me never to fly in your Piper Cub with you, never to go salmon fishing in your boat with you, and never ever go woodcutting with you if there was more than one six-pack in the cooler. So how many six-packs did you load in there?" I asked.

"Just one ... each," he mumbled the last word at whisper under his breath with his hand in front of his mouth. I pretended not to hear the last word.

Soon the three of us arrived at the wood cutting site in a cloud of dust, and Karl ... two beers into the morning ... proceeded to park his ugly truck next to the biggest dead Douglas fir he could find. Then he pulled out his McCullough chainsaw out of the truck and began fueling the tank and oiling the chain. "A couple of trees like that," he said, pointing to the giant Doug fir next to the truck, "and we can head home with a full rack." Karl had built side racks for his beast so that he could load it to the height of the top of the cab.

"Don't you think we're parked a mite close to that bruiser," I asked?

"Naw, it saves a lot of time and energy to park close, makes it a lot easier to load. I wouldn't want you to have to walk too far." There was no conversation for a while after that, as he gave first one and then a second stout pull on the chainsaw and it roared to life in a cloud of blue smoke and a deafening roar.

Karl walked up to the tree, gave the accelerator a squeeze, and the deadly sharp teeth of the chain began biting into the flying bark. I took up a coward's position behind the dusty truck, praying that it would have the strength to protect me from imminent impact and death from the falling tree. Within minutes, that giant conifer lay harmlessly on the ground a full three feet from the tailgate. It was then that I realized I hadn't taken a breath since the chain first hit the bark, and surrounded as I was by the dust stirred up by the falling tree, it wasn't a good time to inhale! My lungs burned from the long delay, but I did the best I could to wait.

As Karl explained it to me, it was my job to take the ax and start climbing the tree from the top down while he worked on the much larger limbs from the bottom up. Then he would begin to cut 16 inch rounds for me to load into the truck bed. Some of the rounds would be too large and heavy to lift. Those, he said, would require a wedge, splitting maul and a beer.

When that first tree lay quietly in perfect 16 inch rounds ... all cut without any formal measuring on Karl's part... the saw went silent, and only the sound of lifting the cooler lid could be heard in the woods. Larry had parked approximately two or three football field lengths away from the tree he wanted to fall, and by the time Karl and I had limbed and segmented our tree, Larry had his tree on the ground, had it limbed, and he was pouring a cup of coffee from his thermos. He ambled over and joined us where we had perched on a couple of 16-inch high rounds. We had saved a third one for Larry. As I sipped on a cold Hamms, Larry began to share the latest gossip. Did we know that there was a new drug infested free-love cult up on Old 99 at Loraine road, he wanted to know?

"Whoa Larry! Where on Earth it you hear something like that?" I asked.

"Mary Beth had lunch with one of her friends at the cafe up in Drain yesterday. I guess the news is all over town by now," he said.

"That's not news, Larry. Somebody is out to spread some vicious rumors at the expense of the good name of Sunapee Farm, and I would be happy to give you a dose of truth to take back to Mary Beth if you are willing. Also, it would be a big help if we could track down the identity of the originator of that garbage. I would joyfully work to re-educate that person. As a matter of fact, if I could find that person, I would take him or her to lunch at the farm," I replied.

"If the farm is not another cult or commune, what is it?" Larry asked.

Karl, to whom I had spoken many times about Sunapee Farm during our time of struggle to get it up and running, chimed in. "It's a private non-profit alcohol and drug rehab center on a farm. Jim's on the board of directors and so is Doc Wiltse. I think it's a terrific idea. I would say it is as close to the opposite of a commune or a cult as you can get."

"Is that right? I'll be damned. Boy, Mary Beth sure got that all screwed up," Larry said.

"No Larry, I'll be willing to wager that she's telling it just the way she heard it, and that's what's bothering me. I hope we can find the source and help that person toward some positive interaction with Bill and Joyce, the couple who are putting their lives into this enterprise. Everyone I've known who has ever spent any time there comes away pretty enthusiastic," I said.

"It might not be that easy to trace back to the source," Larry observed.

"You may be right about that. Maybe we could have a neighborhood open house or something so that more people would have first-hand experience of the farm and could spread good rumors and intercept some of the poisonous ones," I suggested.

"That sounds like an idea with possibilities," Karl affirmed.

What happened in the next few moments is a matter of legend. Before we returned to tree falling, Larry lifted the round red can containing the gas/oil chainsaw fuel mix from the back of his truck and he emptied the contents of that can into his chainsaw's fuel tank. After securing the lids on both his can and saw, he began to walk away in the direction of the next tree he planned to fall, leaving the red can sitting on a stump.

"Better move your gas can Larry. That's where I plan to land our next tree, right there on that stump, "Karl said, with a glint of challenge in his eye.

"That can is not only empty but safe right where it is. Ten bucks says your snag doesn't come within three feet of it," Larry replied and kept on walking.

"Whatever you say Larry, but don't say I didn't warn you." In a flash, Karl cranked up his saw and Larry and I ran for opposite ends of Karl's pick up where we hunkered down to watch. It was a thing of beauty to watch as the bark and wood chips began to fly. A notch here, a little back cut there, and pretty soon that dead jack pine was headed for the earth, coming to rest amid ship on that stump. The red can was now a dead ringer for the letter "U". When the roaring saw gave way to the silence of the forest, Karl said, "Ten bucks please."

On the way home, I felt obligated to swing by the farm to give Bill and Joyce the heads up on the rumor mill, and perhaps brainstorm together about solutions. As usual, they were significantly out in front of the situation. Joyce said, "I can show you the source from our sidewalk. He's right across the Highway ... spends at least half the daylight hours sitting on his porch glaring at our house out of a menacing face. We've all gone out of our way to be friendly, even hospitable. We smile and wave every morning. I make it a point to time my mailbox run to match his, so I can invite him over for coffee or tea. But so far, he is identical to the troll under the bridge in the Three Billy Goats Gruff."

We talked further about a positive rumor strategy and how we might fortify and magnify the goodwill messengers. All agreed to follow a course of prayer, outreach and patience toward the neighbor, to whom we lovingly gave the nickname Mr. Grumpy Butt. Before heading south, Bill had to show me the newly completed Grade-A approved milking parlor for the goats, machines, concrete floor, stations and water run-off systems. And Bill's new pride and joy, there under the long overhang of the barn sat a brand new Kubota tractor. Of course I had to sit on it and play with the controls, like the Walter Middy of tractors. Up went the front end loader, bucket almost to the roof. I scared myself with that maneuver, so soon hopped down and admired this Japanese beauty from the ground.

Upon arriving back at home, I brought Annis up to date on the happenings at Sunapee Farm, and she did her best to bring my attention to her agenda.

Selective deafness was one of the skills that I learned from my parents in childhood, one which has never been a favorite of my beautiful wife. And why should it be? It wasn't her fault that my mother could and sometimes would speak incessantly (youngest of nine children, so go figure!), and my dad was raised by a very taciturn single parent on a dust-bowl era dry land wheat farm in eastern Colorado. "Don't talk, just keep moving," that must have been the motto. Dad's hearing, as a young man, was excellent, but he pretty much ignored mom's pointless babbling, tuning in to only what he thought were the salient points. I am afraid I inherited some of this skill, and for several months I failed to acknowledge the problem Annis was having with the front door of our house... on the flood plain of the Fairhaven neighborhood.

"When are you going to fix the front door? I must have asked you a hundred times," she said in utter frustration. "It sticks or drags and is very hard to open or close."

Mentally reviewing my marriage vows, I don't remember anything about tackling balky front doors. Having worked in canneries and sawmills as a kid, I just might have sought out the mental health profession as a refuge from physical labor. The fact is that we were both still kids when we got married, but we didn't know it at the time. What I do know is that when we decided that we couldn't stand to be apart any longer and I asked her father for her hand in marriage, she hadn't completed her cooking lessons, and I didn't own any tools.

Her dad, being more than willing to walk her down the aisle at the Methodist Church, gave her a quick lesson in how to cut up a whole chicken...which he believed was essential premarital training. Upon hearing that I was serious about marrying this beautiful woman of my dreams, my mother bought some heavy denim material, and from a pattern she must have had in her head, she designed a tool roll and then filled it with the essentials: pliers, screw drivers, a crescent wrench, a hammer and on the side, a hand saw. This, she thought, I must have before I could get married. On this one point, I believe Mom and Annis were on the same page. If there was something wrong with the front door, it was jolly well my job to fix it.

One day, when my selective deafness skill was getting me nowhere, I decided to tackle the sticky, balky door. Our neighbor, Mr. Schwartz, was more than happy to loan me a couple of sawhorses, but I didn't want him to know that I was a complete home repair idiot, so that was the full extent of the help I sought from him. Pulling the pins out of the hinges and getting the door to lie down on the sawhorses was easy enough. With my trusty tool roll unfurled out on the sidewalk beside the horses, I began to ponder which of my many tools might be best suited to the task at hand. By sheer process of elimination...not the pliers, not the screwdrivers, etc...I soon settled in on the hand saw as my tool of choice.

If Mr. Schwartz was watching from behind the fence, laughing his ass off, he was gentleman enough to never say so. With no small exertion of effort, I managed to circumcise the bottom of our door. Surveying the result, there was some imperfection in the outcome. It wasn't as even or as smooth a cut as I would have liked, but by jolly, I was pretty sure that it was never going to stick again. Giving it a second and third look, I was fairly sure I wasn't about to improve on it. So, I hung it back up. Right away, I could see some potential problem with my fix job. While the door swung free and easy, I could see a good patch of daylight here and there at the bottom of the door! "Oh well, it's still summer," I thought, "so the gap won't matter much until we hit late Fall or Winter when the cold could come rushing in. Maybe Annis won't notice. Maybe she'll be happy that she can open and close the door."

I took the sawhorses back to Mr. Schwartz.

Three days later, Bill gave me a call at home while I was in the midst of contemplating the rotten, sagging grape arbor. I was observing that it might possibly collapse and if the children happened to be playing there when it went down, I'd have to find a way to get more kids. "Great news Jim," Bill said. We solved our evil rumor problem."

"How the heck did you do that?" I asked.

"Sarge, Bill and Sally were out picking up trash along the irrigation ditch. Old Mr. Grumpy Butt was out plowing his field and about four passes into the process, his tractor quit on him. Then he yelled at it, banged on it and gave it a swift kick. Nothing worked for him. He couldn't get it going. He stomped back to his house and slammed the door a good one. When our crew came back from their ditch work, they told Joyce and me the whole story.

We decided to crank up the Kubota and finish his fieldwork for him. As soon as he heard us out there, he came flying out on his front porch and stood there like he had the usual stick up his butt. He glared and we plowed. After a while, he sat down and watched with a quizzical smile. When we finished, we chugged on home like nothing had happened. We had a call from your friend Karl a few minutes ago. He says the story is all the way down in Yoncalla, and we haven't said a word to anybody!"

"And God bless you, everyone," I said.

Of Time and Humility
31

The many joys of our autumn coastal interlude to the Powell's beach house and beyond were fondly remembered in early July in the labor and delivery rooms at Mercy Hospital. Baby Lara was born to the musical serenade of my wife's obstetrician. That doctor knew all the notes and verses of the tune "Laura." We went down to the hospital on the 4th of July, thinking that we would have a little firecracker baby, but they said it was false labor and sent us home.

Home by this time was a small green house ... partial brick facade in the Fairhaven subdivision ... on the flood plain of the South Umpqua River. What made this house affordable was the 1964 flood, which had occupied the neighborhood for several days of that fateful year. Come to think about it, this postwar community must have been built on a swamp to begin with, because you could drive a steel pipe into the ground with a sand point on the end anywhere in the Fairhaven and find enough water to run three hoses 24 hours a day.

Our neighbors on the north side were a sweet retired couple, Ed and Martha Schwartz. Some 10 plus years before our first appearance in Fairhaven, Martha had experienced a devastating stroke, which she survived, but which left her wheelchair bound. Their home had a commodious front porch to which Ed had attached a very effective, wide, gently sloping ramp. Our son Aaron, having quickly mastered the three-wheeler, was certain that Ed had built this for him. On warm summer days, Martha loved to sit on her front porch where she was visited and entertained by Aaron, as he was both ramp enthusiast and conversationalist.

"Where is Aaron?" my wife would say.

"If he's not here, he must be on Ed and Martha's front porch," I would reply.

"Well, you better go get him. It's time for dinner and Martha might fill him up on cookies. Besides, sooner or later, he might become a pest."

"The cookies scenario could have some merit, but those two are a mutual friendship society of the first order. He's much more of a pal than a pest, I can assure you," I said. But I was already headed for the door to do the retrieving.

"Hi, Martha, how are you on this pleasant summer evening," I asked.

"I'm fine as can be...with one exception, that is. Aaron and I are having a delightful time out in the fresh air on the front porch," she replied, but then didn't go on to enlighten me as to the exception.

"And what would that exception be that stands in the way of perfection," I asked, as Aaron zoomed down the ramp, made a quick U-turn on the sidewalk and headed up the incline again.

"That baby girl of yours, you know I haven't met her yet ... she's been home for days and I haven't met her yet. And she's not about to walk, run or ride her trike over here, if you get my drift," she said.

"Yes Martha, you are being very subtle and delicate, but I get your drift. I will get Lara over here pretty quick. I promise. She's got a very busy schedule... always eating, pooping and sleeping." Turning to Aaron, I said, "I'll race you back to our house," knowing that he could not resist the challenge of the word "race."

Two days later, for no particular reason that I can think of, I took a little detour through the Health Department section of the building on my way to the mental health section. Dr. Gray's door was wide open, and he had a very somber look about him as he labored on the paperwork on the desk in front of him. Not wanting to disturb him, I observed for a moment in silence before proceeding on down the hall. But in that moment, he looked up and caught my glance. It was a puzzling moment of acknowledgement, and I filled the void with a question. "What has your intense attention so early this morning?" I asked.

He briefly looked down at the papers in front of him, then slowly looked up and held me seriously in his gaze. He took in a very full breath and let it out before he answered. "I am at this moment filling out and signing the death certificate for your neighbor, Martha. She passed away middle of the night last night."

I sat down in the hallway in front of Dr. Gray's door so that I would not fall down. I was stunned and dizzy and to be honest, a bit nauseous. I don't know how long I sat there in silence, but after a while I heard Dr. Gray say, "I am sorry Jim, I didn't know how attached you were to her."

"It's not only that. I am a complete and total arrogant, narcissistic ass," I said, with head hanging down and arms around my knees. "Several times in the past few days Martha expressed the desire to meet our new daughter. She said in no uncertain terms that it was the one thing that would make her life complete. I made a promise to Martha … 'Pretty quick' I said. My God, what did I do? She sat in the shade on her front porch in the warm afternoon sun every day and visited with our son. And I was behaving like I could take our daughter over for an introduction any old afternoon … any old afternoon," I whispered with tears streaming down both cheeks.

"And now you know … the hard way … that there is no time but the present. And I doubt you will ever forget it," came Dr. Gray's compassionate voice.

Fundamentalists and Lizards
32

Life is zipping along at a very creative and eventful clip up at Sunapee Farm. The young adults keep arriving, recovering and thriving. With very few breaks, Bill and Joyce and their natural family keep on embracing the incoming tribe members and giving them meaningful work to do ... hands-on nurturing of the crop and the livestock. Since the slanderous rumors ceased, even more people have joined the ranks of supporting cast.

Once in a great while I get a call to run interference between the farm and some generous but misguided supporting cast member.

"Jim," Joyce is whispering loudly into the phone, "you've got to help me here. Pastor Mel Nixon and his wife from Cottage Grove are parked in our driveway in a large pickup truck. Bill is out there with them right now. They have two brand new twin-size beds in the bed of that truck ... mattresses ... bedding and all... which is fine except for the fact that they want to haul off our old queen-size bed and move the twins into our bedroom ... as if Bill and I are going to sleep on them. It's not going to happen, Jim.

"Nelda Nixon came right out and asked me how I can stand to sleep with that hairy, heavy old beast, pointing at Bill! I want to run them off and Bill is out there being his diplomatic self. He saw how upset I am and sent me back inside. Jim, I've been sleeping with that hairy beast for 37 years, and I'm not about to stop doing so now! What should we do?"

"Don't let that right-wing fundamentalist pastor and his wife lay their pseudo-religious guilt trip on you and Bill. Nowhere does the Bible say 'Thou shalt not sleep in a queen bed... thou must sleep separately and only in twin size beds!' You can bang on the Bible just as good as they can. I suggest that you calmly and confidently march right back out there and tell Mel and Nelda that after you and Bill exchanged vows before God and the minister that officiated at your wedding, that the minister quoted scripture to the effect that no one was to come between the two of you, and that meant then, now and forever. Tell them that they are welcome to contribute the new twin beds to the dorm or find another suitable location for them. How does that sound?"

"I like it!" she offered just before hanging up.

As soon as I hung up the phone, my beautiful wife caught my attention. "Hey mister big problem solver, we have a problem. Come into the living room as quick as you can. There's a foot and a half long lizard just came in under your newly remodeled front door. Right now he's just looking around to see which kid to swallow, but pretty soon he could take off into one of the closets or someplace that might make him difficult to find. He's your lizard, so I want you to remove him!"

I knew I would just be digging my hole deeper to debate whether or not this was my lizard, so I admitted that my door repair work had been a bit over zealous if not misguided. I took one look at the lizard, and said, "Jeez Louise, I had no idea Mount Nebo had dinosaurs running around on her slopes. That's the biggest lizard I've ever seen."

"We're just lucky it wasn't a Mount Nebo rattlesnake come to see what a good job you did on that front door!" she said.

"I get your point. When Uncle Jack comes to remodel our bathroom, I will have him help me with the door. I think it requires a table saw, which by the way, wasn't included in my prenuptial tool kit. I am sure he will be bringing one. In the meantime, I think I can get some weather stripping to tack on the bottom of that door to keep the larger wild animals out," I said with the confidence of a genuine handyman. "Here, you hold this box on its side. I'll take the broom and herd this lizard toward the box."

"No way are you going to sucker me into holding onto that box. That would be like the time you talked me into holding the nail while you lined up to hit it with the hammer. You hold the box. I'll sweep the lizard toward you," she said as she pried the broom out of my grasp.

This activity was beginning to look an awful lot like a Three Stooges routine, with a reptile as the third stooge. However, after several spastic attempts at capture, we finally trapped the lizard and returned him to the great outdoors.

Cars, Planes and Boats
33

During my next visit to Drain, Dr. Wiltse wanted to deliver the good news that Mike had graduated with honors from Drain High School and won an ROTC scholarship to Oregon State University with his proud mother observing and looking quite presentable herself. "This is the longest period of medical and mental stability that Alice has had in the past 12 years. Also, she and Mike have figured out a new post-graduation contract for continuing her medication and aftercare supervision. Now, if only she can remember how much better off she is sane than crazy..." his statement just hung in the air, unfinished.

"I definitely think the combined success of Mike and Alice is worth celebrating. You want to go fishing at Dorena Lake with Karl and me? You deserve a day off," I said.

"Yes, I guess I've earned a day off, but I would like to live long enough to tell about. You go ahead and tempt fate if you like. I think my best option is to just cast a line into the Row from my deck chair with a glass of lemonade on the side table," he replied.

Dr. Wiltse's home sat on the picturesque Row River (Row is pronounced as in the word 'rowdy'), and I could imagine him sitting on his deck reading a medical journal being completely inattentive to his line in the water. "Why be so cautious? You only live once... depending on your theology of course. What would be so dangerous about boating or flying with Karl?"

"Karl, my friend, likes to live on the edge if you haven't noticed. For example, his Piper Cub has the wings over the fuselage design. In other words, the wings are just sitting on top of the body of the plane, being held on by a couple of small struts. On the instrument panel of the plane is a 3 by 5 inch brass plaque, which reads 'This Plane Not Designed For Aerobatic Flight.' And Karl delights in flying that little puddle jumper any which way but straight," he persuaded.

"Aerobatic... as in loops, rolls, flying upside down and stuff like that?" I shivered.

"And stuff like that," Doc said.

"And not designed for aerobatic flight..."

"Yes, that means the wings could just fall off during maneuvers like that," he said calmly.

"But they haven't yet," I said.

"The operative word in this case would be yet. I would say that with each flight, Karl is pushing the odds in favor of the plane's factory specifications or its design limitations. What do you think?"

"How do you know all this stuff about his barnstorming tendencies?" I asked.

"He comes to me for his flight physical, Jim. And he is not modest about what he would call his accomplishments."

"And you sign off on his medical worthiness so that he can keep on doing this?" I asked.

"I can't stop him from flying, Jim. He could get his flight certification physical lots of places, so he might as well get it here when he gets his general physical. I can't stop him from flying. I just make it a rule not to get in there with him."

"OK. What about the boat? Why won't you join us in the boat? It is a beautiful little aluminum sled with seats, a flying bridge, fishing rod holders and a 100 horse Honda. What's not to like?" I asked.

"The operative word here is small. That thing has one motor, no back up. Karl loves to take this little boat out across the bar at Winchester Bay. Have you heard about hypothermia? Given the water temperature along that part of the Pacific, if you capsized, you could last maybe 20 or 30 minutes even with your flotation devices strapped on. And a mile or two out beyond the whistler you could float around out there all day without seeing another boat ... if you get my drift," he said, pun intended. "As I said before, I am very pleased that you two have become good friends, but I would rather not run the risk of losing you both on the same day."

From that moment on, I decided to create a few precautions of my own when spending time with Karl. When he asked me if I would like to fly to Salishan for lunch and a round of golf, I told him I would do it only if he flew straight and right side up. If he felt the urge to make loops and dives, he had to put me on the ground first. He promised to honor this request. My thinking about the boat and the deep blue sea was a work in progress. Catching a 35-pound Chinook was a proposition that had very strong appeal for me, so I was reluctant to set any limits on boat excursions.

I left home before dawn, arriving at Karl's house about 5:30 AM. The boat trailer was already hitched up to his pickup, safety chain properly attached to the bumper. However, I noticed that the Honda had gone missing off the back of the boat and mentioned this to Karl. "Too big a motor for Dorena," he said. "I put the little 10 horse in the boat. We can attach it to the transom when we get to the lake. It's a good little trolling motor."

Very soon, we were heading up the road to Lake Dorena, boat in tow. As the expression goes, we were just rolling along and shooting the breeze. "Oregon State is going to win some games this Fall," Karl said, as he down shifted the transmission to a lower gear on the steep and curvy road. We were nearing the summit before the final decent toward the lake. "The coach made a recruiting trip down to inner city L.A. after the season last year. He signed some really big, mean, black athletes who will be showing up in Corvallis any time now."

"That sounds a lot like DHS recruiting Yoncalla foster parents to care for inner city Portland juvenile delinquents. Maybe you and I should offer... for a small fee... to run a counseling group for these new OSU athletes," I said with tongue in cheek.

"You may have a splendid idea there. Working it into our schedules, that would be the hard part," he replied, as the truck picked up speed on the curvy downhill grade.

Just then, out of the corner of my left eye, I caught sight of a boat passing us on the port side of the truck. Karl must have spotted it at about the same moment that I did because he immediately hit the brakes and said in a loud voice, "Shit, I forgot to tie the boat down!" It had evidently been riding along on the trailer and happy to do so until we hit the steep and crooked downhill stretch. The two of us watched in horror as the sled slipped on by, and in what appeared to be slow motion ballet, the boat made a 180 degree turn in the road and began to slide down the road backwards. Gradually the boat began to lose speed and it came to rest, transom first, against a steel roadside reflector post, a marker strategically placed to warn of the hundred foot drop on the far side of the marker.

We quickly pulled the truck and trailer off the road at the first available wide spot down the hill from the boat, fearing the worst as we huffed and puffed several hundred yards back up the hill to the boat next to the reflector on the precipice.

Karl got there first and it was quiet in the extreme as he slowly took an inventory of the situation. The wind in the trees, and the buzz of a few grasshoppers provided the only break to the absolute stillness that surrounded the sled. After several minutes of inspection, which seemed infinitely longer, Karl declared, "I don't see a damn thing wrong with it. It seems to have slid along on those reinforced ridges on the bottom and the ass end of the boat being the strongest part, it survived the signpost just fine. Now all we have to do is figure out how to reload it here in the middle of the road without getting killed by a passing log truck! Then we'd be back in business, headed for the fishing hole none the worse for wear."

I couldn't believe what I saw, but I concluded that he was correct.

There must be a certain code of ethics among fishermen as among thieves, because we soon had all the help we needed. The small guys halted traffic while the muscular guys with tattoos and camels heaved the boat back up on its trailer. A member of neither group, I supervised.

About Creation and the Corn Snake
34

On Monday morning, I wore my new fisherman's tan to work. Basically, all exposed parts were fried to a nice crispy red. The peeling and itching would arrive later in the week, while the skin cancer on the nose and ear would follow much later.

Down the hall on the second floor of the counseling wing of the Health Department, I could see Dr. John with Hugh and Gary having what appeared to be a serious conversation. From what I could hear at a distance, I gleaned that the general nature of the topic seemed to be why intelligent men did stupid things. Drawn to the subject matter, I wandered down that way to get a better grasp of the exchange. Chairman of the United States House Ways and Means Committee, Wilber Mills, was all over the front page of this morning's Oregonian newspaper surrounded by much unflattering commentary. The paper trumpeted the lurid details of the good legislator's alcohol fueled sexual escapade with a young lass named Fanny Fox, Hugh was saying. They ended up falling off a pier with their clothes on. Gary was saying that it couldn't have been much of an affair if they still had their clothes on.

As I arrived within the cluster of men, Hugh said, "There is political blood in the water, and Republican sharks will be quick to attack his power, influence and position of authority. They will pack him out with tomorrow's trash."

"How could he be so stupid?" a temperate Gary wondered aloud.

"Well, if you want to know the truth, this is an issue that goes all the way back to creation," Dr. John replied in a voice of authority.

"You see, when god created man, She gave him a brain and a penis, but only enough blood to run one of these at a time."

"That makes sense," Hugh said. "Especially when there's not much blood left in the alcohol stream."

I think Dr. John might have resembled Hugh's remark, because I am sure I saw Dr. John wince in response to it. "Boy Howdy am I glad I came to work here. Never a day goes by but what I learn something new," I said, as the group began to wander off in different directions toward our respective schedules.

Lucky for me, a new couple was next up on my calendar ... an almost certain opportunity to refocus and get my head back in the counseling game. Merle and Glenda it said in my appointment book. From the argumentative sounds emanating out of the waiting room and wafting up the stairs, I had a strong suspicion that they had arrived. Simultaneous with this thought came a buzz on the intercom. It was Diane with the quiet but desperate message that my 9:00 AM clients had arrived. "No kidding?" I replied. "I'll be right down."

"It's your damn fault! And you are a damn fool if you think that this counseling shit is going to fix anything," said a loud if not certain Merle as I stepped down to the reception area landing.

As I approached, they both turned quiet and looked up. I took this to be a hopeful sign that my presence in their midst might make a difference.

"Welcome," I said, offering my outstretched hand to first one and then the other. "I'm Jim Henson and I will be your counselor. Please follow me up to my consultation room."

Without hesitation, the couple began following me up the stairs, but when we three reached the second floor, Glenda asked, "Aren't you a little young to be doing this kind of work?"

"Thank you for noticing my youthful appearance," I said. "What do you think would be the right age to be doing what you and Merle need me to do?" I asked, as we closed the door and began to take our places.

"Let me put it another way," Glenda continued with her pre-employment interview. "Are you married?"

"Yes I am and happily so I might add," I replied.

"And do you have any children?" she asked.

"Yes indeed, two healthy and joyful little poopers. You know, I think you are really on to something. That fancy diploma from the University of Chicago and the ACSW certificate next to it up there on the wall don't actually mean that much without some actual life experience. Am I right?" And that is how I maneuvered toward the position of question asker and away from the interviewee.

Both Merle and Glenda nodded in the affirmative, so I decided to go for the closer. "Do you have some more questions about my background or do you think we can get to work and be a team?"

"I'm ready if she is," Merle said calmly, with a glance in Glenda's direction.

"You big liar, less than five minutes ago in the waiting room you said you were against the whole idea of being here and you know, to quote your big mouth, it wasn't going to do us a damn bit of good," Glenda spouted, the veins on her neck become pronounced.

"Somebody told me not long ago that we ought to speak sweetly to our spouses because we never know when we might have to eat our words...sounds like a good philosophy, doesn't it." I left it more as a statement than a question. "What brings you to the point of considering counseling, Merle?" I know about ladies first and all that, but from their opening exchange it seemed to me that his decision to come was weaker than Glenda's. She was the one promoting counseling but wanted to make sure that they had the right counselor. Since it was more her idea, she didn't want it to fail and have him throw it back in her face.

"Because we fight about everything and I am sick and tired of fighting about everything. I didn't think being married would be this hard," Merle replied.

"What made you think it would be easier, Merle?"

"I never saw my parents argue or raise their voices even. They didn't fight about anything that I can recall. I thought marriage would be more like that," he said.

"Your mother was a spineless, gutless wonder from the old school who believed in submission to the dominant alpha male warlord and master. If she had any idea or belief contrary to your dad's, she wouldn't have said anything. That's why she was dead by age 60, after suffering in silence for a year with colon cancer," Glenda said.

"Whoa," I said, hoping to pull back on the reins a bit. "I'm trying to get a little drink of information and it is flowing out at me like a full on fire hydrant! I can see here that one of my jobs with you two will be to manage the volume of the flow and exchange of information. What different family systems you two must have come from... like one from loquacious Italy and the other from inscrutable Japan. Merle, what in the world was it that attracted you to Glenda in the first place?"

"Well, as you can see, she's not bad looking," a very high Norwegian compliment from Merle. "And she was fun, very outgoing and confident," he continued. "I liked that about her."

"And what was your initial attraction to Merle?" I asked Glenda.

"Well, as you can see, he is a strong, good looking guy and he seemed more mature than other guys I had gone out with. He was well on his way to becoming a journeyman plumber. He knew where he was headed. He was kind of quiet, but I just thought he was a great listener," she said.

"Let me see if I understand these things," I said. "Merle, your parents perfected the fine art of sweeping every difference under the rug. Perhaps they feared conflict, but they definitely knew how to avoid it. Part of the attraction to Glenda, in addition to her beauty, is that she is fun and out there with her ideas. Glenda's parents were out front with their differences, occasionally needing a fire extinguisher to get to resolution. However, Glenda is attracted to Merle not only because he is a good-looking, hardworking guy, but also quiet and thoughtful. In short, your parents were compatible with each other, but you two are opposites attracted and frustrated. Does that sound about right?"

"Oh, God yes!" said Glenda.

Merle shook his head in affirmation.

"My wife grew up in San Diego and most of her family still lives right around there. Last time we visited we all went down to the fabulous San Diego Zoo. There is so much to see there, but what completely captured my imagination was an exhibit in the reptile pavilion. They have in captivity a corn snake with a strange genetic anomaly. It has two heads on one body. It's a two-headed corn snake. I was so fascinated that I read the entire caption at the base of the snake's enclosure. It said that genetic anomalies such as this were uncommon, but because the two heads could not communicate or cooperate on the most essential of life activities, like where to go or how to capture food, they didn't survive very long out in their natural habitat. They would just wither and die out there.

I think you are two heads on one body called family, and separate and apart, as individual single people, you each could thrive. Then you went to the chapel or justice of the peace and got married and began to starve to death."

"Do you mean like we are incompatible so we have to get a divorce?" Merle managed to choke out these words as if it was the last thing in the world he wanted to happen.

"No Merle, what it means is that you and Glenda have to accept the fact that you are a respect worthy two headed entity called a couple. You are called upon to learn how to communicate and cooperate for the purpose of thriving and creating a family. The brains inside the heads of the two headed corn snake are about the size of a pinhead. You and Glenda have no such excuse for failure."

"So you think there is hope for us," Glenda asked meekly but with resolve.

"Do you want to keep this guy?" I asked.

"Yes!" she said emphatically.

"Then yes is your answer if you are willing to learn how to put your heads together," I concluded.

They decided to make another appointment and left my office, hand in hand speaking through smiles, chatting about snakes and brains. "He's a strange guy, our counselor," I overheard Glenda saying. "Yeah, I like him too," was Merle's reply.

We would have a long way to go, Merle, Glenda and I, but they had made a decision to continue their counseling and to succeed as a couple, and it doesn't get much better than that.

And Then There Were None
35

Persistence, Thy name is Glenda and Merle. They just kept coming back. "We don't agree on anything. How to raise our two kids, how to spend or save our money, who's going to do what, what to do with our relatives, whether we are going to make love or not and when, should we move or stay put... it's all a contest every day," said Merle.

"You agree to be here every week until you learn to communicate and problem solve together successfully. You agree that you come to each other from opposite ends of the family system spectrum. You agree that you are so different that you cannot assume that you know anything about your partner until you hear it from them personally, and you may soon come to believe that being different has its benefits. For instance, you are sometimes upset with each other, but never bored. Your marriage has known problems, not insidious hidden ones. You can have respect for the fact that neither one of you is a pushover, so that when you arrive at a compromise or a consensus, you can count on it being a genuine and lasting one," I observed, not willing to accept Merle's all or none construct.

"How can our differences become benefits?" Glenda challenged.

"Which of you is right 100-percent of the time?" I countered.

It was fun to watch them look each other over, as if to see who would blink first. Although each of them had expressed belief in the superiority of their positions, neither wanted to fall prey to trap of claiming to be perfect. The silence built over several seconds.

"OK, I'm not," said Glenda, "but I would like to be."

""I'm not and I don't even want to be, but I will be damned if I am going to be brow beaten into accepting her as the almighty authority on everything," Merle conceded.

"Speaking of The Almighty, that One who must have a tremendous sense of humor, it would appear to me that our differences and limitations were built in from the day of creation, and it was on purpose, not an oversight. Would you two be willing to indulge in a brief experiment?" I asked. I figured if that backsliding Catholic, Dr. John, could come up with a creation story, so could I.

"OK," said Glenda. Merle, the talkative one, nodded his consent.

"Here we go then. If you're willing, lift your arms up from your sides straight out from your body until they are even with your shoulders...like this (I demonstrated). Now rotate your wrists until your thumbs point up like this. Imagine that family life is going on around you in a perfect 360 degree circle. Your arms in this position are marking the middle or 180 degree point in that circle. Looking straight ahead, can you see either of your hands?"

"Not me," said Glenda.

"Me neither," Merle said.

"So are you willing to admit that the way we were created, none of us can see half of what is going on in this room or anyplace else for that matter?" They are both watching me intently, and beginning to accept their lack of omniscience. "Now very, very slowly move your arms forward until you can first see both of your hands at the same time. What percent of the 360 degree pie is left, as measured by your out stretched arms?" I asked.

"Not more than 140 to 160 degrees," observed Merle.

"Exactly, without the help of others, we can't take in half of what's going on around us. This is what they mean when someone says, "I've got your back." We have to accept our limitations and trust the information that we are giving to each other. You can put your arms down now. If yours are anything like mine, they are starting to get a bit heavy. Then, in the field of the 140 to 160, each of us will pay attention to different things. We've trained from birth to notice different things. Close your eyes for a moment, if you would please. Take a minute to reflect on the first thing you noticed as you came into this room today?"

"I noticed that your desktop is all neat and organized and I thought you might be somewhat compulsive," Glenda said without hesitation.

"Somewhat compulsive, she says. Glenda, I am more compulsive than a left handed surgeon, and I am a pale compulsive compared to the group of raccoons that raised me! Merle, what did you notice when you walked in here today?"

"That matted print on the wall over there with the blue County Fair ribbon on it... it kind of looks like flying snails. What the heck is it really supposed to be?" Merle asked with as much tact as he could muster.

"Merle, you may not be the first person to notice that woodblock print, but you are the first person to have the courage to ask about it. What you see there are genuine flying snails, possibly the only ones ever presented in this manner. Our boss, you see, sent us out to man a booth at the health fair. And it was boring as hell to sit there and hand out brochures about depression and addiction. To be honest, they weren't selling very well, and we were trying to give them away. "The 10 warning signs" or something like that and another one titled: "You know you are an alcoholic if..." Fortunately, I took along some wood and my wood block cutting tools.

"All the children and I were bored out of our minds, you see. The only action in the whole place was the siren on the ambulance and trips on a medical bed that could make a complete rotation with a kid strapped into it. So, I started drawing and thinking about what to carve, and then pretty soon, eight or 10 kids surrounded me... wanted to know what I was doing. I tell them I am drawing and trying to decide what to carve, and I could use some ideas. We pushed all the brochures to one side of the table and we all began to draw and attempt to come up with a theme befitting of this so-called health fair. One bright little sandy haired kid piped up and said he thought the event reminded him of a snail race... in a hurry to go no place. We all laughed and then came up with this design of the flying snails. About that blue ribbon, one day I came to work and that print had gone missing from my wall. I wondered who in the heck would want that piece of personal memorabilia. A few days after that, I got a note from the County Fair Board that the snails print had won a blue ribbon in its category. My boss's wife had hauled it out there for the judging! Frankly, I think it must have been the only piece in its category!

"The point is, we don't see very much of the field and we don't see the same thing when we are looking at the same field. I may not like what my partner sees, and I may not like what she has to say about it, but I can't imagine parenting or strategizing our social or financial life without her.

"Does this give you any ideas for some possible homework?" I asked.

"This is like the two headed corn snake all over again, isn't it?" Merle replied. (And I am feeling elated that he has made this connection, but playing dumb, I asked him to elaborate on his observation.) "You know, one snake sees the mouse running to the right, the other snake can't see it. The first head doesn't say anything to the second head. He just struggles to pull the entire body to the right all by himself. And he misses and they starve."

"Yes, it is the corn snake, and to beat the old pattern, we have to practice sharing with each other what we see in our individual zones. We have to practice receiving the information we get from each other so we can put together the big picture." Glenda really nailed it.

"So we can be a functional team." Merle nailed it too.

"And pretty damn quick you won't need to hang around me. I'm not old enough to be working with you people anyway," I concluded, and we all had a good laugh.

Later in the day, came an unexpected call from Drain. Mike's mom, Alice was on the phone to arrange a medication review. Her confidence has risen many percentage points in the months preceding and following Mike's graduation. "Dr. Wiltse says he would like me to see a real psychiatrist for my next medication review, and I think I'm up for a trip to the big city," she said, and she meant Roseburg, not Portland or Eugene. It was my business card she had, and it was my familiar face with which she wanted to deal, not some unknown character in the appointment center.

"I'll get it set up and call you back," I assured her. After hanging up, I hit the intercom, hoping to catch Diane with the appointment book open to Dr. John's schedule.

Instead of Diane, Betty answered, sounding a bit overloaded and befuddled, which is quite unlike her. If anyone in administration is organized and on top of her game, it's Betty, but she did manage to ask what she could do for me.

Knowing Diane was assigned the task of fielding the intercom messages downstairs, I jokingly said, "Don't you have any help down there today?"

"That is correct. I have no help down here today!" Her voice had a somewhat exasperated quality to it.

"Where the heck is Diane, on vacation, sick day or something?" I asked.

"Or something, that would be the answer. About 10 minutes ago, I have a call from her. She and Dr. John are evidently in Montana where the two of them apparently are planning to take up residence. With Dr. John, nothing that man did would surprise me, but I thought Diane had better sense."

"Wait just a minute. Let me get this straight in my mind. Diane and Dr. John took off together to Montana? And what about Jane and what about their jobs here?" I said, sitting bolt upright in my desk chair for the first time ever.

"It would appear that Jane and here are history, and this took a bit of planning on someone's part, because Diane said Dr. John already has a job in Bozeman... and that they are, 'Oh, so happy.' By the way, what was it you called about?" Betty was really in the mood to unload now.

"This is just crazy. Somebody has been consuming too much of the grape or pharmaceutical products. I was calling to find out when I could line up an aftercare medication review appointment with a real psychiatrist for my favorite Drain schizophrenic in remission. Guess we can forget about that, unless perhaps we can get Forest Miner from the V.A. to see her." This I knew was grasping at straws.

"You haven't seen today's paper, I take it," Betty said, with accompanying gallows laugh. "Forest is in secure hold at Douglas Community, accused of killing his wife. EMT staff answered a call from his house last night and found him beside her body completely incoherent."

"I don't want to hear this stuff, really I don't. Is Hugh around? I think I need a counseling session!" I sputtered.

"I think it needs to be a group session for all of us, and the sooner the better. Hugh's door is open. I'll send him up," her wisdom shining through.

"Thank you and wonderful idea about a group session. You are right, of course. We should invite Dr. Gray to the group session. This is going to hit Dr. Gray like a ton of bricks too. That man has tried so hard to get some medical help on his team." I am more slumped than upright in my chair now.

Hugh was up the stairs within a few minutes. I was at the door to my consult room when he arrived, and we exchanged a full body hug and exhale right there before moving to the interior space and sagging into chairs. "We shouldn't be all that surprised about today's revelations, Jim. We have been standing on greased grape leaves through this entire chapter. Dr. John was a lot more active and entertaining than Dr. Puhak. (I nodded) And we shouldn't forget the essence of psychiatry, Jim. Psychiatry is for people who get all the way through their medical training and find out that they are blood and bodily fluids phobic. Then they have to search out a medical profession in which they don't have to touch any of these."

"I guess you're right. If there is anyone I feel bad for in this situation, it's Dr. Gray. He has worked so damn hard to line up some medical help," I replied.

"He'll be OK. He's a survivor of WWII and Korea, and he is very observant. He likely saw this coming long before it ever smacked us in the face," he said. Then we set a time for an all clinic staff meeting that would include Dr. Gray.

With feelings of gratitude for my clients, family and co-workers, this day, like others I had known, came to an end.

Courage: Liquid and Real
36

Sometimes small talk is just the thing to help clear your mind of the current and serious important stuff. Just when I am thinking gloomy thoughts about the clinic and all things related to psychiatry, into my consult room pops the head of Gary. "Can we talk for a couple of minutes?" he asks.

Given the clinic climate de jour, I say "Sure." However, I am afraid some other bad shoe is about to drop.

After settling into one of my cushy bottomed stack chairs, he says," I been thinkin about getting a Toyota like yours... different color of course. And I was wondering what you think of yours."

"Well, it has a comfortable ride and it gets 32 MPG on the highway, and it has only tried to kill me three times thus far."

"You gotta be kidding. What happened?" he asks.

"For starters, on my way home on Stevens Street ... we are talking about three months into ownership ... something went haywire with the accelerator linkage. Whatever holds the accelerator pedal up gave up the ghost, leaving the pedal on the floor and the car revving at full throttle! Since it is an automatic with power steering and steering wheel column lock, I was initially scared shitless, not sure what to do. I couldn't just turn off the ignition. The column would lock and I would be unable to steer. In a few seconds, I decided to shift into neutral and started to pump the brakes. The brakes, by the way, worked pretty good, but my tires and my underwear took a beating.

"Then there was the night Annis Rae, Aaron and I drove down to Medford to visit my parents. Somewhere south of Canyonville, we began to smell an unholy stink from the front end of the car. My intuition was telling me something's gone wrong in the engine compartment. So, I coast to a stop beside the Interstate, pop the latch and lift up the hood. The hood and the hood latch, by the way, work fine. It was then I realized that I didn't have a flash light, and in the dark of night I couldn't see what was going on under there, but the stink was obvious... and no smoke, just a smell like somebody had left a wrought iron skillet on the stove and absentmindedly walked away with the burner left on high. I am still under warranty, and I am one third of the way to my destination. The car has made it this far. So I close the hood and keep going.

"Near the second turn off to Grants Pass, everybody is complaining about the stink, so I stop again and pop the latch and lift the hood one more time. I can't see a blooming thing in the dark of night. Honestly, the stink didn't seem any worse to me... and I was still under warranty and three quarters of the way to our destination.

"When we arrived at my parents' house, dad came out to greet us and help carry stuff into the house. But as he approached the car he wanted to know where all the stink was coming from. We backed his Plymouth out of the garage and rolled Toyota in there. It was my good fortune that Annis Rae and Aaron were safely in the house with mom when dad and I hung the mechanic's light over the engine and started the car. She might have killed me for putting our lives at risk. Toyota Motors of Japan had run a straight aluminum pipe between the fuel pump and the carburetor. Every time the engine revved or giggled on the motor mounts that aluminum tube was flexing.

"Metal fatigue had finished off the pipe, and it had separated from the carburetor. That car has a great fuel pump. It was shooting gas in the direction of the carburetor over a quarter inch gap and was still getting enough gas to run the engine at 70-mph for eighty five miles!"

"With gas flying on the hot engine block, one spark would have set the whole engine compartment ablaze," Gary said, with hand to mouth. "You could have all been cooked alive!"

"You got that right, and it only cost 10 cents worth of small gage surgical tubing to fix... something to take care of the flex and vibration. Are you sure you have time to hear the rest of the story?"

"I doubt I have anything waiting for me that beats this," he said.

"OK, here is the clincher. New Year's Eve, you may recall, Annis Rae and I went over to Sunriver. A dear old friend invited us over there for a small celebration. Temperatures reached 14 to 15 below zero that night. Aaron and Lara had wisely stayed home with friends in our babysitting co-op. At the highway sign which reads '1 mile to Sunriver exit' the engine died and the car rolled to a stop. Since we had planned to drive pretty much door to door, neither one of us had worn hats or gloves. Stupid thinking I know ... not the Boy Scout living up to the Boy Scout motto. We hiked into the Sunriver village gas station on the verge of frost bitten ears and noses and fingers, there we sought warmth and made a phone call to our friend, Fred. We decided to just leave the damn car on the side of the road until the next day, when we had it hauled into Bend. The diagnosis ... a frozen carburetor. The cure ... let it thaw out, then drive away. You want to buy a cute little fuel efficient Toyota Corolla, light blue? I got one I'll sell you. Good horn, good headlights, nice body, excellent glass, no dents or significant scratches, low mileage, and always serviced on time."

"OK, no sale," he said. "You talked me out of the deal."

"Wait, Wait, it has a great horn, turn signal lights and radio..."

Further conversation was interrupted by the ringing intercom bell. Betty asked if I could take a call from Dr. Wiltse. "He sounds pretty upset," she said. I told her I would take the call even if he didn't sound upset. Gary waved good-bye, taking his leave and closing the door behind him as he went.

"Jim, we have ourselves a situation here. Did you know Karl was a member of the Elks Club?" he asked. I told him it was news to me. Karl had never mentioned it. "Last night he must have tried to empty their well drink reservoir. Just South of Curtin, on the old highway, he cut his car in half on the guardrail and he doesn't even remember it. I kept him over night at the hospital in Cottage Grove for observation of possible internal injuries, but I had to discharge him this morning. Other than a few bruises and a small cut on his forehead, he didn't sustain any injuries."

"His sudden promotion from teacher/counselor to District Superintendent appears to be a gift from Hell," I said. "It seems to have set off a binge of self-destructive proportion. When I mentioned to him what the job of Principal had done to Larry Mack, he just laughed at me. He said his marriage to Maureen was rock solid, that he was a prince of a family man compared to his father-in-law, implying that she would easily accommodate any hardship he might dish out."

"Well, that's the other thing I was going to tell you. This morning, Maureen and the kids moved out of that farmhouse they bought a few months back. She is staying with friends in Sutherlin or Winchester. She told me she didn't know what she would do next, but she said that she was certain that she was not going to raise her children in circumstances similar to the ones in which she was raised."

"Hopefully, Maureen's moving out will be the shock Karl needs to consider sobriety and/or a treatment program. From what he told me and more importantly, what he had been telling himself, her leaving with the children is not anything he expected. I will make time to go by his house this evening after work ... see if I can persuade him toward a program. I haven't seen the farmhouse yet. That will be my excuse for stopping by his place."

"My suggestion is that you wait until you can go in the morning," Doc said. "Larry informed me that after discharge, Karl went home and began drinking. By now, I expect he wouldn't remember any visit you might make."

"Good point. Wish me luck," I said before hanging up. In the back of my mind was lurking the thought that blackouts are a late stage not an early stage symptom of alcoholism.

"Forget about luck. Take your Higher Power along with you. And call me after your visit," he said. I assured him that I would.

When I arrived home that evening, I told Annis Rae how worried I was about Karl. His recreational alcohol use seemed to have suddenly exploded into something family and life threatening. Maybe to those around him on a daily basis it wasn't a sudden thing at all. Perhaps others saw a more gradual descent from a brilliant loving, caring, playful Karl to a person lost in the denial of his full-blown addiction. "I'm going to go up there and see if I can have a conversation with him, probably Saturday or Sunday morning."

"Don't forget that your mom and dad are coming this weekend. You too could have marriage problems if you took off and left me here to entertain them without your help. I know Karl is important to you, but so are we," she said, in a practical, not terribly judgmental tone of voice.

"Thanks for reminding me," I said. I failed to clarify whether the thanks was for jogging me about my parents visit, about the fragile nature of all marriages including my own, or for helping me keep my priorities straight. She didn't ask for clarification.

Life transitions, whatever they are and whenever they occur, can be jarring and can set off surprising skirmishes. Dad, as I may have mentioned, came out of the Eastern Colorado dust bowl and Great Depression with an exceedingly strong work ethic. For over 40 years, he always worked at least five very long workdays and sometime six. He took few vacations, for as a self-employed optician he didn't make much money and when on vacation he would not be making money. He would be spending it. I think of him as a good father, engaging in both discipline and playfulness, but he spent a ton of hours in his optical shop.

Mom was primarily a domestic engineer, running the home front, making delicious meals, keeping an immaculate home, being crafty and riding heard on my sister and me. As parents, they seemed to agree on most things.

My sister and I found little daylight between them to exploit.

When my dad decided to sell the shop and retire, a large seismic shift occurred between them for which they, in retrospect, may have been ill prepared. Except for his weekends and noontime pool games at the Elks Club, he didn't have much practice at leisure pursuits.

Mom was definitely not used to having dad under foot on her turf. It's an educated guess on my part that the bickering and mean-spirited verbal back biting that occurred around this time in their relationship was either a poorly understood result of this awkward transition in their lives, or a misguided effort to reset the distance and control mechanisms in their changed lives.

Whatever the true cause, it was damned difficult to hear and observe. They were both strong-willed people with too much ambition for perfection and the need to be correct.

"John, what's the matter with you? Let me show you how I do it," she might say.

"You want to show me how to breathe while you're at it," he might answer.

It was during this visit, the one in which Annis Rae let me know very emphatically that it would not be in the best interest of our marriage for me to take off and check up on Karl and leave her alone with mom and dad, that real courage happened. In the midst of this particularly uncivil exchange, Annis Rae interrupted. "Excuse me," she said. "You two are a lot more fun to be around when you are being kind to each other." Her delivery couldn't have been more heart-felt and well meaning.

"Do you want us to go home now?" asked my mom in a short, sharp package.

Standing her tender ground, Annis Rae replied, "No. no, please don't miss my point. We really enjoy your company when you are kind to each other. It's just a fact."

We four never spent a second discussing the cause or the cure for this behavior. They never even acknowledged its existence, but a very real and important change occurred in their communication when they were in our presence, which we very much appreciated. I hope they did too.

After mom and dad got on the road for Medford, I had Annis Rae's blessing to make the trek to Yoncalla. I gave him a call first to make sure he was going to be at home. He asked me why I wanted to come up, and I decided to play it absolutely straight. "Our mutual friends called me at the end of this last week. They told me about the bifurcation of your car, the blood level in your alcohol stream and about Maureen and the kids moving out. I was thinking, with all that good news hanging around your neck, I should come up there, see your new house and kick your ass."

"In that case, I'm gonna be home. You might as well come on up." If his voice was any indication of his present state of consciousness, he sounded fairly sober.

It wasn't easy to focus on my driving. I have many times thought of Karl as my mentor. In all of my experience of him, I think of him as having equal or superior intelligence and vastly wider experience. I admire his skill and profoundly appreciate the friendship we have developed. Now he is in deep stink. How did he reach late stage alcoholism so quickly...not coming home at night, not remembering what he is doing and where he has been? A few months back I can see him as a fun-loving problem solver. Am I blind? What is the status of my own denial? What kind of a friend am I? Am I kidding myself about my capacity as a therapist? Wait a minute. I am not nor will I ever be Karl's therapist. I have only been a loving and imperfect friend.

As I pull into the gravel driveway in front of Karl's recently acquired old two-story farmhouse, I see him waving to me with his open right hand. He's sitting on his sun shaded front porch in a cane rocker, left hand firmly holding a can of beer on the arm of the rocker.

"Hey partner, good to see you. Come on up here and have a beer with me before I show you around my new place," he said.

"It's good to see you too. Nice place you found, a lot roomier than the old one, far enough away from the school to be way less of a fishbowl than the old place," I replied.

"Yeah, that last one, that's the best part about it. I've got some privacy here. Have a seat here in the shade. I'll get you a beer."

"Lemonade or water would be good. My body is less and less tolerant of beer as time goes by. My eyes get itchy, my nose stuffy and it wants to fly through me like bread through a goose," I said.

"If beer treated me like that, maybe I wouldn't drink so much of it. As it is, I like the taste and it doesn't cause me any grief like it does you. Hard liquor, that's a different story. I drink that stuff and I'm down for the count. That's what I was drinking the night I cut my car in half. Once I get going on it, something clicks off in my head and it's like I am drinking on autopilot. Beer... I can take it or leave it. Hey, now that I am thinking about it, Maureen and the kids left some A&W root beer in the fridge. How does one of those sound?"

"That'll be fine, thanks," I said.

"OK, let me get you one of those, then we can do a walk about the place," and he was off his rocker and on his way into the house. I followed him into the house. I am not sure precisely how many days Maureen and the kids have been gone, less than a week is my estimate. But the interior already has a musty odor of neglect and stale beer.

Together we wandered around the large, mostly empty place. "There's a lot of potential here Karl... probably twice the space you had in the old house. What does Maureen think of it?"

"She likes the house all right. It's me she... she's unhappy with me, not the house. She wants me to quit drinking and go with her to see a marriage counselor. I told her I would go with her to see a counselor if she set up the appointment. I told her I have quit the hard liquor, but don't see the beer as a problem. She says that's not good enough.

So that's where it stands at this moment."

"You're going to put that can of beer ahead of your marriage?" I asked.

"I don't look at it like that. One shouldn't necessarily get in the way of the other. That's what I think," Karl said.

"But Karl, suppose she sees liquor and beer as all part of the same dog...you haven't left her any starting place. Alcoholism is a mean disease...once you cross that invisible line, you can't go back for the ears, tail or hair of that dog. Maureen knows that as well as anyone. And your theory about her being willing to put up with any crap that you dish out, that one is surely a shoot down," I said.

"You may be right about the booze. I know you are right about my crackpot theory, like I was the hero that rescued her from the drunken Indians. But hey, let me show you my new airplane hangar." His change of subject was abrupt and astounding.

We walked out the back door, Karl leading the way, can in hand. As we approached the tall weather-beaten barn, I could see Karl's Piper Cub through the wide open doors. "Have you been doing some flying?" I asked. But as we got closer, I could see that the plane was in pretty rough shape and partially disassembled. The house, the barn and the plane, each could have been a simile for the man ambling in front of me.

"No, it needs some work. Until it's up and running again and recertified, it's cheaper to keep it here than to pay rent at the port," he said. And I am thinking that the plane and all the joy that it brought the pilot have come to this resting place to die. I was shocked at my thought.

He entered the barn through a squeaky side door and as he did so, empty beer cans fell out at his feet. The room that door opened into must have been littered two or three feet deep with empty returnable cans. Karl let out a none-too-convincing laugh and said, "This here is my retirement fund." Now I've gone from shock to numb, the hair rising on the back of my neck. I sense that he is telling me, in a not so subtle way, that this is the entire retirement program he is going to need.

I muttered something like, "Educators don't have great pay, but they have some of the best health insurance and retirement packages to be had," hoping against the odds that he would change his mind.

Shortly after the tour concluded, so did our visit. We exchanged a terrific bear hug as we stood beside the Corolla wonder car ... wonder when it is going to try to get me next ... but I felt an almost overwhelming sadness. I knew in my gut that this attempted intervention, if that's what it was, had ended in failure.

Monday morning, I made the call I dreaded but promised to make to Dr. Wiltse. Cecilia, cheerful and efficient as always, soon had the good doctor on the line. "How went your visit with Karl," he asked, going straight to the point.

"It may have been the toughest 45 minutes of my young life," I said. "I think he is on a collision course with death and knows it. And I feel powerless and kicked in the gut."

"I think you are right. I have seen it coming for years...not just the drinking, but all the thrill-seeking, death-defying stunts. But listen to me. You didn't cause any of it. In fact, I think you extended his life a little, because when he was around you he moderated some of his excesses. That's my opinion."

"Your opinion means a lot to me," I said. And, though our conversation was at an end, I felt some relief from my sorrow and shame, not because of his expressed opinion, but because he offered a continuing and lively friendship.

Hot Tub Head Hunters
37

Continuing education opportunities have always had a rejuvenating effect on my professional spirit. And Salishan Resort, on the Oregon coast, knows how to host a conference in such a manner that no one ever needs to suffer... no matter how esoteric the topic or how mentally challenged the presenter. In October every year for nearly a decade, the Mental Health Director's Association sponsored an educational event at Salishan, and this year was no exception. The brochure that came in the mail announced that Dr. Irving Berlin, a renowned psychiatrist on the faculty of the Medical School at the University of Washington would be the keynote speaker. The topic of his address was "Prevention in the Field of Community Mental Health." This raised some curious flags for me, the first of which was that our presenter was an academic, not a practitioner in "the field."

Secondly, why would anyone want to teach practitioners in the field how to prevent mental health? And why would anyone with a terrifically musical name like Irving Berlin want to be a psychiatrist?

Neither these questions, nor the predicted inclement weather, came even close to dampening my enthusiasm to attend this year's Salishan event. Thanks to Hugh and Fran's encouragement of my fledgling talent as a woodblock print carver, I packed my chisels and blocks. I tossed in my swim trunks and my tennis rackets, and as I did so, I could just feel the rejuvenation surging back into my professional spirit! Did I mention the 5-star Executive Chef?

As I drove up to the resort, the wind driven rain was pouring down and the participants were sweeping into the parking lot and making a mad dash to the registration desk. Umbrellas were left in cars because the blowing gale wanted to turn them inside out. It seemed odd to be without my Umpqua valley peers, but I assumed that the presenter and his topic had been a turn off to them. Or perhaps it was the typhoon-like weather forecast. If the parking lot was any gauge for the conference turn out, the event was going to be a sellout.

Those covered walkways between buildings are a marvelous sight to behold in such a storm as this, but with the wind sending the rain sideways, they were only a partial solution. After a light, late dinner, I lit the logs in my fireplace and settled in for a quiet evening of jazz on the stereo and woodcarving.

Chisels in hand, I began working on a hardwood block, trying to bring a Viking ship out of the grain. Carving is a great meditative activity, especially if you are not overly perfectionist about it. Though I have never done any knitting, I surmise it to be somewhat like that, but messier. As a matter of fact, after a while, I found myself wondering what the housekeeping crew will think when they see this room in the morning.

"Now they are renting rooms to beavers!" Estelle might say to Nicole. Then I rationalize that it is a clean kind of messiness as opposed to a dirty kind. And soon after that I was asleep.

Sometime during the night, the howling wind subsided and the enormous downpour transformed into a persistent mist. On my way to breakfast, I decided to leave my glasses in my raincoat pocket until I was completely inside the breakfast buffet room. These "one price, all you can eat" situations are eventually going to be the death of me. Being a tightwad, I always arrive early and have to see how much food I can put away, so that I can make sure that the meal is a bargain. But my rationalization is that early arrival equates to freshness. Not immediately seeing anyone I know (who else is going to get up early just to get a breakfast bargain), I picked up a complimentary copy of the Oregonian to place beside my overloaded plate. By the time I finished up the sports section and all the comics, I had to let my belt out a couple of notches so that I could accommodate the last of my cinnamon roll and bacon before going back for a second plate. Pushing my chair back from the table, I felt the sudden onset of a need to get in a good long waddle before the keynote speaker took to the podium. Miracle of miracles, I decided to forego the second plate.

I think the waddle did me some good, because as I located a seat in the last row of the conference hall, I didn't have to unbutton the top button of my Dockers in order to sit down. My thought about occupying a seat in the last row is, if the speaker is a dud, my escape will be that much easier. It will make it easier to slip out without causing a scene. To my horror, the hall is rapidly filling up, and conference organizers are beginning to set several rows of chairs behind me, and several more out to the side of me as well.

Here comes Dr. Irving Berlin, three piece gray striped suit and burgundy print tie, slightly taller than wide. Perhaps he knows more about the all you can eat buffet that I do. In a short while, he has himself organized at the lectern, and begins.

"Today, as community mental health professionals, we are going to be focusing on the communities in which we practice to determine whether or not these communities in which we live and work have an impact on the psychopathology of the clients we see in our clinics every day. And furthermore, as the day progresses, we shall explore the ways in which we can impact the health of the communities in which we live, and thereby enter the realm of prevention," he said. Then he took his first breath followed by a sip from the water glass he had precariously balanced on the top of the lectern.

Right about this moment, I am thinking this could be far worse than even I had imagined. I will bet you all my marbles and chalk, the honorable Dr. B has never been anywhere near the community in which I live and practice, which for sure looks nothing like Seattle. Everyone in this room already has a full time job doing the triage that counselors do with their clients every day. We don't need a new job as community organizer. I would be happy to leave community organizing to the community organizers and planners. It is going to be awkward with all these new bodies and chairs to climb over, but the time has come for me to get out of here… and put on my suit. I am talking about my swim trunks.

After ducking quickly back into my room for my swimsuit and a towel, I gently closed the door behind me and proceeded down the hall. With my head down, I slipped as quietly as possible past the housekeeping crew, hoping they would not identify me as the resident beaver in room A221. My myopia being what it is, I cannot see worth a darn without my glasses. In the warm humid air of the pool house, they would have immediately fogged up anyway.

As I entered the pool house, there didn't appear to be another soul in the pool. The two guys in the Spa pool were invisible to me as I slid into the lap pool and began to chart my course at a moderate pace, swimming up and back. This felt incredibly more useful than the non-activity proceeding without me in the conference hall. After a half dozen or more round trips up and back, with some crawl stroke, sidestroke and a bit of butterfly, I pulled my exercised body out of the lap pool, walked a few steps to the spa pool and eased myself into the spa. At this close range, I could see two laid back gentlemen that I had not noticed as I entered the pool house. They were already enjoying themselves in the large oval hot tub.

Over the rumbling noise of the aqua jets, I distinctly heard the shorter of the two men say to his companion, "I think we've found our man!"

"Yes indeed!" said the taller fellow.

"Are you guys referring to me?" I ask in a dubious manner. I did not recognize either one of them. If my memory wasn't failing me, I had never laid eyes on either one of them before this very moment.

"Yes, we are referring to you, my man," said the jovial bewhiskered shorter fellow. "Let us introduce ourselves. I am Charles Whitchurch, Director of Mental Health Services for Deschutes County. And this is my friend Harry Danielson, a psychiatrist from Medford."

"And I am Jim Henson, a psychiatric social worker from Douglas County. I grew up in Medford. Have I ever met either one of you before?"

"I don't believe I've had the pleasure," Charles replied.

"My office is located in the Medford Center Building, just a hundred feet or less down the hall from your father's," Harry offered. "You look much like the picture your dad keeps of you at his desk. Of course, in that one, you have your clothes on."

"Can you tell me then in what context it is that you think you have found your man?" I asked.

"Just before you arrived," said Charles, "I was telling Harry that I think I am going to cast my lot into the private practice sector, which will leave a vacancy in the directorship in Bend. And I was sharing with Harry that, this conference being a prime example, many people in our profession, to quote Steve Martin," don't appear to know shit from Shinola." And that's about the time you showed up here at the pool, within a couple of minutes of our own arrival. We are convinced that you are the best possible candidate for this opening."

"So while you were swimming laps, Charles and I independently came to the same conclusion. You should be the next Mental Health Director in Deschutes County," Harry said.

"You gentlemen are making some stupendous cognitive leaps here. What do you know about me? Have you seen my resume? What leads you to believe that I could or would want to shoulder that much responsibility?" I asked.

"Let's see. A Master's Degree in Clinical Social Work from the University of Chicago, Jim, it doesn't get any better than that. And you've got, what, about four year's post graduate experience? That's plenty, Jim." Harry said.

"Everybody wants to come to Bend, Jim. It's the new Aspen. The job itself doesn't require a high degree of effort. At least not the way I do it. I can show you the shortcuts. Yes, there will be 200 some applicants, but the total number is rather inconsequential since we are only going to interview three candidates. You will be one of those. All you have to do is get your application in ahead of the deadline. I can take care of the rest," said Sir Charles, with an air of absolute confidence.

"Can he do this?" I asked Harry, with skepticism and incredulity dripping from my lips.

True to his profession, Harry blithely answered my question with a question: "How fast can you pack your stuff?"

As I let myself sink deeper into the hot tub, I murmured, mostly to myself, "I'll be damned. This I have to see."

When I arrived back at our little Shangri-La on Nebo Street, I told Annis Rae all about the storm, Irving Berlin, and the attempted shanghai by the hot tub headhunters. I think she could tell that I was still somewhat under the spell of the sales pitch those headhunters cast. She peppered me with realistic questions about the workload, the staffing, the budget, and the political support behind the Deschutes County Mental Health program. These critically important questions bounced off me like hailstones off a tin roof. "I'll find out about that. I'll look into that. I'll think about that one." I countered.

One of her best suggestions was, "ask Hugh what he thinks." I did, of course, but I took my tin roof with me. My emotions about Hugh were terribly thick and complex. He was a terrific friend. The skirmishes that we had won, the outings that we had survived, the clinical challenges that we had undertaken... these are the things of which enduring friendships are made. Deep in my guts, I knew he was the best boss that I would ever have, and I admired him for who he was and how he did things. His respect of me was something I greatly prized. I wanted to do things like he did things, including his passion for fun, and his unstinting egalitarianism. I wanted to steal and try out some of his ideas as an administrator and manager of people. If I stayed on the staff at Douglas County, I knew that I could continue to grow, explore and have fun. Hugh said he would write a good reference letter for me, but he didn't want me to go. When I look back on it now, I believe that my tin roof was an amalgam of youthful energy, ambition, naiveté and arrogance. If it doesn't kill you, cockeye optimism is not an altogether bad thing to have, is it? Surely, if you are going to be stuck with an ism, it must be among the better isms to have. So apply I did.

Weeks rolled by until nearly two months had piled up since I mailed my packet to Charles. By now, I was pretty sure that my new friends, Charles and Harry, were full of that well known highly processed sandwich meat and were just having some fun at my expense in the hot tub. Besides, I thought, who in their right mind would want someone as green as I knew I was running a program in a medium sized county. I had no budget or managerial background in a county of any size. Dick Takai, the handsome Hawaiian whose place I had filled in the Douglas County Clinic, had gone all the way to the far eastern town of La Grande, to assume his first directorship. Only a wheat farmer would want to live that great a distance from the beach!

"This letter came in the mail today. I had to sign for it. It looks very official and appears to be from the Deschutes County Board of Commissioners," Annis Rae said, as she placed both the letter and sweet baby Lara into my hands in the same fluid motion. Talk about mixed messages. It seemed as though she was saying that the former was important, but the latter certainly trumped all. And, of course, she was right as usual.

While Lara and I sat down to open and eat the correspondence, Aaron was operating his wooden log truck on the floor. He delighted in the practice of running it over the floor furnace grate, which created an enormous racket and made everyone jumpy. Annis Rae disappeared into the kitchen without further comment. Actually, Lara was quite satisfied with the envelope, so I had the letter pretty much to myself. The cat had already assumed ownership of the most comfortable chair. Lara and I settled for what was left.

It was a brief message. Getting to the meat of it didn't take long to discern. "Honey," I said. "It says here that I am one of three remaining candidates for the position in Bend. They want me to go over there for a personal interview in front of their mental health advisory board a week from Friday! Isn't that great?"

Poking her head around the corner, she looked me in the eye and said, "I hope you know what you are getting into." Of course, following the great canoe mess up in the Alsea River estuary, she has every reason to have her suspicions. And in the next instant, as if to underscore the point, Lara made a prodigious rumbling noise in her cotton all natural home delivered diaper, while Aaron hit the floor furnace grate with his log truck at full speed, creating a deafening exclamation point.

The next 10 days zoomed by with the speed of an earthbound asteroid. Or perhaps it was just a hot breathed meteor. But I managed to find out a few things about the Deschutes County mental health advisory board.

The chairperson was pastor of the 1st Lutheran Church. Don Beake was his name.

Vice chair was a social justice activist from the United Methodist Church by the name of Jane Poor. Jane was a very spirited, slender, cheerful and approachable woman with the energy of any three normal people rolled into one. "This is a good place to live and work and raise a family," she said, with obvious love and enthusiasm for the community in which she raised her own family. "The mental health program here in Central Oregon is kind of a scrappy skin and bones affair, but all the people involved in it are long on skill and heart. I think you will like it here. You keep your application in the pot!"

"Are you going to become the next chairperson of the advisory board," I asked, because she just felt like a powerhouse even if it was just a voice on the phone. If I ended up being hired to be the next Deschutes County mental health director, I could tell she was definitely someone important to have on my side.

"That's a good possibility," she replied.

I couldn't help but wonder what my competition looked like, after Charles had finished trimming it from 200+ down to three. Since he accomplished this elaborate feat somehow, I wondered what possible strategy he could have up his sleeve to move my candidacy past the last couple of applicants. "You won't know until it's all over. Relax and enjoy the ride," was all that he would say.

One of the items that had not caught my attention until the day of the interview was the fact that the State of Oregon Mental Health Mental Health Division would be sending a delegate to participate in the hiring process. Out of public view, a power struggle was unfolding. Not until after the fact did I know that the Mental Health Division delegate had rather heavy handedly dismissed one of the three remaining candidates, the "local favorite son" applicant, as not possessing sufficient credentials to hold the job. "This candidate lacks the proper degree and credentialing. He might be a good program manager, and you my like him, but his clinical skills are nowhere in evidence. We think his work history is not what we would like to see in a candidate for mental health director. We (the Mental Health Division) would withhold the State matching funds if the County hires him," the State bureaucrat said forcefully.

Chairman Abe Young of the Deschutes County Board of Commissioners was not used to being told who he could or could not put on his payroll; and furthermore, he was not about to be browbeaten or blackmailed by some officious twit from Salem. When he weighed into the conversation, it was later reported to me, he only asked one brief question; "Well young man, which of the candidates do you think the Mental Health Division would endorse for this position?"

"It is obvious that David McTarter, the candidate from the Multnomah County mental health program, is the only applicant with a well-rounded resume, with good balance in both clinical and administrative experience," said the twit.

"Let's go forward with the interviews then, but we fully intend to bring all three of our candidates before the advisory board hiring committee, whether or not you like the three that we have selected to interview," said Chairman Abe Young.

And that is how the best qualified candidate on paper received the kiss of death on his attempt to become the next Deschutes County mental health director. There was no possible way that the chairman of the board of County Commissioners would consider hiring the candidate recommended by the State twit. By the time the committee ushered me in for my interview, the three had been reduced to one. I could have been covered in plaid and wearing a clown's red nose and floppy shoes. It wouldn't have made the slightest bit of difference.

"Mr. Henson, please give us a brief introduction, some background on yourself, and what you think might be your strengths and weaknesses," Chairperson Beake asked.

"I've just come through the waiting room, and from that experience, I've gleaned from the clinic staff that I am by far your tallest applicant. I'm an Oregonian, born and raised. For eight joyful years, my wife and I have been married now, and we have two energetic preschoolers to keep us challenged and fully exercised. My clinical education and experience, including supervision and practice, have given me a terrific base from which to work successfully with lots of different kinds of client needs. Having assembled a satellite clinic for the north end of Douglas County, I have had a chance to create and manage community mental health services. As Charles Whitchurch would most likely confirm, I have had the opportunity to work for one of the best director role models in the State. I do plan to steal as many of his great ideas as I can. Never have I had to craft and manage the annual program budget. That has to be my biggest deficit. With a little tutoring and a little time, those are skills that I believe I can add to my tool kit. With the staff and advisory board, we can continue to build the mental health service that Deschutes County citizens need.

I guess that about covers it," I said.

I was looking at a room full of smiles. It was time for me to be quiet. Don Beake looked at Abe Young, and then they both looked around the room. "Does anyone have any questions for Mr. Henson?" Don Asked.

Again, a brief pause filled the smiling room. They all looked like cats with canary feathers on their lips. I didn't know that the State and the County had already cancelled out the other applicants. Finally, Abe said, "I have one. When can you come to work?"

About Jim Henson

Born in the Rogue River Valley in 1944 at the community hospital, which was condemned shortly after his birth, Jim left the center of the pear-shaped universe at the earliest possible opportunity. He attended college in San Diego, where he majored in psychology, and met and married his beautiful bride of 45 years and counting. They moved to Chicago in 1966, and stayed through the deepest snowfall in recorded history and the Democratic Convention/Police Riot in 1968. Jim has worked in the field of mental health for the past 40 years. He is the co-parent of two beautiful adult children and has four gorgeous and brilliant grandchildren. After four years in Oregon's Umpqua Valley, he and his family moved to become residents of Central Oregon's high desert where he currently resides.

Jim has a BA degree in psychology from California Western

University. He was admitted to the dual degree program at McCormick Theological Seminary and the University of Chicago. After completing one year at McCormick, Jim transferred to a full time student position at the University of Chicago, where he completed his Master's degree in clinical social work.

Jim completed the requirements for ACSW and Diplomat status with the National Association of Social Workers. Additional postgraduate studies lead to Clinical Member status in the American Association of Marriage and Family Therapists and Certified Sex Therapist and Diplomat in Sex Therapy in the American Association of Sex Educators, Counselors and Therapists.

Jim is a Licensed Clinical Social Worker in Oregon and served under the appointment of four Oregon Governors on the State Clinical Social Work Licensing Board. Jim was elected to serve as Chair of the licensing board for five of his 11-year appointment.

He was elected to serve on the national board of Directors of the American Association of Sex Educators, Counselors and Therapists, and to serve as the Chair of the Ethics Committee of the Oregon Association of Marriage and Family Therapy.

At the local level, Jim served on the Deschutes and St. Charles Home Health Advisory Board as well as the St Charles Mental Health Advisory Committee. He was a long-time member of the Deschutes Alcohol Council and served as its President for two terms.

Subsequent to his graduation from the University of Chicago, Jim worked for the Family Service Bureau of Chicago before moving to Oregon. Jim worked as a Psychiatric Social Worker for Douglas County Family Service Clinic, a full service outpatient mental health service for just under four years. In the fall of 1973, Jim moved to Bend Oregon where he served as County Mental Health Director for four years. In 1977, Jim moved into full time private practice, from which he retired on Halloween, 2008. As of mid-2010, he continues to do some clinical case consultation and education work and is an active Mental Health Examiner for Circuit Court for Deschutes County.

Jim began writing for pleasure in the early 1990's when he and his wife became empty nesters.

Jim's professional interests and activities have reached across a wide spectrum of mental health concerns due to his curious nature and the opportunities his professional life have offered him. At the University of Chicago, his first year field placement was at Jane Adams Hull House, where he and his supervisors and peers established a community based therapeutic elementary school which required parent participation. Group therapy and family therapy were a required part of the curriculum for elementary age students who had already been suspended from neighborhood schools. The second year field placement was with Family Service Bureau on the South side of Chicago. This was another opportunity to work with a broad range of people, diverse in age and issues of concern.

While in graduate school, Jim also held down a mental health job at Onward House, a settlement house on the near West side, which offered everything from Headstart to job placement and sports. Once in Oregon, Jim began an eight-year stint in rural public mental health clinics, which further stretched the scope of his interests and skills, because in both Douglas County and Deschutes County, these outpatient mental health clinics were essentially the only mental health services available. There was not the luxury of becoming a symptom specialist even if he had been drawn in one direction. He was determined to become a skillful generalist even when one part of his practice attempted to push out others.

By 1977, the job description of County Mental Health Director was becoming more and more administrative in nature, which was not a good fit for Jim. This emotional and cognitive dissonance helped propel Jim into private practice. It was move on or go crazy. A new medical building with a four-year lease beckoned him, and he found himself surrounded on three sides by Obstetrics/Gynecology and on the fourth side by Pediatrics. This position propelled Jim into a seven-year training program with ASSECT, which led him to certification as a Sex Therapist... the only one between Portland Oregon and Boise Idaho (about 600 miles of sagebrush and 100 thousand people).

The Oregon laws, which sent drunk drivers to county mental health programs, pushed Jim to seek training in addiction and chemical dependency recovery work. A contract to do aftercare for Serenity Lane, an excellent residential treatment program in Eugene, created more necessity and opportunity for professional growth in this area. In time, Jim came to enjoy all the connections that these human conditions have with each other. And, bring an array of skills to address the needs of persons, couples and families, not just chase the symptoms they bring.